ENGLISH AND HINDI
RELIGIOUS POETRY

STUDIES
IN THE HISTORY OF RELIGIONS

(SUPPLEMENTS TO *NUMEN*)

XXIII

ENGLISH AND HINDI RELIGIOUS POETRY

AN ANALOGICAL STUDY

LEIDEN
E. J. BRILL
1973

ENGLISH AND HINDI RELIGIOUS POETRY

AN ANALOGICAL STUDY

BY

JOHN A. RAMSARAN

LEIDEN
E. J. BRILL
1973

ISBN 90 04 03648 2

PRINTED IN THE NETHERLANDS

for
My Wife, Margaret
and
My Daughters, Susan & Janet

CONTENTS

PREFACE

This work was accepted by the University of London for the degree of Ph. D. in the Faculty of Arts; and its publication now gives me the opportunity to express in some measure my deep gratitude to all who, in one way or another, helped, guided or encouraged me during the period of my research. I wish I could name them all individually, and I hope that those friends whose names do not appear in this preface will excuse the omissions made necessary by the limited time and space at my disposal.

To Professor Geoffrey Bullough, D. Litt., Emeritus Professor of English of the University of London, I owe the greatest debt as one of his students. Over a period of more than twenty-five years he has been my teacher and friend. It is largely to his active support and guidance that the completion of this work is due. Besides reading the thesis himself, he enlisted the help of two members of his staff at the University of London King's College, Mr R. F. Hill and Mr R. A. Waldron, whom I should also like to thank for reading portions of my work and making helpful comments.

Dr R. S. McGregor of the University of Cambridge kindly read several chapters and made useful observations on the Hindi aspects of my study. Mr J. G. Burton-Page of the University of London School of Oriental and African Studies discussed the plan of my work in the initial stages and I am grateful for his advice on a number of points. Whatever failings there may be in this study—in either the English or the Hindi aspects—are entirely due to my own lack of perception, and in no way to that of the scholars I have named whose excellent counsel, I am sure, has saved me from many a pitfall.

Two eminent Hindi scholars, Āchārya Pandit Paraśurāma Caturvedī Jī and Āchārya Dr Hazārī-Prasāda Dvivedī Jī (both of Uttar Pradesh, the province from which my forebears came), have been my constant inspiration in the study of Bhakti Poetry during the last twenty years. It was my great privilege to meet them when I visited India in 1964 on study leave from the University of Ibadan, Nigeria. Of their profound scholarship others better qualified than I may speak; but of their generosity no one has had better proof than I. Since that visit I have been overwhelmed by the continued kindness of Āchārya Paraśurāma Caturvedī Jī who has so readily undertaken the supervision of a Hindi translation of my thesis to be published in India.

Mr K. D. D. Henderson, C. M. G., obtained for me a grant from the Spalding Trust when I was setting out for India. To him, for many favours, and to the Trustees of the Spalding Trust I shall always be indebted. To a friend of long standing, Professor E. G. Parrinder, I should like to say how thankful I am for encouragement during the course of my researches. Among friends who sustained me during a difficult period, I must mention Professor and Mrs Adegoke Olubummo, Mr and Mrs Charles M. Casey, Mr and Mrs Lawson Ilegbodu, Mr Femi Shobande and the late Professor Joseph Anene.

I would also like to record my warm appreciation of the friendly assistance rendered me at all times by various members of library staffs in the British Museum, the School of Oriental and African Studies, the University of Ibadan and the University College of Swansea.

Finally, to my wife (to whom this work is in part dedicated) I owe more than I am able to express; but I can, at least, say I am most grateful for the willingness with which she has relieved me of a variety of burdens connected with the preparation, at many stages, of the MS. of this work.

The memory of my mother and my father has been to me like a living presence during my years of reading in Bhakti Poetry. And in my parents is symbolised for me the beauty that two languages and two religions can together provide. I therefore count myself in few things so fortunate as in being able to pay this humble tribute to my parents by presenting this work for the sympathetic consideration of readers of English as of Hindi religious poetry.

Brown's Field,
Ightham Common,
Sevenoaks, Kent,
England
April 1972

INTRODUCTION

The subject of this comparative study is the poetic expression of religious belief and practice in two cultures: one, European; and, the other, Indian. There are doubtless many analogies between the spiritual experiences of the West and the East which may be drawn from the literatures of various languages; but this study examines mainly what is typical in English and Hindi poetry as representatives of the European and Indian religious traditions.

The history of the period, from which the literary examples are chosen, provides striking parallels in the intellectual and religious life of Europe and India. After passing through the Middle Ages, the West saw the full flowering of the Renaissance which gradually spread from Italy northwards through Europe into Britain; it experienced, too, the conflicts of the Reformation and the Counter-Reformation and all that these movements imply as regards the social and religious life of Europe from the late fourteenth to the seventeenth centuries.

The same period saw the spread of Islam in North India and the establishment of the political supremacy of the Muslim invaders. In the face of foreign domination and religious persecution, the Hindu masses turned more and more to sectarian worship of the theistic Brahman for spiritual refuge and consolation. So there developed the popular cults of bhakti or loving devotion to a personal God as manifested in His incarnations, especially the *avatāras* Kṛṣṇa and Rāma. (An attempt has been made in Hindu theology and poetry to distinguish between *saguṇa* bhakti having as its object of worship the godhead with qualities, and *nirguṇa* bhakti directed towards the divine Absolute not associated with qualities or incarnations). The golden age of bhakti poetry in the modern Indian languages extended approximately from the end of the fourteenth to the middle of the seventeenth century, and produced in Hindi a long line of religious poets from Kabīr (d. 1518) to Tulasī Dāsa (1532-1623) who stand at the limits chosen for the Hindi aspect of this study.

Although this wave of bhakti poetry was largely the immediate reaction of Hindu piety to Muslim persecution, intellectually bhakti has affinities with earlier Vedic religion, in the theistic strand of which the concept of bhakti may have had its origin. During the

Middle Ages, Indian theism had begun developing as a protest against the sterility of metaphysical speculations and came to a climax in such later movements as Vaiṣṇavism, which provided its adherents with a religion charged with devotional ardour. Similarly, the aridity of European scholasticism was challenged by a Christianity of love and service which found its most intense emotional expression in the raptures and songs of mystics and saints.

A brief preliminary survey of some of the intellectual and religious ideas of the Middle Ages, is, therefore, necessary to an understanding of the European and Indian backgrounds of religious poetry in English and Hindi. The philosophical and theological concepts of Western scholasticism in the one case, and, in the other, medieval Vedantism and the revival of anthropomorphic Hinduism in the face of the heretical doctrines of Buddhism and Jainism, contributed in a large measure to the environments in which the works to be discussed flourished.

The course of metaphysical speculations in Europe from the neo-Platonism of the pseudo-Dionysius to its Renaissance exposition by Marsilio Ficino (1433-1499) is paralleled by the long line of debates on Hindu monism (*advaitavāda*, literally "non-duality") and qualified monism (*viśiṣṭādvaitavāda*, literally "modified duality" the equivalent of Western theism). And as St. Thomas Aquinas put Aristotelian dialectics to the service of Christian theology, so Hindu scholars like Rāmānuja (b. 1017) justified the doctrines of a warm theistic religion by means of Vedānta philosophic method. The result of these intellectual currents in the West and in the East was the infusion of a new spirit into religion during the later Middle Ages and early Renaissance period, so that discussions on the nature of reality, and questions about the relationship of the Many and the One, were no longer the occasion of mere logomachies, but contributed to the spiritual quest for a living communion with God, or identification of the human spirit with the divine Absolute, in a religious experience which forms the central theme of much of the poetry to be considered in the following chapters.

The religious orders founded in Europe during the twelfth to the fourteenth centuries contributed much to the life of Christian fervour whose influence was felt among the laity. For example, the *laude* of St. Francis, through his disciples and imitators, fostered the Italian *laudesi*; and their hymns in the vernacular found ready acceptance among the untutored masses. In this way, too, religious enthusiasm contributed to the growth of Italian literature. (The Indian counterpart of the *laudesi* is the *kīrtana* or hymn recitals in Vaiṣṇava worship). English as a literary medium received a new stimulus in the thirteenth century from the writings of European and British saints and mystics; and the principal themes of divine love in Latin hymnology were adopted by vernacular poets and translators. Devotion to the Blessed Virgin and love of Jesus, for example, inspired some of the finest imitations of the mood of love-longing in the theme of the human soul's yearning for union with the divine. Festivals of the Christian Year and the daily rituals and ceremonies of the church, likewise stimulated many to compose hymns which were used both in public and private worship. A tradition of systematic meditation gradually developed, and the stages of contemplation in the soul's progress towards God were codified in the light of the Christian mystic's experience. The result in the literary field was the composition of numerous manuals of devotion setting out various spiritual exercises. At first these were in Latin, but several were translated into the vernaculars and their influence is to be seen in the form and content of many religious lyrics composed in English.

In the Indian scene the late Middle Ages witnessed similar events in connexion with the spread of Vaiṣṇavism, that is, the most popular form of Hindu theism centred on the worship of Viṣṇu, one of the triad or *trimūrti*—Brahmā, Viṣṇu, Śiva—generally accepted as different aspects of the unconditioned Brahman, which are associated with creation, preservation and dissolution in the cycle of existence. Vaiṣṇavas are devotees of the benevolent aspect of the Brahman, that is, Viṣṇu, and worship his *avatāras* especially Kṛṣṇa and Rāma. The various *avatāras* of Viṣṇu are celebrated in scriptural *Purāṇas* written in Sanskrit, the most famous being the *Bhāgavata Purāṇa* (c. 900). This was composed in the Tamil country of South India where the worship of Viṣṇu had been introduced from the north. The popularity of Vaiṣṇavism in this region was due in a large measure to the religious fervour of the Āḻvārs, poet-saints, whose devotion to Kṛṣṇa inspired, in Tamil, numerous hymns which appealed to the masses. The temples of the Śrī-Vaiṣṇava sect were erected in the later Middle Ages, and the images of Kṛṣṇa placed in them became the focus of daily rituals and worship. The *Bhāgavata Purāṇa*, the Āḻvār compositions, and the lyrical *Gītagovinda* by Jayadeva (c. 1200) in Sanskrit, have inspired many lyrics in several modern Indian languages, especially among adherents of the Kṛṣṇa cults in which music, dancing and singing play a prominent part.

The songs of the Āḻvārs together with the teaching of Rāmānuja and his disciples, spreading to the north, inspired Vaiṣṇavas there, especially the Gauḍīya school of bhakti in Bengal of which Caitanya (1486-1533) was the prime mover. His love of Kṛṣṇa and his sojourn in Vraja, the country of Kṛṣṇa's earthly existence, led his disciples to reclaim the sacred sites from neglect and to establish the modern temples and shrines of Vrindābana on the banks of the Jumna river. This work was carried out under the leadership of the sixteenth-century Goswāmins of the Kṛṣṇa cult who, in their scholarly Sanskrit works promulgated, on the basis of orthodox Sanskrit poetics, a spiritual aesthetics of bhakti. Their elaborate descriptive analysis of the nature of Vaiṣṇava sensibility and devotion has set the pattern for bhakti poetry criticism in the modern Indian languages.

Another significant aspect of the religious life of North India was the establishment of the Ṣūfī religious orders after the Muslim conquest. Spreading from the north-west during the thirteenth and fourteenth centuries, Ṣūfism by the tolerance and virtuous living of its followers, won many Hindus to a sympathetic consideration of its monotheistic principles founded upon Islam. And it is possible that in this way it was able to exercise some influence upon the *Rāma-bhakti* cult, which avoided the erotic excesses of *Kṛṣṇa-bhakti*, especially of the Gauḍīya school. Eventually, Hindi Ṣūfī poets made their literary influence felt in the sixteenth and seventeenth centuries through their allegorical romances on the theme of the soul's quest for the ideal beauty in God.

Turning to a comparison of the theology of Vaiṣṇavism and that of Christianity, one finds that there are basic differences in their doctrines regarding reality, God and incarnation. Strict Hindu monism or *Brahmavāda* identifies the human soul and all creation with the Absolute; and there is no place for theistic ideas. But bhakti seems to vacillate between monism and theism, *nirguṇa* bhakti inclining towards the former, and *saguṇa* bhakti towards the latter and belief in incarnations or *avatāras*. Literally, *avatāra* is a "descent" of Viṣṇu in flesh among the creatures of this world to deliver them from oppression, and to secure the soul's ultimate salvation from the cycle of rebirths. But whereas the Christian doctrine of salvation maintains that there is only the unique incarnation of God in the person of Jesus Christ, Vaiṣṇavism upholds several incarnations.

Further, Christian salvation works through the redemptive love of God shown in the sacrifice of Himself through the passion, death and resurrection of Jesus Christ; but Vaiṣṇava *avatāras* do not sacrifice their lives for the sake of mankind: they rescue and defend their devotees from cruelty and oppression through their supernatural power, prowess of arms or superhuman strength. However, both Christianity and Vaiṣṇavism preach a doctrine of grace as indispensable for salvation, the aim of which is final union of the human soul with God. Although the Hindu belief in metempsychosis generally presupposes more than one existence before this consummation is achieved, it is, nevertheless, possible for the Vaiṣṇava believer, because of his intense love for Kṛṣṇa or Rāma, to be granted instant and final release through the grace of God, from the cycle of rebirths.

These basic differences between the tenets of Christianity and Hindu theism are reflected in the English and Hindi religious poetry under review in this study, whose chief aim is to show that in spite of differences in attitude to fundamental theological questions, the poets of both cultures have much in common as regards the theme and treatment of similar religious subjects in their poems. Starting with the Middle English nativity lyrics, one finds that the adoration of the Christ Child lying in the manger or in the arms of the Blessed Virgin, is analogous in intention to the Vaiṣṇava's joy in contemplating the baby Kṛṣṇa or Rāma being fondled and caressed by his mother. The religious practice in both cases, of the worshipper's mind dwelling on the charms of the infant's beauty and innocence in such a *compositio loci* (of the medieval and Renaissance spiritual exercises), aims at evoking in the devotee a tender love which reaches out towards communion with the divine. There is a similar appeal to the sensuous in many of the rituals of daily worship, and in the observance of various festivals in the calendar of the Christian and the Vaiṣṇava Year. Incidents from the lives of Jesus and the *avatāras* providing the focus for communal or private contemplation thus direct the soul towards God. There is therefore an unmistakable resemblance between Hindi bhakti lyrics and Middle English or Renaissance poems in which are uppermost the simple, unsophisticated feelings of love, joy, longing and hope which spring, as it were, from the immediate apprehension of the physical particularities of characters and scenes from scriptural accounts.

But there is, on the whole, a gradual shift in English poetry from this unsophisticated involvement in the Gospel story with its concrete details, to a more intellectual approach. Therefore, though the sensuousness of the Middle English lyric persists in a modified form in Renaissance lyrics (for example, in the baroque richness of Southwell and Crashaw), by the seventeenth century English religious poetry like that of Traherne and Vaughan, influenced by the philosophical and scientific temper of their times, seems partly occupied with the metaphysic of religious experience in their treatment of the theme of virtue, sin, love, death, and immortality. In Hindi, on the other hand, there are always two streams: one whose current is strongly sensuous, and another that is distinctly speculative. These seem to run side by side most of the time, sometimes mingling in the works of one and the same poet, as in Sūra Dāsa; in contrast to whom stands Kabīr whose *nirguṇa* bhakti is expressed with a metaphysical terseness that has something of the concentrated quality of Donne's poetic wit.

Another general difference between English and Hindi religious poetry may be recognised in the extent to which the individual personality of the poets is felt in their compositions. It is to be expected that, in both languages, lyrics intended primarily as hymns for communal use do not allow for obtrusion of the composer's personality to any noticeable degree. This is borne out by the characteristics of translations and adaptations of Latin hymns, the Middle English carols and, to a large extent, the metrical psalms. The same thing is true of the majority of *saguṇa* bhakti *bhajans* or hymns intended for use in Kṛṣṇa worship. However, in the late sixteenth and the seventeenth centuries, English religious poetry more often has the characteristic tone of the individual poet, as in the case of George Herbert, some of whose lyrics are still to be found in modern hymn books. The bhakti poetry closest to Herbert's in certain moods and sentiments is that of the poetess Mīrāṃ Bāī; but although she seems to establish a distinct personality of her own in the total effect of a large body of her lyrics, they are singly very typical in diction and imagery of the *saguṇa* poets of her own and later times. She is more like Crashaw, whose devotion in the full tide of Catholic fervour seems to engulf his individuality. This effect is due to the poetic vision which finds expression through similes and metaphors of a generalised sensuousness, in which scriptural allusiveness is not subtilised to an abstraction of philosophical dialectics, since it is reinforced by a faith that seldom questions or doubts. Such poetry is not therefore inclined to psychological analysis of the devotional state of mind; nor is it consciously didactic though occasionally sententious in tone. Much of Kabīr's poetry, unlike Mīrāṃ Bāī's, has the obvious sententiousness of a master composing extempore verses inspired by homiletic fervour while instructing his hearers, as well as the speculative ardour of a philosopher who has recourse to analogies from the experiences of everyday life in which emotions play a large part. His personality is therefore felt both in the colloquial terseness of his language, and in the sudden insights gained through commonplace images transformed into metaphysical analogies.

Lyrics of penitence and supplication may have the quality of confessional exercises in communal worship, or the distinctive accent of individual voices in a dialogue with God as judge and redeemer. Tulasī Dāsa's prayers in the *Vinaya Patrikā*, like Donne's *Divine Sonnets*, have the individual tone of a personal experience. But even here, in the treatment of very similar themes, Donne's personality is established more vividly than Tulasī Dāsa's since there is an ambivalence in the latter's treatment of the Hindu preoccupation with the essential unity of all beings and the desire of the Vaiṣṇava devotee to enter into the human-divine communion with a retention of the sense of individual existence.

Finally, turning to some longer religious poems of both languages, one finds that the emotional and the intellectual are combined in varying degrees in the overtly didactic poem, the allegorical romance and the epic. Spenser, in his *Hymn of Heavenly Beauty* and *Hymn of Heavenly Love*, expresses his beliefs with a personal warmth pervading an eclectic philosophy that is partly Christian and partly neo-Platonic; and in *The Faerie Queene* he produces a sensuously rich allegory together with a syncretism of all the pagan and Christian metaphysical ideas current in his times. Milton, in *Paradise Lost*, writes a Christian epic in which he exploits the resources of the Bible and the history of Christianity and European philosophical thought, in exploring the moral law of the universe. At the same time, the allusive wealth of his literary imagery gives the narrative in some passages a highly emotional quality. Similarly, Tulasī Dāsa in his Hindi epic, the *Rāma-carita-mānasa*, puts all Hindu scripture to the service of Vaiṣṇavism, and in his story of Rāma, the recitation of which is in itself an act of devotion, he combines the lyricism of bhakti with the abstractions of philosophical disquisition. Attitudes may differ according to the theological and philosophical beliefs held by the poets, but in all these works the individual voices of the poets find an echo in the hearts of sympathetic readers to whom they speak of spiritual longings common to all humanity.

CHAPTER ONE

THE EUROPEAN BACKGROUND

Medieval European philosophy and theology are inseparable from the intellectual and religious life which found expression in Middle English literature. Even when some feature of general Christian theology or scholastic thought, for example, the neo-Platonism of the pseudo-Dionysius, was not the specific subject matter, or the direct inspiration of English writers, the ideas of the philosophers from Erigena in the ninth century to Ockham in the fourteenth,[1] contributed very largely to Christian dialectics and the world view generally accepted among scholars in Britain. It is therefore important in a study of English religious verse, to bear in mind the principal philosophical and theological concepts of the Middle Ages which continued to form to some extent, through reinterpretation or modification during the Renaissance, the basis of much Western thought.

John Scotus Erigena's transcendentalism deriving from neo-Platonism remained a cardinal conception in Christian theology even after Abelard (1079-1142), the proto-scholastic, influenced by the extreme nominalism of Roscellinus had questioned its validity by his cogent and uncompromising logic in the Aristotelian spirit. And Abelard's controversy with St. Bernard is further proof that the strands of rationalism and idealism (I am using a term in the Platonic nomenclature instead of the scholastic "realism") were closely intertwined in European thought of the Middle Ages. Indeed, it was the synthesis of the rationalistic and idealistic in the writings of Duns Scotus and Thomas Aquinas which brought scholasticism to its peak of philosophic achievement, and established the *via antiqua* of the Scotist and the Thomist schools of the thirteenth and fourteenth centuries. These were, however, to be eventually challenged by the logicians of a new movement, the *via moderna*, of which Ockham (c. 1290-1349) was the leader.

But, as Fr. Copleston has observed, Ockham was a Franciscan

---

[1] This was also the period in India from Śankara, the champion of monism, to the rise of medieval Hindi bhakti poetry.

theologian, not a modern radical empiricist;[2] and his aim, therefore, was not to undermine Christian doctrine, but to safeguard it against the concept of universals which he saw as attempting to limit the omnipotence of the transcendent godhead of Christian theology. He maintained that "the existence of the universal consists in an act of understanding and it exists only as such. It owes its existence simply to the intellect: there is no universal reality corresponding to the concept".[3] The subtleties of Ockham's disciples, nevertheless, ultimately led away from the Thomist integration of metaphysics and theology to the arid field of mere logic-chopping, with the consequent drying up for many of the spiritual springs of Christian religious experience; or, as Martz puts it, "during the late Middle Ages the scholastics threw a deep shadow over the affective life, a shadow which led some, such as Thomas à Kempis and his Brothers of the Common Life, to renounce scholastic subtleties as the brood of folly and the bitter fruit of that *curiositas* which St Bernard had denounced as the father of sin." [4] The real danger of divorcing philosophy from theology lay in two extremes: either, subservience to rationalism resulted in a futile scepticism with loss of faith in the logically undemonstrable truths of Christian religious experience; or, blind, unintelligent belief regarded sincere intellectual probings as mere *curiositas*.

In England, Thomas Bradwardine (c. 1290-1349), Archbishop of Canterbury, in his *De Causa Dei* rebutted the scepticism of the Ockhamites and sought to reinstate divine authority in place of human reason. "The outstanding feature of *De Causa Dei* was its refusal to concede anything to fact or to natural evidence. Bradwardine, on the contrary, saw all truth as revealed truth, and in this sense his outlook may well be described as the doctrine of authority. He judged everything in divine terms; and the effect of his system was to make all creation merely the extension of the divine will." [5]

Apart from theological reaction against scepticism, another way out from the sterilities of scholastic subtleties was shown by speculative

[2] Frederick Copleston, *A History of Philosophy* (London, 1953), III, 48. Cf Etienne Gilson, *History of Christian Philosophy in the Middle Ages.* (London, 1955).

[3] *Ibid.*, III, 57.

[4] Louis L. Martz, *The Poetry of Meditation* (New Haven, 1954), p. 112.

[5] Gordon Leff, *Medieval Thought: St Augustine to Ockham* (London, 1959), pp. 297-298.

mysticism and affective devotion. Those who followed this way sought through faith a more intimate experience of the Divine Absolute, an experience which found one means of expression in religious poetry. The current of medieval mysticism that had been generated by the neo-Platonism of the pseudo-Dionysius through Latin translations, as early as 850 by Erigena, became stronger and more evident in the religious life of the twelfth and thirteenth centuries in various parts of the Continent of Europe and in Britain. It was chiefly in the religious orders that the contemplatives, through a system of teaching and spiritual discipline, developed the mystic life; but it is not possible to enumerate or describe those orders within the strict confines of geographical or political boundaries. They were orders of a universal Christian church, hence English mystics were in the mainstream of the intellectual and spiritual life of medieval Europe. At the same time, it is convenient and useful to speak of the orders, centres of learning or religious activity, since these give a peculiar quality to the contemplatives associated with them.[6]

Among those who combined a life of contemplation with social service were St Francis (1182-1226) and his followers: Jacopone da Todi (1228-1306), Angela of Foligno (1248-1309) and St. Bonaventura (1226-1274). Quite in contrast to these compatriots of his was a Dominican, St Thomas Aquinas (c. 1225-1274), the chief exponent of Aristotelianism in Christian theology, whose mysticism was marked by a profound intellectual quality. Among the German Dominicans was Meister Eckhart (1260-1327) whose passionate quest for the Absolute, through philosophical probings and Christian devotion, has striking resemblances to that of one of India's greatest scholars and mystics, Śankara (c.800), whose monism, *advaitavāda*, did not prevent him from being a votary of the goddess Durgā. Prominent among the Flemish mystics was John Ruysbroeck (1293-1381) who, though deriving much inspiration from Eckhart's teachings, made his own peculiar contribution to European mysticism.

An important centre of Christian thought and worship in the twelfth century was the Parisian abbey of the Augustinian Canons of Saint Victor, founded in 1108 by William of Champeaux, from which centre Hugh (1097-1141) and Richard of St Victor (c.1123-1173), the

---

[6] Evelyn Underhill, *Mysticism*, 12th ed., (London, Methuen Paperback, 1960), pp. 457 *et seqq*.

latter born in Scotland, wielded much influence on medieval mysticism through their philosophical and devotional prose. Adam of St Victor, their distinguished contemporary, is better known for his Latin hyms, especially the celebrated Sequence in honour of the Blessed Virgin—*Salve Mater Salvatoris*. The Victorines who, like the pseudo-Dionysius had accepted the concept of an approach to the Absolute through the *via negativa*, gave a fresh impetus to the contemplative life of Christian devotees which reached a climax in the fourteenth century both on the Continent and in Britain.

Medieval English prose and verse were influenced, like the European vernaculars, by the life and writings of the saints and scholars mentioned above. However, there is no denying the fact that "the continuity of English prose [from Old to late Middle English] is to be found in the sermon and in every kind of devotional treatise";[7] for, as Professor Chambers has convincingly shown, the quality of such a translation as *Sawles Warde* (c.1200-1250), from the Latin of Hugh of St Victor, must have had a literary tradition of the vernacular behind it. Certainly the devotional manual, *Ancren Riwle* (c.1200), intended for a religious community of women recluses, is original English prose of striking literary quality.[8] But the fact remains that, from the thirteenth century onwards, devotional writing in English received a fresh stimulus from the religious movements which were giving new life to the Western Church.

The *Sawles Warde* which is really a free rendering, with elaborations, of a portion of the *De Anima* of Hugh of St Victor, appeared in the thirteenth century. Another anonymous English translation of a devotional treatise by an unknown thirteenth-century French mystic appeared later, probably in the fourteenth century, under the title of *The Mirror of Simple Souls*. This work, too, was clearly influenced by the Victorines. But the most notable of such writings of the fourteenth century in England were *The Cloud of Unknowing* and *Privy Counselling*. The anonymous author of these works has acknowledged his indebtedness to the works of the pseudo-Dionysius which had been commented upon by, among others, Hugh of St Victor and St Thomas Aquinas (c.1225-1274).

[7] R. W. Chambers, *On the Continuity of English Prose from Alfred to More and his School* (London, 1932), p. xc.

[8] *Ibid.*, p. xcvi.

Professor Hodgson, however, has this to say about thematic influences in connexion with these works:

> It is often impossible in *The Cloud* and *Privy Counselling* to determine whether the author was influenced in a particular theme by the tradition of Dionysius or by that of the Western Church, since many of the Dionysian conceptions were based ultimately upon the Scriptures, and many of the same ideas were developed independently by such Fathers as St. Augustine and St. Gregory. Moreover, in many passages the author of *The Cloud* blends the Dionysian conception of prayer with the traditional teaching of the Church on contemplation.[9]

Similar caution is necessary in estimating probable European stylistic and thematic influences on Middle English religious lyrics. Professor R. M. Wilson has made the following observations:

> There is no direct evidence for the existence of lyric poetry in England before the twelfth century, and even then only odd fragments of it have been preserved before the following century. When it does appear in writing it is already in many respects highly developed and its ultimate origins are not to be traced. Some of the influences which have gone to its development are obvious enough; there can be no doubt, for example, that it has been influenced to a considerable extent by the lyric poetry in French and Latin, though whether it owes its primary inspiration to these two literatures is a different question. There is little in the Middle English lyric which we can claim as an unmistakable development from Old English, but since we know nothing of Old English lyric poetry—not even whether it existed or not—the fact that we can trace no connexion is of little value as evidence.
>
> Whatever may have been the origin of the Middle English lyric there can be no doubt of its close connexion with the contemporary French lyric and with the Latin accentual poetry. It is much more doubtful whether the courtly lyric, which had been developed in Provençal at the beginning of the twelfth century, exerted any direct influence.... Whilst some of the ideals of courtly love may occasionally be reflected in the Middle English lyric, the technical vocabulary of love is largely absent and there is not the same delight in sentimental analysis. The influence of the Provençal lyric is more apparent in such technical details as the construction of the stanza or the distribution of the rhymes.[10]

He goes on from this to a discussion of the early English carols, maintaining the view that if they were in fact due to the French

[9] Phyllis Hodgson (ed.), *The Cloud of Unknowing and the Book of Privy Counselling*, E.E.T.S. o.s. 218, 1st ed. 1944 (reprt. London, 1958), p. lxix.

[10] R. M. Wilson, *Early Middle English Literature* (London, 1939), pp. 250-252.

carole, its introduction found a ready welcome in England because here music and part-singing had been well developed by the twelfth century. But very little of the lyric poetry composed during the twelfth and early thirteenth century has survived; and the largest portion of the existing lyrics, after the middle of the thirteenth century, is religious because they were written down, in most cases, by members of the religious orders in their abbeys, convents and monasteries. And obviously the majority of these religious lyrics owe much to Latin hymns and Latin religious poetry.

Vernacular lyrics were more specifically influenced by the particular form of the Latin Sequence which began to develop about the beginning of the tenth century. The pattern followed in Germany was that of Notker (c.840-912), who was practically the inventor of the Sequence; in England the French model was preferred. The eleventh century saw the transition from the Notkerian type to the regular Sequence of the twelfth century when Adam of St Victor (c.1100-c.1180) dedicated his poetical talent to the adornment of the liturgy, quietly following the offices and composing Sequences for the festivals of the church. To him "tradition assigns the glory of having brought to perfection this most characteristic achievement of medieval poetry." [11] There was throughout the Middle Ages a large output of Sequences which gradually declined in quality so that only four were retained in the Roman Missal of 1570.[12] Yet the Sequence never entirely ceased to influence English religious poetry, and as late as 1648 Richard Crashaw, in his *Steps to the Temple* included free translations and adaptations, in his characteristic vein, of several Latin hymns among which were the *Lauda, Sion, Salvatorem; Dies Irae;* and *Stabat Mater.*[13]

Another Latin hymn form, that of the *Laudi Spirituali*, was perhaps next in importance to the Sequence in shaping the medieval lyric. According to Greene

> ... the greatest flowering of religious popular song took place in thirteenth-century Italy. Towards the end of the preceding century there had sprung up a popular zeal for devotional singing, fostered by the organisation of musical fraternities calling themselves *laudesi*. These guilds were of the greatest service, not merely to religion, but to the

[11] F. J. E. Raby, *A History of Christian-Latin Poetry* (Oxford, 1953), p. 348.
[12] *Ibid.*, p. 229.
[13] Richard Crashaw, *The Poems English Latin and Greek of Richard Crashaw*, ed. L. C. Martin (Oxford, 1927), pp. 285-301.

> cause of vernacular poetry as well; being composed of layfolk, they naturally preferred to sing in their own tongue rather than in the Latin of the church ritual. The result was that in the thirteenth, fourteenth, and fifteenth centuries thousands of *laude* were composed and sung, varying widely in form and content, but alike in their popular character.[14]

The history of the *Laudi Spirituali* is closely associated with the Franciscan Order, the members of which first came into England in 1224. The Friars Minor influenced by the warm humanity and humility of St Francis, himself a writer of *laude*, and the intense devotion of Jacopone da Todi who was the greatest of the early Franciscan composers of *laude*, spread their lyrical ardour throughout northern Europe. In England, too, the Franciscan influence was felt in Latin compositions; in the numerous translations, and adaptations of Latin hymns; in the carols of James Ryman; and in the lyrical pieces of William Herebert (d. 1333). The poetry of these and other writers, many of them anonymous, has fortunately been preserved in several manuscripts; and the Early English Text Society (E.E.T.S.) provides excellent printed texts of these. Carleton Brown's anthologies give a selection of the best that is available from the thirteenth to the fifteenth centuries.[15]

The English Franciscan, John Pecham (1225-1292), who became Archbishop of Canterbury, wrote the *Philomena* in Latin. This is one of the loveliest of Latin devotional poems and Pecham's masterpiece in which he employs the Goliardic four-lined stanza of thirteen syllables, with a mono-rhyme. A brief summary of the substance of this poem and its symbolic meaning is given in Raby's *Christian-Latin Poetry* in the following paragraph:

> ... It is a purely lyrical poem, unfettered by the conditions imposed upon a liturgical composition, personal in its emotion, and filled with the new inspiration which was the secret of the gospel of Assisi. The subject of the poem is the nightingale, the forerunner of the spring, the bird who, 'in her saddest, sweetest plight', sings a song which typifies the crying out of the soul for the heavenly country. For the nightingale, when she perceives that she is near to death, flies to a tree top, and at

---

[14] R. L. Greene, *The Early English Carols* (Oxford, 1935), p. cxx.

[15] Carleton Brown (ed.) *English Lyrics of the XIIIth Century* (Oxford, 1932); *Religious Lyrics of the XIVth Century* (Oxford, 1924); *Religious Lyrics of the XVth Century* (Oxford, 1939). Hereafter references to these anthologies will be given briefly as Brown XIIIth Cent., Brown XIVth Cent., and Brown XVth Cent.

> dawn pours forth her song. When the day begins to break, she sings without pause ever louder at the hour of prime, and at tierce the joy and passion of her song increase, until it seems as if her throat must burst with the torrent of melody. Then at last when noon arrives, her body can endure no longer; *Oci, Oci,* [16] she cries, and in the anguish of her song she sinks and fails. At none she dies, her tiny body shattered and broken. The nightingale is the type of the pious soul, which longs for the heavenly country, and, longing, beguiles itself with song. So it lives, as it were, through a mystical day, the hours of which correspond to the stages of its redemption. Dawn is the stage of man's creation; Prime the season of the incarnation of Christ; Tierce is the period of His life on earth. Sext represents the hour of His betrayal, scourging, and crucifixion. None of His death, and Vespers of His burial. Stage by stage the soul follows in meditation, and out of its meditation fashions a song. The sweetness and sadness of the meditation increase as the hour of the Passion approaches, and the soul remembers the sufferings of the Redeemer, in which it longs to share, until, at the hour of the *Consummatum est,* it fails and dies in the ecstasy of love and compassion.[17]

This poem is an example of Latin devotional poetry blending the inspiration derived from the hours of worship of the church with the medieval habit of allegorising divine love through the commonplace experiences of everyday life. Ten Brink has said that "divine love (*die Gottesminne*), in the medieval sense, became a new theme in English literature, before secular love poetry . . . could take root there." [18] His opinion is supported by G. R. Owst who suggests that "in its first beginnings, indeed, the religious love-lyric in this country may well have been a direct product of homiletic fervour, rather than a mild imitation of worldly love-songs." [19] Whether the English vernacular religious lyrics antedate the secular or not, the influence of Latin hymns on Western vernacular poetry generally is indisputable.

As far as Middle English religious lyrics are concerned, a

---

[16] See Frederick Brittain, *The Penguin Book of Latin Verse* (Harmondsworth, 1962), which contains only the first part of this poem, and where *Oci, Oci* is translated 'Kill, kill.'

[17] Raby, *op. cit.*, pp. 426-427.

[18] Quoted in E.E.T.S. no. 241, *The Wohunge of Ure Lauerd* (London, 1958), p. xx.

[19] G. R. Owst, *Literature and Pulpit in Medieval England* (Cambridge, 1933), p. 16. Cf. Ruth E. Messenger, *The Medieval Latin Hymn* (Washington, 1953), p. 76: "Celtic churchmen were pioneers among medieval Latin hymnists, their earliest contribution dating from the sixth century. Religious lyrics in the Celtic tongue must have been produced and recorded before the Danish invasions although the destruction of these manuscripts delayed the compilation of new vernacular collections until the eleventh century."

knowledge of the favourite Latin hymns must be presupposed on the part of the laity who must have understood, for example, Chaucer's use of *Angelus ad Virginem* in the *Miller's Tale* and the Sequence *Alma Redemptoris Mater* in the *Prioress's Tale*, as well as at least some of the more popular examples of macaronic verse as in the Christmas carols, and Latin refrains like "quia amore langueo" an understanding of which was necessary for a full appreciation of the poems in which such refrains occur. Seldom did macaronic verse, however, achieve the integration of English and Latin as in a thirteenth-century lyric in praise of the Blessed Virgin of which the following is the first stanza:

Of on that is so fayr and briȝt
velud maris stella
Briȝter than the day-is liȝt,
parens & puella,
Ic crie to the, thou se to me,
Leuedy, preye thi sone for me
tam pia,
That ic mote come to the
maria.

(Brown XIIIth Cent. p. 26 MS Egerton 613).

The three principal themes of early Latin hymnology are the nativity, crucifixion and resurrection, in all of which the Blessed Virgin figures prominently. But there are also numerous Marian hymns in which she is addressed directly, for example, the anonymous *Ave Maris Stella* (c. seventh or eighth century) of which Frederick Brittain writes:

> The most famous of all Marian hymns, owes much of its charm to the simplicity of its language and construction. Apart from proper nouns, only four words in it have more than two syllables, and most of its lines are end-stopped. It contains some of the favourite word-play of the Middle Ages; e.g., the word 'Mary' is supposed to mean 'star of the sea'; and Gabriel's 'Ave', which brought salvation to man, is an anagram of 'Eva', the first woman, who brought about man's fall.[20]

The *Ave Maris Stella* is extant in several English versions, but that of MS. Bodley 425 consisting of twenty-eight four stress verses *aaaa* follows beautifully the Latin, stanza for stanza. The original Latin and

---

[20] Brittain, *op. cit.*, p. xxi; text of *Ave Maris Stella*, pp. 129-130.

the English version may be usefully compared to show how the vernacular was being established as a suitable, flexible medium for lyrical expression.

AVE MARIS STELLA
(MS. Bodley 425)

AVE maris stella,
Dei mater alma
Atque semper virgo,
Felix caeli porta.

Heile! sterne on the se so bright,
To godes holi modir dight,
and euer maiden made of miht,
that seli yate of heuen is bright.

Sumens illud Ave
Gabrielis ore,
Funda nos in pace,
Mutans nomen Evae.

Takand and hailsand was thou faine,
Thurght gabrols mough and maine;
In pais thou put vs out of paine,
Turnand the name of eue againe.

Solve vincla reis,
Profer lumen caecis,
Mala nostra pelle,
Bona cuncta posce.

Vnles bandes of sinful kinde,
Thou bring forth liht vn-to the blind,
Oure iuels put thou alle bi-hinde,
Alkine gode that ve mowe finde.

Monstra esse matrem;
Sumat per te precem
Qui pro nobis natus
Tulit esse tuus.

Show the for modir als tou is,
Oure preiere take the thorou thi blis;
He that for vs and for oure mis
be-come thi sone, thou moder his.

Virgo singularis,
Inter omnes mitis,
Nos culpis solutos
Mites fac et castos.

Onely maiden and no mo,
A-mang vs all so meke to go,
Vs of sake lese of wo,
Meke thou make and chaste als so.

Vitam praesta puram,
Iter para tutum,
Ut videntes Jesum
Semper collaetemur.

Clene lif in land vs lene,
and seker gate vs graȝe be-dene,
That we Ihesu seand so shene,
Euer faine we vs be-twene.

Sit laus Deo patri,
Summum Christo decus,
Spiritui sancto,
Honor tribus unus.

To god fadir be louyng,
til holi crist wurschipe als kyng,
The holi gost wold of hem spring—
Thise thre haue oure wurcheping.

Amen.

(Brown XIVth Cent., no. 45)

Alliteration distantly reminiscent of O.E., and M.E. head rhymes on which the accentual rhythm moves in many of the verses (e.g., 1 and 3 of the first stanza), gives the English a crispness quite unlike the softness of the original (which is due in large part to the vowel quality of the Latin); but there is a more consistent use of end rhyme throughout the stanzas of the English version. The *Ave Maris Stella* has only a few of the stock images associated with medieval Marian verse. It is not unusual in several other lyrics both in Latin and in English to find a catalogue of nominal phrases descriptive of the Blessed Virgin's charm and virtue. Marbod (c.1035-1123) provides characteristic examples in the following hexameters written in couplets with internal rhymes:

Stella maris, quae sola paris sine conjuge prolem,
Justitiae clarum specie super omnia solem,

Gemma decens, rosa nata recens, perfecta decore,
Mella cavis inclusa favis imitata sapore. . .

Star of the sea, who alone without a husband didst bear a child who is the sun of righteousness, shining bright in beauty above all things,

Beauteous gem, fresh-blown rose, perfect in thy beauty, in savour like honey enclosed in the hollow comb.[21]

Middle English religious lyrics influenced by the Latin tradition,[22] are replete with examples of symbolic titles for the Blessed Virgin as in the following:

Hymn to the Virgin by William Huchen (MS c.1460) [23]

Swete and benygne moder and may,
  Turtill trew, flowre of woman alle,
Aurora bryght, clere as the day,
Noblest of hewe, thus we thee calle,
  Lyle fragrant eke of the walle;
Ennewid with bemys of blys,
In whom neuer was founden mys.

---

[21] Brittain, *op. cit.*, p. 189.

[22] In this connexion it is important to remember that the Middle English religious lyric was influenced not only by Latin hymns written on the Continent since the early Middle Ages, but also by English poets of Latin hymns and lyrics as late as the thirteenth century. The Golden Sequence, *Veni, sancte Spiritus*, for example, has been attributed to Stephen Langton, Archbishop of Canterbury (c.1150-1228). Other English writers of Latin religious poetry in the thirteenth century include Alexander Neckham, John Garland, and John Howden.

[23] E.E.T.S. o.s.15. *Political, Religious and Love Poems* ed. Furnivall (1866 revd. 1903), p. 291.

Or the following selections from

A Hymn to the Virgin Mary to Preserve King Henry [24]
(Lambeth MS. 306).

1.

O blessed mary, the flowre of virgynite!
O quene of hevyn Imperyall!
O empres of hell, and lady of chastyte! . . .

2.

Heyle, bryght starre of Ierusalem!
Heyle, ruddy roose of Ierico!
Heyle, clereness of bethlehem!

* * * * * * * *

3.

O clere porte of paradyse!
O spowse of Salamon so eloquent!
O quene of most precyous pryce!
Thou art a pyller of feyth excellent! . . .

4.

Heyle flece of gedion, with vertu decorate!
Heyle plesaunt lyly, most goodly in bewty! . . .

5.

O plesaunt olyue with grace circundate!
O lemyng lawmpe, in light passing nature! . . .

6.

Heyle blasyng starre withowte peere! . . .

These titles of the Blessed Virgin sprang from the devotion to her which developed during the Middle Ages, but which was not evident during the earliest centuries of the Christian Church. It has been suggested that the spread of the cult of the Virgin was due to a number of forces including Eastern pagan influences, and the *Protevangelium of James* with its affirmation of her perpetual

[24] *Ibid.* pp. 112-113.

virginity supported by the teachings of Ambrose, Jerome and Augustine on the spiritual value of virginity. Once the cult had been universally established in the West by the eighth century, the Virgin's praises were celebrated in the offices of churches raised specially in her honour. By the twelfth century "the custom was widespread in the monasteries of reciting the *Little Office of the Blessed Virgin* before the canonical office, and to add to Compline the *Salve Regina* or other anthems in her honour. By this date the cult of the Virgin had assumed such proportions and evoked so much fervour that the figure of the Mother of Christ began to eclipse that of her Son and of all the apostles and saints." [25] The Sequences composed in the twelfth century employed all the epithets and titles, in the Latin and M.E. lyrics quoted above, deriving the majority from the Old Testament prophecies of the birth of Christ, the Canticles, and the writings of the early Church Fathers.[26]

The medieval habit of allegorising scriptural allusions and episodes as so many *exempla* of spiritual truths, nurtured, in conjunction with scholastic wit, a symbolic theology of the cult of the Blessed Virgin which is well demonstrated in the imagery of the Marian lyrics. By the end of the Middle Ages most of the images had become so trite that they had lost a great deal of their effectiveness in religious poetry. But it was quite otherwise in the twelfth century with Adam of St Victor whose Marian hymns, composed for liturgical purposes, were inspired by the speculative mysticism of the Victorines who saw an intimate connexion between the earthly and the heavenly.

In the *Ave Maris Stella* of Marbod, who also was similarly fascinated by the symbolism of nature, the "star of the sea" is linked with the prayer for a safe voyage through life (*iter para tutum*).This is an image that elicits an immediate response and makes superfluous such an exegesis as the following by Luis de la Puente in the early seventeenth century: "Shee is the Starre of the sea, for that shee is light, consolation, and guide of those, that sayle in the sea of this worlde, tossed with the greate waves, and tempestes of temptations." [27] This archetype of human existence as a perilous ocean occurs frequently in Hindi poetry in which Kṛṣṇa or Rāma, incarnations of the Divine, are pilots of the human soul; but the

[25] Raby, *op. cit.*, p. 365.
[26] *Ibid.*, chapter xi. See also, R. T. Davies, *Medieval English Lyrics: A Critical Anthology* (London, 1963), pp. 371-378.
[27] Quoted in Martz, *The Poetry of Meditation*, p. 232.

notion of a guiding star is absent. However, several of the other Marian symbols, like "fleece of Gideon" and "Daniel's mountain", are so involved in medieval pedantry that they fail to make their original impression on a modern reader.

Like the Marian hymns there were also many others translated or adapted from Latin whose subject was the love and beauty of Jesus. Some of these will be discussed later, but mention may here be made of the celebrated *Jesu Dulcis Memoria* which is of peculiar interest because of its disputed authorship. It was formerly ascribed to Saint Bernard of Clairvaux (c.1090-1153), but recently rival authorships have been suggested. According to Gillmore,[28] a manuscript of the eleventh century ascribes it to a Benedictine abbess; but according to Brittain,[28] it is now presumed to be the composition of an unknown English Cistercian.

The original *Jesu Dulcis Memoria* has forty-two stanzas, but when the feast of the Name of Jesus was instituted in the fifteenth century the first seven and last two stanzas were adopted as a Sequence for the Mass. Although there is a forty-nine stanza English version (very freely adapted) in Harley MS. 2253, the eleven-stanza Hunterian Museum MS. version (late fourteenth century) [29] is independent of the text in Harley 2253, closer to the Latin reading in some verses, and more in tone with other English poems of love-longing for Jesus.[30]

Only the first two stanzas of the Latin are here quoted because from stanza 3 the English poem shows only slight verbal resemblances to the original, and suggests a more personal response to the love of Jesus.

JESU DULCIS MEMORIA

(Hunterian Museum, MS. V. 8. 15.) [31]

Jesu dulcis memoria Dans vera cordi gaudia, Sed super mel et omnia Dulcis ejus praesentia.	Ihesu, swete is the loue of thee Noon othir thing so swete may be; No thing that men may heere & see Hath no swetnesse aȝens thee.

[28] F. J. Gillmore, *Evolution of the English Hymn* (New York, 1927), p. 81. Brittain, *Penguin Book of Latin Verse*, p. xxxi.

[29] Brown, *Religious Lyrics of the XIV Century*, No. 89, on pp. 111-112 and notes pp. 272-273.

[30] E.E.T.S., o.s. 117. *The Minor Poems of the Vernon MS* Pt II ed. F. J. Furnivall, (London, 1901), pp. 449-462.

[31] Brown, *op. cit.*, p. 111-112.

Nil canitur suavius,	Ihesu, no song may be swetter,
Auditur nil jucundius,	No thing in herte blisfullere,
Nil cogitatur dulcius	Nouȝt may be feelid delitfullere,
Quam Jesus, Dei filius.	Than thou, so sweete a louere.

Stanzas 8-10 of the English are as follows:

Ihesu my god, ihesu my kyng,
Thou axist me noon othir thing,
but trewe loue & herte ȝernyng,
And loue teeris with swete mornyng.

Ihesu my loue, ihesu my lyȝ[t],
I wole thee loue & that is riȝt;
Do me loue thee with al my myȝt,
& for thee moorne bothe day & nyȝt.

Ihesu, do me so ȝerne thee
That my thouȝt euere vpon thee be;
With thin yȝe loke to me,
And myldely my nede se.

This is strikingly similar in tone and diction to the following original English lyric in the Vernon MS.[32]

Swete Ihesu, now wol I synge
To the a song of loue longinge:
Do in myn herte a welle springe
The to louen ouer alle thinge.

Swete Ihesu, kyng of blisse,
Min herte loue, Min herte lisse:
In loue, lord, thou me wisse,
And let me neuere thi loue misse.

Swete Ihesu, myn herte liht,
Thou art day with-oute niht;
ȝive me both Grace and miht
ffor to loue the ariht.

Swete Ihesu, my soule bote,
In myn herte thou sette a Roote
Of thi loue that is so swote,
And weete hit that hit springe mote!

[32] E.E.T.S., *op. cit.*, p. 449.

Swete Ihesu, myn herte gleem,
Brihtore then the sonne Beem:
As thou weore boren in Bethleem,
Thou make in me thi loue-dreem.

Swete Ihesu, thi loue is swete—
Wo is him that hit schal leete!
ȝif me grace for to wepe
ffor my synnes teres wete...

There are nine further stanzas in this strain.

Besides translations and imitations of Latin hymns, there gradually appeared original vernacular poems of Christian experience. Apart from those religious lyrics which were more specifically expressions of an intimate and private character springing from the spiritual discipline of the recluse or the ecstasy of the mystic, there were many others which were inspired by a personal response to forms of worship laid down in the missals: prayers, collects, liturgical responses, processional hymns, rituals connected with the offices and precise hours of worship, and the festivals of the Christian Year. Some of these will be discussed later alongside analogues from Hindu worship as they are found in bhakti poetry.

It has already been observed in passing that some religious lyrics may have resulted from the homiletic fervour of preachers when their alliterative prose acquired a singing cadence like that of the prose lyric, *The Wohung of Ure Lauerd* of the thirteenth century, in which the surging fervour of the devotee breaks into waves of rhythmic alliterative phrases:

Iseu swete iesu. mi druth. mi derling.
mi drihtin. mi healend mi huniter.
mi halivei.[33]

Jesu sweet Jesu. my darling, my darling.
my lord. my saviour.
my honey-drop. my balm.

Private and corporate worship in their various ways contributed to the religious poetry of M.E. literature. Robbins has said that "we are only beginning to realise the important position which vernacular

[33] E.E.T.S. no. 241. *The Wohung of Ure Lauerd* ed. W. M. Thompson (London, 1958), p. 20.

prayers played in the religious life of the later Middle Ages." [34] The literature embodying such prayers and the M.E. religious lyrics reached a wide circle outside the religious orders because of the extensive use of the vernacular during the thirteenth and fourteenth centuries. But ironically enough, the vernaculars nursed in the bosom of the Church became one of the most effective means of attack on Catholic theology and hierocracy which culminated in the Reformation during the late fifteenth and sixteenth centuries. Although there had been in the thirteenth century English translations of the Psalter and various portions of the Bible in verse, it was John Wyclif (1320-1384) who incited, and probably participated in, the translation of the entire Bible including the Apocryphal books, although the work was not completed during his lifetime.

Wyclif was determined to make the Scriptures available to lay folk in their own tongue. He vehemently asserted the Bible to be more authoritative than Church dogma and ecclesiastical law; therefore his teaching was anti-sacramental and anti-sacerdotal. He instituted his "poor priests" as a crusade against the friars; denounced pilgrimages and indulgencies; inveighed against statues and paintings in churches, though it appears that he was not entirely opposed to icons as aids to worship; and expressed unorthodox opinions on the sacraments.

However, in spite of the popularity of Wyclif and his disciples, the devotional life of the time still retained much of its emotionalism which drew its warmth and significance from the symbols of the Church in the form of ritual worship and its concrete appurtenancies of icons, rosaries, paintings and other aids to worship. In short, the affective life of a great many true and ardent Christians continued to draw inspiration from the pre-Wyclifite practices of the Church. And the religious lyrics of the fourteenth and fifteenth centuries express this continuity more strikingly than any other aspect of the cultural life of the late Middle Ages in England.

That this continuity of religious experience and expression extended beyond the fifteenth into the sixteenth century, Carleton Brown thinks can be substantiated by the evidence of the religious lyrics that continued to be written:

---

[34] R. H. Robbins, "The Gurney Series of Religious Lyrics", *PMLA*, LIV (1939), p. 338.

> Even a casual reading of these fifteenth-century lyrics is sufficient to demonstrate that no real line of cleavage exists between the fourteenth and fifteenth centuries. When one crosses the threshold of the sixteenth century the continuity may seem to the reader somewhat less obvious. However, the lyrics of the century, if studied attentively, supply evidence of a development from the fifteenth to the sixteenth century almost as constant as that traceable from the fourteenth to the fifteenth. The apparent break in continuity was to a large extent the result of new external conditions—the extension of printing, the introduction of the new learning, and the change of religion. And, though changes in external conditions materially modified conventional forms, they did not quell the essential spirit of the earlier lyrical tradition, but merely opened new channels for its expression.[35]

This continuity was made possible by the fact that, in spite of attempts to stifle the emotional life of the Church, the devotionalism associated with ritual and sacrament was far from quenched even in the full tide of the Reformation. On the contrary, religious persecution only intensified the spiritual discipline which Jesuit priests inculcated through manuals of contemplation, notably *The Spiritual Exercises* of St Ignatius Loyola (1491-1556). The resurgence of devotional enthusiasm in the reigns of Mary and Elizabeth enhanced the beauty and attractiveness both of the panoply of religion in the external aids to worship, and of the living communion with saints and martyrs through prayers and colloquies of Christian meditation.

In this way, too, the seductiveness of Renaissance pagan poetry was counteracted by the richness of the Roman Catholic imagination expressing itself in the emotional extravagance of such a poet as Robert Southwell in the late sixteenth century. His poetry marks a stage in the Christian baroque spiritualising of the senses [36] in the human-divine dialogue of love, which is essentially the chief theme of the religious poetry that turns upon the fixed centre of Catholic faith during the sixteenth and seventeenth centuries.[37]

---

[35] Brown, *Religious Lyrics of the XVth Century*, p. xxxi.

[36] Mario Praz, "Baroque in England", *Modern Philology*, LXI (1964), p. 177. This phrase "spiritualising of the sense", I have adapted from Praz's "that spiritualisation of sense which is the aim of Baroque art at its best."

[37] This does not mean that all Christian baroque poetry was Jesuit inspired, or that there were not Protestant poets like George Herbert whose poetry expresses a personal love of God in terms as warm and confident as the Catholic singers.

The Laudian Movement in the Church of England was a return to Catholic rites and ceremonies; and the scholarship as well as the saintliness of some Caroline Protestant divines matched those of the Jesuit Counter-Reformation.

Though it is broadly true to say that religious poetry of the seventeenth century was "a resurgence of traditional piety in an ambience of new philosophical and scientific thought and new artistic fashions",[38] it is necessary to observe that this "traditional piety" operating in an intellectual environment of growing complexity, itself became more complex in its literary manifestations. It acquired a more sophisticated philosophical quality, than it had earlier, in the interplay of intellect and emotion as well as in the poetic technique employed for its expression. This statement is generally true only of the religious lyrics; for, certainly the long elegiac poem, *The Pearl* (c.1370), is highly sophisticated in its structure and its impassioned logic of the religious sensibility pervading the arguments on theological questions like the equal dispensation of God's grace. And yet something of this more obviously distinctive poetic quality was already discernible, as it were in embryo, in a few theological lyrics of the fifteenth century which were sophisticated in tone and characterised by verbal conceit and clever paradox. For example:

A God and yet a man?
A mayde and yet a mother?
Witt wonders what witt Can
Conceave this or the other.

A god, and Can he die?
A dead man, can he live?
What witt can well replie?
What reason reason give?

God, truth itselfe, doth teach it;
Mans witt senckis too farr vnder
By reasons power to reach it.
Beleeve and leave to wonder.

(Brown, *Religious Lyrics of the XVth Century*, p. 187)

Between these earlier lyrics and what are usually called the "metaphysical lyrics" of the seventeenth century, there was the poetry of the English Renaissance as expressed in much Elizabethan verse in which the pagan *Eros* was more clamant than the Christian *Agape*. The rivalry between these two had been evident in the late medieval

[38] Frank J. Warnke, *European Metaphysical Poetry* (New Haven, 1961), p. 63.

literature of courtly love on the one hand, and Christian poetry on the other. As already mentioned, the medieval religious lyrics may have an origin independent of secular verse, but there is an obvious similarity between the themes of loyalty and devotion to an idealised mistress in the convention of courtly love, and the Christian devotee's adoration of the Virgin Mary and longing for union with God.

But courtly love, in spite of its refinement of emotion in the exaltation of woman, was no substitute for the Christian ideals of chastity and a loving devotion to God. And though early Elizabethan poetry was much influenced by the form and spirit of the courtly love convention, there is a tendency in the later works of Sidney and Spenser to turn away from earthly love to heavenly love; or, at any rate, to use earthly love and beauty as a step in the progress towards the ideal beauty and truth of Platonic philosophy as reinterpreted by Ficino during the Renaissance in Italy.

In contrast to the philosophical and ethical poetry of the sixteenth century there was the poetry of Christian propaganda: "There was a movement to substitute divine poetry for the secular poetry which was coming off the presses in the sixteenth century, a movement to substitute Biblical story for secular story, to substitute a Christian mythology for a pagan mythology, as well as to substitute prayer and praise of the Christian God for poetry addressed to an unkind mistress." [39] Robert Southwell's aim to show "how well verse and virtue suit together" must be set in this context, where the baroque extravagance of his poetry utilised the sensuous in the service of Christian meditation.

So it may justly be contended that there is a certain continuity in English religious verse from the M.E. lyrics to the metaphysical poetry of the seventeenth century. But it is a continuity marked by increasing variety and complexity. And in the first half of the seventeenth century these qualities are heightened because "the new philosophy calls all in doubt", as a result of the conflicts caused by political, social, religious and scientific upheavals of the period. In reality, however, as far as religious poetry is concerned, the scepticism of the "new philosophy" was but a step towards the reaffirmation of the medieval synthesis of reason and faith as exemplified in the philosophy of St Thomas Aquinas.

---

[39] L. B. Campbell, *Divine Poetry and Drama in Sixteenth-Century England* (Berkeley/London, 1959), p. 5.

CHAPTER TWO

THE INDIAN BACKGROUND

The history of the development of bhakti poetry in several North Indian languages bears a striking resemblance to that of English religious verse, because of similarities in the social, religious, and linguistic forces that emerged in the Middle Ages both in the East and the West. In India and in Europe the metaphysical abstractions of the early medieval philosophers were challenged by the spirit which sought expression in the worship of a personal God through religious discipline and contemplation, or through a popular fervent devotion to a human manifestation of that God.

This spirit found a simpler and more wide-spread medium in the language of the masses than in the classical languages of antiquity: the vernaculars came to be extensively used both by scholars and popular preachers for evangelisation and religious reforms. As Latin hymns gradually gave way to translations, adaptations and original compositions in English, so Sanskrit and Prakrit were in time superseded by the Middle and Late Aryan *Apabhramsas*[1] and Old Hindi (among other vernaculars) which built up a corpus of religious verse evolving from Buddhist *caryagiti* ("mystic practice songs") [2] and the couplets and *padas* of the Nāth *yogīs* into the kind of verses composed by the *santa* poets of whom the most famous was Kabīr who appeared in the fifteenth century.

Some account of the history of the concept of bhakti, and the growth of theism in medieval India, is therefore a necessary preliminary to a discussion of Hindi bhakti poetry from the fourteenth to the seventeenth century. In the light of recent research such an account must take note both of Aryan and non-Aryan elements which contributed to the idea of bhakti or a loving devotion to the theistic Brahman. It used to be generally maintained that this idea was of Aryan origin since it could be traced as far back as the

---

[1] Sukumar Sen, *History of Bengali Literature* (New Delhi, 1960), pp. 27-36. Much of what is said in these pages applies, *mutatis mutandis*, to Hindi poetry as much as to Bengali poetry.

[2] *Op. cit.*, p. 27. Cf. Paraśurāma Caturvedī, *Mīrāṃ-Bāī kī Padāvalī* 7th ed. (Allahabad, 1956), pp. 248-255.

hymns of the *Ṛg-veda* and showed more clearly in the later Upaniṣads of the pre-Christian era. The probable subsequent influence upon the cult of bhakti of Islam and Christianity has also been suggested to account for strengthening of the monotheistic trait of bhakti in some quarters, and for the similarity of certain episodes in the Kṛṣṇa story and the biography of Hindu saints to the life of Jesus.[3]

But more recent research suggests that the earlier, non-Aryan Dravidian influence made a greater contribution to the cult of bhakti (to the Kṛṣṇa legend specifically and Vaiṣṇavism generally) than has been usually recognised by Western and Eastern students of Hinduism. Esoteric tantrism operated in Kṛṣṇa bhakti worship as it also did in Buddhist belief, practice and cryptic vocabulary. All these elements of the tantras were certainly incorporated, in some form or the other, into other theistic cults besides Vaiṣṇavism, for example, in Śaivism and Śaktism. The tantras are esoteric texts outside the strict scope of the Vedic teachings; and relate to the worship of such deities as Śiva, Viṣṇu and Śakti, all probably of Dravidian origin. They have a complex symbolism of letters, and employ, along with images, mystic diagrams called *yantra* or *cakra*. S. K. De says that "Tantra is a term which has been very loosely applied, and its later distorted forms have obscured its proper significance. Whether Buddhist, Vaiṣṇava, Śaiva or Śakta, it implied in its essence a mystic worship of Śakti or Female Energy, exalted in conjunction with Male Energy in the universe. Its origin is lost in obscurity, but it assumed various forms, and its doctrines spread not only to decadent Buddhism but also to the various sectarian systems of Hinduism." [4] The implication of all this is that the idea of Indian bhakti may not only be not entirely Aryan (or Semitic as some scholars have suggested); but that its origin may really be Dravidian, since the Indus Valley Civilisation has strong resemblances to Dravidian Culture and antedates the Aryan invasion of North India. An alternative theory is that there were two distinct sources of bhakti in India: one non-Aryan and the other Aryan which gradually merged into one.[5]

---

[3] Surendranāth Dāsgupta, *A History of Indian Philosophy*, (Cambridge, 1952), IV, 92-93.

[4] Sushil Kumar De, *The Early History of the Vaiṣṇava Faith and Movement in Bengal*, 2nd ed. (Calcutta, 1961), p. 27.

[5] Malik Mohammad, *Āḷvāra Bhaktoṃ kā Tāmil Prabandham aura Hindī Kṛṣṇa-Kāvya* [The Influence of the Tamil Poetry of the Alvar Saints on Hindi Kṛṣṇa Poetry] (Agra, 1964), p. 4.

Emotionally bhakti is not necessarily a uniquely Indian phenomenon.[6] However, it is certainly possible to trace some kind of a development of bhakti in Vedic literature. Before the ninth century, Hinduism had gone through the stages of Brahmanical sacerdotalism, philosophical speculation, and a belief in *avatāras* or incarnations of the theistic Brahman, that is, one of the three aspects of the Absolute Brahman: Brahmā, Viṣṇu, Śiva. Although these stages are regarded as broadly succeeding one another, there was naturally some overlapping of the stages. In the first of these, worship was a matter of sacrifice, rituals, and ceremonies prescribed by the *Brāhmaṇas* of the Vedas and expounded by the priests. The effective means of approaching Brahman, the Absolute, was therefore *karma-yoga* or the way of action. In the philosophical period which followed, the *Upaniṣads*[7] (the third and last division of the Vedas) laid emphasis on *jñāna-yoga* or approach to Brahman by the path of pure intellect, the goal being the realisation of the identity of the individual self with the Absolute Brahman: *tat tvam asi*—"That art thou". This identity, one of several doctrines in the *Upaniṣads*, represents the culmination of philosophical thought in the Vedas, and is variously referred to as *advaita* vedantism, monism, non-dualism. Perhaps the most brilliant exposition of *advaita* vedantism is that of the ninth century by Śankara who was writing his commentaries on the *Upaniṣads* about the same time that John Scotus Erigena was translating the Greek writings of the pseudo-Dionysius into Latin at the court of Charles the Bald.

The period of the *avatāras* or incarnations (roughly extending from 500 B.C. to A.D. 200) overlapped with the philosophical. It was now that the two great epics, the *Rāmāyaṇa* and the *Mahābhārata* were composed with Rāmacandra and Kṛṣṇa as their respective protagonists. They represent the seventh and eighth incarnations of Viṣṇu, the benevolent aspect of the Absolute Brahman. It was this period that saw, too, the emergence of rivals to orthodox Brahmanism in the form of Buddhism and Jainism which had no

---

[6] A. C. Bouquet, *Comparative Religion*, 6th ed. (London, 1962), p. 140. "Intellectually it [the rise of bhakti] is the natural consequence of the theistic trend in Indian thought, but emotionally it belongs to a zone of human aspiration which extended round the whole planet during the Middle Ages in Europe."

[7] M. Hiriyanna, *Outlines of Indian Philosophy* (London, 1958), p. 51. "Standing thus at the end of the Veda, the Upaniṣads came to be known as 'Vedānta' or 'end of the Veda'—much as the Metaphysics of Aristotle owed its designation to its being placed after Physics in his writings."

place in their systems for the worship of Vedic deities, belief in Brahman or any manifestations of its theistic aspect as incarnations.

In the face of opposition from these heretical systems, orthodox Hinduism (or Aryan Vedic religion as most Hindi scholars prefer to call it) had to make certain modifications, for example, the abolition of ritual animal sacrifice. But at the same time it reasserted the importance of the anthropomorphic Vedic pantheon, the worship of which now absorbed more and more tantric elements from local, indigenous cults, and, gradually assuming the Bhagavat form, culminated as Vaiṣṇavism. The *Purāṇas*,[8] composed at this period, played an important part in the resurgence of orthodoxy, and gave a new emphasis to theistic devotionalism in the age of Pauranic Bhakti from the first century B.C. to the beginning of the sixth century of the Christian era.[9] This bhakti took two forms: one in the tradition of *jñāna-yoga* was contemplative, the other in the tradition of *karma-yoga* was emotional; but both were theistic.

The external marks of the emotional bhakti were to be seen in the form of numerous shrines and temples which sprang up throughout India as centres of worship in which music, singing and dancing were important factors. The quiet, contemplative form of bhakti was based on the fact that the Brahman of the *Upaniṣads*[10] was

---

[8] Sarvepalli Radhakrishnan, *Indian Philosophy*, 2nd ed. (London, 1951), II, 663-64: "The Purāṇas are the religious poetry of the schools, representing through myth and story, symbol and parable, the traditional view of God and man, cosmogony and social order. They were composed with the purpose of undermining, if possible, the heretical doctrines of the times. They are eclectic in their character, mixing up philosophical doctrines with popular beliefs. . . .Their main object is to convey the lessons of ancient thinkers, especially those of the Vedānta and the Sāṁkhya. Their name indicates that they are intended to preserve ancient (purāṇa) traditions. They are theistic in character, and recognise the distinctions of matter, soul and God. The conception of *trimūrti* [Brahmā, Viṣṇu and Śiva] comes into prominence, though each Purāṇa is interested in emphasising one particular aspect. . ."

[9] Paraśurāma Caturvedī, *Uttarī Bhārata kī Santa Paramparā* [The Santa Tradition of North India] 2nd ed. (Allahabad, 1964), p. 24.

[10] The first mention of bhakti is in the *Śvetāśvatara Upaniṣad* 6, 23: Yasya deve parā bhaktir yathā deve tathā gurau, tasyaite kathitā hy arthāḥ, prakāśante mahātmanaḥ, prakāśante mahātmanaḥ.

R. E. Hume, *The Thirteen Principal Upanisads*, 2nd ed. (Oxford, 1954), p. 411, gives the following translation of the above:

To one who has the highest devotion (bhakti) for God,
And for his spiritual teacher (guru) even as for God,
To him these matters which have been declared
Become manifest [if he be] a great soul (mahātman)
Yea, become manifest [if he be] a great soul.

conceived both as *nirguṇa* (unconditioned), and as *saguṇa* (conditioned):

> *dve vāva brahmaṇo rūpe, mūrtaṁ caivāmūrtaṁ ca, martyaṁ cāmṛtaṁ ca, sthitaṁ ca, yac ca, sac ca, tyac ca.* (*Bṛhadāraṇyaka Upaniṣad* II. 3.1)

> Verily, there are two forms of *Brahman*, the formed and the formless, the mortal and the immortal, the unmoving and the moving, the actual (existent) and the true (being).[11]

> *tad ejati tan naijati tad dūre tad vad antike*
> *tad antarasya sarvasya tad u sarvasyāsya bāhyataḥ.*
> (*Īśa Upaniṣad* 5)

> It moves and It moves not; It is far and It is near;
> It is within all this and It is also outside all this.[12]

> *aṇor aṇīyān mahato mahīyān ātmā guhāyāṁ nihito'sya jantoḥ.*
> (*Śvetāśvatara Upaniṣad* III, 20.)

> Subtler than the subtle, greater than the great is the Self that is set in the cave of the (heart) of the creature.[13]

In short, Brahman is *sarva-rūpa*, that is, "having all forms", which includes the formless, the unconditioned, the unmanifested. In so far as Brahman may be experienced or apprehended by human feeling and thought, it may be said to be *saguṇa* (conditioned); but in its transcendence Brahman, because of the inadequacy of language, is said to be *nirguṇa*, without form and unconditioned. In the final analysis, the highest affirmation in language can paradoxically be but negative, as stated in the words of the classical expression of the third *Brāhmaṇa* of the second Adhyāya of the *Bṛhadāraṇyaka Upaniṣad*:

> *athāta ādeśo na iti na iti [neti], na hy etasmād iti, na ity anyat param asti.*

> Now therefore there is the teaching, not this, not this for there is nothing higher than this, that he is not this [*neti*].[14]

Thus it can be seen that it was quite possible in the Upanishadic period for the intellectual approach to take two different paths

---

[11] Sarvepalli Rādhākrishnan, *The Principal Upaniṣads*, (London, 1953) pp. 192-93.
[12] *Op. cit.*, p. 571.
[13] *Ibid.*, p. 730.
[14] *Ibid.*, p. 194.

leading to the same end: one that entirely ruled out the emotional and the other which combined the emotional with the intellectual. It was the latter path that Vedic bhakti followed; and it became the philosophical duty of the opponents of pure monism to justify their own qualified monism by showing that it was not dialectically unsound. This is what the four Vaiṣṇava schools of Rāmānuja, Nimbārka, Madhva and Viṣṇuswāmin attempted to do after the ninth century, when some followers of the absolute monism of Śankara by tending to substitute the mechanical *advaita* formula of identity with Brahman, *Tat tvam asi* ("That thou art"), ruled out the ardour of religious worship which Śankara himself had endorsed by observing the Vedic injunctions of ritual and ceremony, *smārta.*[15]

Today the concept of bhakti is not only regarded as dialectically sound by Hindu scholars, like Professor Siddheśwar Bhattacharya, but as reaching the peak of Hinduism in its ascent through *karma-yoga, jñāna-yoga* and *bhakti-yoga.*[16] During the Vedic period the emphasis lay on sacrifice, *karma-yoga,* that is, worship through the offering of one's material possessions. This gradually gave way to the idea of offering oneself by identification on the purely intellectual plane with the Cosmic Self, or Brahman, through the concentrated meditation of *jñāna-yoga.* In the earlier *Upaniṣads* the predominant concept of Brahman is a philosophical abstract, the Absolute Reality, larger than the largest in which the self of the sacrificer was merged and lost its identity. But in the later *Upaniṣads* there is also the concept of a personal God who is the manifestation of some aspect of the Absolute Brahman. This is more explicitly stated in the *Bhagavad-Gītā.*

Surrender to this theistic Brahman by bhakti or loving devotion is

---

[15] Rādhākrishṇan, *Indian Philosophy* II, 661-662.

"Though Śaṁkara did not mean by jñāna theoretical learning, there was a tendency among some of his disciples to make religion more an affair of the head than of the heart or will. . . The mechanical repetition of the formula "I am Brahman" is a sorry substitute for intelligent devotion. Hence the emphasis on bhakti by the theistic systems, including the four Vaiṣṇava schools. Despite doctrinal differences, these are all agreed in rejecting the conception of māyā, in regarding God as personal, and the soul as possessed of inalienable individuality, finding its true being not in an absorption in the Supreme but in fellowship with him."

Cf. Sushil Kumar De, *Early History of the Vaiṣṇava Faith and Movement in Bengal,* 2nd ed. (Calcutta, 1961), pp. 3-4.

[16] I gratefully acknowledge my indebtedness to Professor S. Bhattacharya of Banaras Hindu University for the help and inspiration I derived from him when I visited India in 1964.

not an act of annihilation; for in this loving surrender the individual soul sublimates itself: it is an act of infinite expansion of the individual. It is an act, not of self-extinction, but of self-expansion into the *puruṣottama* ("the supreme person") of Viṣṇu, incarnate as Śrī Kṛṣṇa of the *Mahābhārata* and Śrī Rāmacandra of the *Rāmāyaṇa*. Vaiṣṇava bhakti aims at the final and complete surrender of the devotee's "I" to Hari or Viṣṇu in the form of Kṛṣṇa and Rāma.

Dāsgupta has observed that "though the monotheistic speculations and the importance of the doctrine of devotion can be traced even to some of the *Ṛg-veda* hymns and the earlier religious literature such as the *Gītā* and the *Mahābhārata* and the *Viṣṇupurāṇa*, yet it is the traditional songs of the Āṛvārs and the later South Indian philosophical writers beginning with Yāmuna and Rāmānuja, that we find a special emphasis on our emotional relation with God. This emotional relation or *bhakti* differentiated itself in many forms in the experiences of various Vaiṣṇava authors and saints".[17]
The Āḻvārs were Tamil singers who flourished from about the middle of the seventh century to the middle of the ninth century.[18] Their lyrics were marked by a fervent devotion to Kṛṣṇa and were introduced into the worship of the Śrī-Vaiṣṇava temples of South India where the cult of Viṣṇu as practised in the North had been imported by Brahmin immigrants to the South.[19] The influence of the Āḻvārs repaid this debt by the inspiration their hymns gave to the Vaiṣṇava sects that spread to the North through the teachings of the disciples of Rāmānuja and other Tamil religious leaders of the next few centuries. The hymns of the Āḻvārs were probably one of the channels through which Vaiṣṇavism acquired its non-Vedic medieval quality of an excess of erotic emotionalism, and tantric associations. Later Buddhism which had spread to the South was also affected by the Dravidian environment, as it had already been affected by the Brahmanism of the North against which it had started as a reaction and subsequently lost the hold it had initially.[20]

[17] Surendranāth Dāsgupta, *A History of Indian Philosophy* (Cambridge, 1952), III, ix.

[18] *Ibid.*, p. 68.

[19] Śaivism, a rival of Vaiṣṇavism, was also wholly or partly an importation. They both faced the opposition of Buddhism and Jainism.

[20] Sarvepalli Rādhākrishnan, *Indian Philosophy*, 2nd ed. (London, 1951), II, 470-71: "It is said, not without truth, that Brahmanism killed Buddhism by a fraternal embrace. We have seen already how Brahmanism silently assimilated many Buddhist practices, condemned animal sacrifices, accepted Buddha as an avatār of Viṣṇu, and thus absorbed the best elements of the Buddhist faith. Though the accidents of its first

It was in this amalgam of orthodox Hinduism, later Buddhism and Jainism, and Dravidian influences that the Āḻvārs operated as a catalyst to give Vaiṣṇavism a form attractive to the various theistic sects of the Middle Ages. The *Bhāgavata Purāṇa* (c. A.D. 900), written in Sanskrit and translated into the vernaculars, owes a great deal of its attractive power to the intense emotionalism of the Āḻvārs. This book is the most sacred scripture and source book of the bhakti movement and vernacular bhakti poetry of the later Middle Ages. Farquhar writes of it in the following words:

> The *Bhāgavata* is really a great work. What distinguishes it from all earlier literature is its new theory of *bhakti*; and therein lies its true greatness. Some of its utterances on this subject are worthy of a place in the best literature of mysticism and devotion. . . .
>
> Bhakti in this work is a surging emotion which chokes the speech, makes the tears flow and the hair thrill with pleasureable excitement, and often leads to hysterical laughing and weeping by turns, to sudden fainting fits and to long trances of unconsciousness. We are told that it is produced by gazing at the images of Kṛishṇa, singing his praises, remembering him in meditation, keeping company with his devotees, touching their bodies, serving them lovingly, hearing them tell the mighty deeds of Kṛishṇa, and talking with them about his glory and his love. All this rouses the passionate bhakti which will lead to self-consecration to Kṛishṇa and life-long devotion to his service.[21]

Both Farquhar and Dāsgupta admit the influence of the Āḻvār poets on the *Bhāgavata Purāṇa*, but while noting similarities between the bhakti of the Āḻvārs and that of the *Bhāgavata*, Dāsgupta also notes an important difference:

> The spiritual love which finds expression in their songs is sometimes an earnest appeal of direct longing for union with Kṛṣṇa, or an expression of the pangs of separation, or a feeling of satisfaction, and enjoyment from union with Kṛṣṇa in a direct manner or sometimes through an emotional identification with the legendary personages associated with Kṛṣṇa's life. Even in the *Bhāgavata-purāṇa* (XI, XII) we hear of devotional intoxication through intense emotion, but we do not hear of

---

immediate form disappeared, Buddhism became, partly through Śaṁkara's influence, a vital force in the life of the country. Buddhism created in the region of thought a certain atmosphere from which no mind could escape, and it undoubtedly exercised a far-reaching influence on Śamkara's mind. An Indian tradition opposed to Śaṁkara holds that he is a Buddhist in disguise and his māyāvāda but crypto-Buddhism."

[21] J. N. Farquhar, *An Outline of the Religious Literature of India* (Oxford, 1920), pp. 229-30.

> any devotees identifying themselves with the legendary personages associated with the life of Kṛṣṇa and expressing their sentiment of love as proceeding out of such imaginary identification... The idea that the legend of Kṛṣṇa should have so much influence on the devotees as to infuse them with the characteristic spirits of legendary persons in such a manner as to transform their lives after their pattern is probably a new thing in the history of devotional development in any religion. With the Āṟvārs we notice for the first time the coming into prominence of an idea which achieved its culmination in the lives and literature of the devotees of the Gauḍīya school of Bengal, and particularly in the life of Caitanya [1486-1533].[22]

Apart from general observations of such scholars as Dāsgupta and S. K. De on the influence of the Āḻvārs on southern bhakti, there was for a long time no full and satisfactory treatment of what Farquhar described as the "fresh element" in the *Bhāgavata Purāṇa* which developed into the explosive, erotic emotionalism in the Kṛṣṇa school of bhakti, of which the Bengali Gauḍīya is the outstanding example. But recent works in Hindi, for example, those of Viśvambhara Nātha Upādhyāya and Malik Mohammad, give a fuller treatment of the subject which supports the theory that the Dravidian influence spread through pre-Vedic practices of indigenous cults, and that these were transmuted into the worship and compositions of the Āḻvārs during the early Middle Ages.[23]

In his preliminary chapters Viśvambhara Nātha Upādhyāya goes over much the same ground as that worked by European pioneer scholars of Vedic literature, in showing that pre-Dravidian and Dravidian cultures [24] account for the nature and characteristics of the demons and some of the gods of the Vedic pantheon; for the superstitions of the *Atharva Veda* involving the use of charms and mystic diagrams and formulas; and for tantric sexualism in the conception and worship of female and male energy as a primordial

---

[22] Surendranāth Dāsgupta, *A History of Indian Philosophy* (Cambridge, 1952), III, 81.

[23] Viśvambhara Nātha Upādhyāya, *Santa-Vaiṣṇava Kāvya para Tāntrika Prabhāva* [Tantric Influence on Santa-Vaiṣṇava Poetry] (Agra, 1962). Malik Mohammad, *Āḻvāra Bhaktoṃ kā Tāmila Pradandham aura Hindī Kṛṣṇa-Kāvya* (Agra, 1964). Cf. S. K. De, *op. cit.*, p. 12. "The Rādhā legend and the exuberant development of its erotic possibilities, which supplied inspiration alike to Jayadeva [12th century], Nimbārka [? 12th century] and writers of such late Purāṇas as the *Brahmavaivarta*, must be traced to a different and earlier unknown source."

[24] He has the advantage over them in being able to make use of references to the Indus Valley Civilisation to demonstrate some of his points.

force mystically integrated in the manifestations of the theistic Brahman. Then he proceeds to enumerate those characteristics of later Jainism and Buddhism which were obviously derived from or influenced by tantric practices, for example, mental and physical austerities, the use of esoteric formulas and *yantras*, and the belief in and the making of the images of *Tīrathkaras* and *Bodhisattvas*. He pursues the same lines in writing of Śaivism and Śaktism.

All the foregoing aspects of Hinduism, he attempts to show, in some degree contributed to the two schools of Hindi *nirguṇa* and *saguṇa* bhakti poetry: *Nirguṇa* poetry was specially influenced by the ideas and terminology of the *yoga* practices of Buddhist *bhaktas* and *siddhas*, and of the Nāth *yogīs; saguṇa* poetry by the demonstrative emotionalism and obviously sensual rites associated with debased tantric cults. The fact that Rādhā is not mentioned in the *Bhāgavata Purāṇa* seems to give some support to the author's theory that Rādhā was the female energy of the male Kṛṣṇa, and the hypothesis that her actualisation as a legendary figure in the Kṛṣṇa story is due to the tantric element in Vaiṣṇavism.

Whereas Viśvambhara Nātha Upādhyāya's contentions consist, on the whole, of a reassessment of old material with the addition of some passing observations on the Indus Valley Civilisation as corroborating the theory of pre-Vedic elements in Vaiṣṇavism, Malik Mohammad's search for prototypes of Rādhā and Kṛṣṇa is based on an examination of Tamil writings from the Sangha Period (c. 500 B.C.—200 B.C.) to the Bhakti Period of the South when the *Prabandham* of the Āḻvārs and the *Bhāgavata Purāṇa* (c. 900) were composed. In advancing his arguments he discounts the theory of Christian and Islamic influence on the bhakti of the Āḻvārs, maintaining that the concept of bhakti existed among the Dravidians before the advent of the Aryans into North India.[25]

Early Tamil literature speaks of a forest deity of the primitive Dravidians called by the various names of Mayona, Tirumāl and Kaṇṇan, who also appears in the songs of the Āḻvārs, and certainly bears a resemblance to Kṛṣṇa of Hindi *saguṇa* bhakti poetry. He is dark-hued like a rain-cloud and is specially worshipped as a youthful god like Bāla Kṛṣṇa; and as Kṛṣṇa sports with the milkmaidens of Vrindābana in North India, so Mayona sports with the pastoral tribe of the Tamil Ayars. According to Malik Mohammad and other South

[25] Malik Mohammad, *Āḻvāra Bhaktoṃ etc.*, p. 9.

Indian scholars Nappinnāi,[26] (in Tamil stories represented as an incarnation of Lakṣmī, consort of Viṣṇu), is probably the prototype of Rādhā. She appears in the hymns of the *Prabandham* as the beautiful favourite of Kṛṣṇa although she is not mentioned in the *Bhāgavata Purāṇa*. A reading of Hooper's translation [27] of the hymns of the Āḻvārs shows how closely "Kaṇṇan" or "Tirumāl" and "Nappinnāi" are associated in tone and imagery with the Kṛṣṇa legend. In the following verses the poet Nammāḻvār imagines the devotee as Nappinnāi, (the name literally means "the one with beautiful hair"—Hooper, p. 16), longing for Kaṇṇan or *tuḷasī*, i.e., Kṛṣṇa:

> Long may she love, this girl with luring locks,
> Who loves the feet that heavenly ones adore,
> The feet of Kaṇṇan, dark as rainy clouds:
> Her red eyes all abrim with tears of grief,
> Like darting Kayal fish in a deep pool. . .
>
> (Hooper, p. 61)

> Hot in this village now doth blow the breeze
> Whose nature coolness is. Hath he, this once,
> The rain-cloud hued, his sceptre turned aside
> To steal the love-glow from my lady, lorn
> For tuḷasī, with wide eyes raining tears?
>
> (Hooper, p. 63)

In a later stanza of this poem "the Āḻvār finds at last some who are directing their course to God and pleads with them not to forget the needs of others; he urges his own crying need as a first claim on them. He suggests that if his devotion brings no enjoyment of God, it will be better for his affection to be withdrawn, that so he may at least be free from the pain of unrequited love." [28]

> The flying swans and herons I did beg,
> Cringing: "Forget not, ye who first arrive,
> If ye behold my heart with Kaṇṇan there
> Oh, speak of me, and ask it 'Sir, nor yet
> Hast thou returned to her? And is it right?'
>
> (Hooper, p. 69)

---

[26] *Ibid., passim*. The author, in this well documented book, mentions several of these South Indian scholars.

[27] J. S. M. Hooper, *Hymns of the Āḻvārs*, "Heritage of India Series", (Calcutta, 1929).

[28] Hooper, *op. cit.*, p. 69.

In another of the *Prabandham* compositions the poetess Āṇḍāḷ takes upon herself the role of one of the *gopīs* or milkmaids who awakens Nappinnāi, the beloved of Kaṇṇan, to go with her and greet him at dawn.

Daughter of Nandagōpāl, who is like
A lusty elephant, who fleeth not,
With shoulders strong: Nappinnāi, thou with hair
Diffusing fragrance, open thou the door!
Come see how everywhere the cocks are crowing,
And in the *māthavi* bower the Kuyil sweet
Repeats its song.—Thou with a ball in hand,
Come, gaily open, with thy lotus hands
And tinkling bangles fair, that we may sing
Thy cousin's name! Ah, Ēlōrembāvāy!

Thou who art strong to make them brave in fight,
Going before the three and thirty gods,
Awake from out thy sleep! Thou who art just,
Thou who art mighty, thou, O faultless one,
Who burnest up thy foes, awake from sleep!
O Lady Nappinnāi, with tender breasts
Like unto little cups, with lips of red
And slender waist, Lakshmi, awake from sleep!
Proffer thy bridegroom fans and mirrors now,
And let us bathe! Ah, Ēlōrembāvāy! [29]

(Hooper, p. 55)

The songs and inspirational teachings of the Āḻvārs were directly responsible for the shaping of the philosophies of Yāmuna, Rāmānuja (b.1017) [30] and others who attempted to give the devotionalism or bhakti of the Āḻvārs a dialectical basis. And although there were differences of opinion, as regards the cardinal principles of religious faith, among these Aragiyas (the scholars influenced by the Āḻvārs) they were all opposed to the absolute monism of Śankara. The Ālvār approach to God by self-surrender or *prapatti* was acceptable to them all; but their interpretation and emphasis differed regarding the nature of God's grace, and the

[29] Hooper, *op. cit.*, p. 49, gives the following note: "The refrain at the end of each stanza, "Ēlōrambāvāy,' is of doubtful meaning, and is best left untranslated. Kingsbury and Phillips (*Hymns of the Tamil Śaivite Saints*, p. 101) also leave it untranslated, and suggest the meaning 'Receive and ponder what I say, O Lady.' Among other suggestions is 'Hail, O thou unique lady!' "

[30] The works of the Āḻvārs were collected together by the disciples of Rāmānuja at his special request. See Dāsgupta, *op. cit.*, p. 80.

obligations to or exemption from scriptural duty. "*Prapatti* is defined as a state of prayerfulness of mind to God, associated with the deep conviction that He alone is the saviour, and that there is no other way of attaining His grace except by such self-surrender. The devotee is extremely loyal to "*Nārāyana* [Viṣṇu] and prays to Him and no one else, and all his prayers are actuated by deep affection and no other motive. The virtue of *prapatti* involves within it universal charity, sympathy and friendliness even to the most determined enemy." [31]

This fundamental doctrine of love and salvation, spread throughout South India as well as in the Hindi-speaking areas of North India by Rāmānuja and his disciples, caught the imagination of the Hindu masses when India was suffering under Muslim domination. The Mussulman invaders having swept down from Afghanistan in the north-west towards the Punjab and Delhi, in time covered the entire Indo-Gangetic plains and even extended their rule southwards into Tamil country.

The intensity of the Muslim attacks dates from the establishment of the Ghazni sultanate in Afghanistan towards the end of the tenth century, when Maḥmūd of Ghazni began his incursions on the Rajput princes, sacking towns and looting the wealth of the temples which he rased to the ground. A magnificent temple in Mathurā, a city sacred to Kṛṣṇa, and the rich temple of Somnāth, on the sea-coast of Kathiawar, were among the objects of his depredations. After the death of Maḥmūd of Ghazni in 1030, the sultanate declined rapidly and Ghazni itself was destroyed by a rival Muslim conqueror, Mohammad Ghori who became the next scourge of Hindu India. By 1192 he had captured Ajmir, Delhi and Banaras, and laid the foundation of the sultanate of Delhi. In the next six or seven years the Muslim conquest was extended beyond Bihar as far as the Bay of Bengal. The sultanate of Delhi lasted from 1211 to 1524 about the time of Babur, the first of the great Mogul emperors.

During this period of three hundred years the country had seldom enjoyed peace and security because of warring factions among the Muslim rulers and threats of invasion from the north-west.[32] The Hindu populace besides experiencing the tyranny of foreign overlordship and the various calamities attendant on the political squabbles of the Muslim conquerors, were also victims of a bigoted

[31] Dāsgupta, *op. cit.*, p. 86.

[32] Timur-i-lang (Tamberlane) actually invaded India in 1398 and sacked Delhi.

monotheistic religion proselytizing both by argument and force. The militant Muslims, intolerant of images and pictorial representations associated with Hindu worship whether idolatrous or not, were ruthless in their iconoclasm and vandalism wherever they came upon shrines or temples dedicated to the incarnations of Viṣṇu as Rāma or Kṛṣṇa as well as to other figures of the Hindu pantheon. Nor had they any sympathy with the idea of "holy places" or pilgrimages to those places dear to the heart of millions of Hindus.

Yet Islam was not wholly destructive in its effect on Hinduism, if the theory is right that the severe example of Islamic monotheism helped to purge Vaiṣṇavism of some of its gross eroticism in the excesses of the Kṛṣṇa cults. It is suggested that the purer worship of the Rāma cult was probably due in part to the influence of Muslim preachers, more especially to the precepts and lives of the Ṣūfī ascetics and mystics who mingled with the Hindu people in the north from the Punjab to Bihar. Certainly Ṣūfism and the Ṣūfī poets had a decided influence on bhakti poetry in Hindi;[33] and it is therefore important to know what is implied by Ṣūfism.

In *A Literary History of Persia*, E. G. Browne states a number of theories about the origin of Ṣūfism: that it represents the esoteric doctrine of the Prophet Muhammad; that it is the reaction of the Aryan mind against a Semitic religion imposed upon it by force; that it has been influenced by neo-Platonism; and that it is of independent origin. The second is the most relevant for the present purpose.

> This theory has two forms, which may be briefly described as the Indian and the Persian. The former taking note of certain obvious resemblances which exist between the Ṣūfī doctrines in their more advanced forms and some of the Indian systems, notably the Vedānta Sāra, assumes that this similarity (which has, in my opinion, been exaggerated, and is rather superficial than fundamental) shows that these systems have a common origin, which must be sought in India... The other, or Persian, form of the 'Aryan Reaction theory' would regard Ṣūfism as an essentially Persian product.[34]

Whatever may be said for the various theories, there is no doubt that the early Ṣūfīs were Muslim mystics who attempted to reconcile their religious theory and practice with the teachings of the Prophet.

---

[33] See Saralā Śukla, *Jāyasī ke Paravarttī Hindī Ṣūfī Kavi aura Kāvya* [Hindi Ṣūfī Poets and Poetry after Jāyasī], (Lucknow, 1956).

[34] Edward G. Browne, *A Literary History of Persia* (London, 1919), p. 419.

However, by the end of the eighth century Ṣūfism had developed a strong element of loving devotion. Rābi'a, poetess and mystic of this period, could say, in dispensing with the Prophet as mediator between herself and the object of her devotion, "Apostle of God who does not love thee? but love of God hath so absorbed me that neither love nor hate of any other thing remains in my heart." [35] In her verses she employs the lover-beloved relationship to symbolise the human-divine communion. This subsequently became a convention in both Arabic and Persian poetry, but the asceticism of the early mystics was not always evident in the lives of many who posed as Ṣūfīs later.

It was in the ninth century that Ṣūfism attained its theosophic heights through the teaching of Bāyazīd Būsṭāmī (d. 875) whose concept of *fanā*,[36] annihilation of the human self through union with God in ecstasy, became the basis of a particular school of Ṣūfism. This found its extreme expression in the life and teaching of al-Ḥallāj whose mystical formula of the human-divine identity was "I am the Truth" (*ana'l-ḥaqq*).[37] Although al-Ḥallāj was condemned as a heretic and finally executed, the ultimate effect of "the monistic doctrines of Bāyazīd and al-Ḥallāj was to reinforce orthodox Islam by re-establishing the principle of Unity, on the basis of mystical experience, and thus to effect a rapprochement between the *Sharī'at* and the *Ṭarīqat* [the observance of scriptural duties and the way of meditation]." [38]

After the Muslim conquest of northern India in the twelfth century, several Ṣūfī orders were established in Kashmir, Sindh, Gujarat and Uttar Pradesh. Among the more influential were the Chishtī, Suhrawardī, Naqshbandī and Qādirī. Most of the Hindi Ṣūfī poets were of the Chishtī order which gave prominence to music and song in their worship. The founder of this order, Khwāja Chishtī, arrived in India in 1190 and made a pilgrimage to the tomb of an earlier Ṣūfī, al-Hujwīrī, in Lahore which had been a centre of Muslim influence since the time of Maḥmūd of Ghazni. Popularly known in India as Hazrat Dātā Ganj,[39] al-Hujwīrī was among the first Ṣūfīs to settle in India. He died sometime between 1063 and 1072.

---

[35] R. A. Nicholson, *A Literary History of the Arabs* (London, 1907) p. 234.
[36] This is reminscent of Buddhist *nirvāṇa*—see, Saralā Śukla, *op. cit.*
[37] Cf. the Vedānta formula, "I am Brahman".
[38] Yusuf Husain, *Glimpses of Medieval Indian Culture* (Bombay, 1959), p. 35.
[39] P. Caturvedī, *op. cit.*, p. 66.

In the introduction to his translation of al-Hujwīrī's *Kashf al-Maḥjūb*, R. A. Nicholson makes the following observations:

> ...al-Hujwīrī, like many Ṣūfīs before and after him, managed to reconcile his theology with an advanced type of mysticism, in which the theory of "annihilation" (*fanā*) holds a dominant place, but he scarcely goes to such extreme lengths as would justify us in calling him a pantheist. He strenuously resists and pronounces heretical the doctrine that human personality can be merged and extinguished in the being of God. He compares annihilation to burning by fire, which transmutes the quality of all things to its own quality, but leaves their essence unchanged. He agrees with his spiritual director, al-Khuttalī, in adopting the theory of Junayd that "sobriety" in the mystical acceptance of the term is preferable to "intoxication". He warns his readers often and emphatically that no Ṣūfīs, not even those who have attained the highest degree of holiness, are exempt from the obligation of obeying the religious law. In other points, such as the excitation of ecstasy by music and singing, and the use of erotic symbolism in poetry, his judgment is more or less cautious. He defends al-Ḥallāj from the charge of being a magician, and asserts that his sayings are pantheistic only in appearance, but condemns his doctrines as unsound. It is clear that he is anxious to represent Ṣūfism as the true interpretation of Islam, and it is equally certain that the interpretation is incompatible with the text. Notwithstanding the homage which he pays to the Prophet we cannot separate al-Hujwīrī, as regards the essential principles of his teaching, from his older and younger contemporaries, Abū Saʿīd b. Abi 'l-Khayr and 'Abdallah Anṣārī. These three mystics developed the distinctively Persian theosophy which is revealed in full-blown splendour by Farīd al-dīn 'Aṭṭār and Jalāl al-dīn Rūmī.[40]

Ṣūfism spread widely in the thirteenth and fourteenth centuries through the orders established in northern India, where they encountered the ideas of Rāmānujist theism. There was a spiritual kinship between the Ṣūfīs and the Rāmānujists, since the essence of their faiths was love and universal brotherhood. The Ṣūfīs, unlike militant Muslims, exercised tolerance and showed sympathy for their Hindu neighbours whose respect they won by their virtuous living. Thus Ṣūfism and Hindu theism came to influence each other more and more. It was in this milieu of religious interaction that they both found popular expression in the modern Indian languages through the work of preachers and poets.

---

[40] 'Alī b. 'Uthmān al-Jullābī al-Hujwīrī: *Kashf al-Maḥjūb* (The Oldest Persian treatise on Ṣūfism) trans. R. A. Nicholson (London, 1911), pp. xx-xxi.

In the fourteenth and fifteenth centuries Hindu theism in the form of Vaiṣṇavism was popularised in the Hindi-speaking area of Banaras by the Rāmānujist leader Rāghavānanda and his disciple Rāmānanda.[41] Both these religious leaders were Rāmānujists, but Rāmānanda was more liberal in his attitude to caste than his *guru* or Rāmānuja had been. Though he was a Sanskrit scholar well-versed in the vedānta *advaita* of Śankara, Rāmānanda preached the doctrine of bhakti in Hindi to the common people. During his extensive pilgrimages he must have come in contact with Islam and the liberal ideas of Ṣūfism, for on his return to Banaras he was no longer acceptable to the order to which he had belonged. He seems to have fallen foul of them because he criticised their rigid adherence to rituals in the matter of eating and drinking.[42] So Rāmānanda founded his own sect of Rāmavat, or the Rāmānandī sect as it is more popularly known, with Rāma and Sītā as the focus of devotion. To this he admitted as his disciples people of all castes and classes, the learned and the ignorant, the rich and the poor. One of these was the weaver, Kabīr, who became the honoured saint and poet of the fifteenth century.

In the poetry of Kabīr and that of the contemporary poets of the *Ādi Granth* of the Sikhs is to be seen the synthesis of the best from Islam and Hinduism. And so the long history in India of the human aspiration for establishing a meaningful relationship with the numinous by way of the intellect and the emotion, through paths as devious as those of the Vedantists, the Ṣūfīs, the Āḻvārs, and the various sects of Vaiṣṇavism, culminated in the vernacular poetry of bhakti.

---

[41] Rāmānanda's dates are most uncertain. I am inclined to accept a much later date than the thirteenth century usually quoted. See Baladeva Upādhyāya, *Bhāgavata Sampradāya* (Banaras, 1953), pp. 248- 253, for arguments in favour of the fifteenth century.

[42] See P. Caturvedī, *op. cit.*, p. 225.

CHAPTER THREE

RELIGIOUS PRACTICE AND POETIC EXPRESSION

As indicated in the preceding chapters, medieval philosophy and theology in the West and the East were concerned with two kinds of experience: one associated with the intellectual exploration of and identity with the unconditioned Absolute, the other with the spiritual endeavour to effect a union of the human and the divine or the conditioned Absolute. Dr. Radhakrishnan has observed that "the central problem of Christian Platonism or any mystic religion is the reconciliation of the two presentations of the Supreme, the Absolute One without distinctions and attributes, and the personal God who knows, loves and freely chooses." [1] This reconciliation may be accepted as the philosophical or theological problem; but mysticism itself is the spiritual experience which poses the problem for intellectual analysis.

Professor Zaehner has described mysticism as 'the realisation of a union or a unity with or in (or of) something that is enormously, if not infinitely, greater than the empirical self.' [2] In the emotive definition of Miss Underhill, "It is the name of that organic process which involves the perfect consummation of the Love of God: the achievement here and now of the immortal heritage of man. Or, if you like it better—for this means exactly the same thing—it is the art of establishing his conscious relation with the Absolute." [3] It will be noticed that whereas Zaehner attempts a general definition of mysticism as either a *union* or a *unity*, Miss Underhill defines it as a process or art with but one end in view, her basic assumption being that "the perfect consummation of the Love of God" and a "conscious relation with the Absolute" are identical and the only aim of mysticism.

Zaehner's definition allows, but Miss Underhill's does not, for different types of mysticism. According to Dāsgupta there are several kinds of Hindu mysticism corresponding to the *karma, jñāna*, and *bhakti yoga* mentioned in the last chapter, as well as the Buddhist

[1] Rādhākrishnan, *Eastern Religions and Western Thought* (London, 1940), p. 241.
[2] R. C. Zaehner, *Hindu and Muslim Mysticism* (London, 1960), p. 5.
[3] Evelyn Underhill, *Mysticism* (London, 1960), p. 81.

type of *Nirvāṇa.*[4] However, these may all be logically reduced to the two main categories of the intellectual and the emotional employing varying spiritual disciplines which aim at either an identity or unity with the formless, unconditioned Absolute, or a union with the conditioned Absolute as a loving God manifested in the unique incarnation of Jesus Christ or in the many *avatāras* of Viṣṇu und Śiva. It is important to bear these two forms of mysticism in mind when studying Hindi bhakti poetry, because they form the groundwork of the *saguṇa mārga* associated with the principal *avatāras*, Rāma and Kṛṣṇa; and the *nirguṇa mārga* which deals with the unconditioned Absolute.

The mystical art or process varies with the goal of the mystic. When it is the unconditioned Absolute, the way of the mystic is the *via negativa* of the pseudo-Dionysius, the *Cloud of Unknowing*, and the *neti* of the Vedānta. The mind must be emptied of all conceptions of the Absolute as having qualities or attributes—the analogies for the desired end of unity with the Absolute must employ the language of men, but it eschews the more concrete associations of mundane affairs such as historical or legendary persons, places and events. When the focus is the conditioned Absolute manifested as a loving God, the aim of the mystic is union with an incarnation as Jesus, Rāma, or Kṛṣṇa through the mind dwelling on the scriptural or legendary accounts associated with these incarnations.

The spiritual exercises of saint and ascetic in the religious orders of medieval Europe had developed gradually through the centuries from the precepts and practices of the early Fathers of the Church. But under the influence of such mystics of the twelfth century as the Augustinian Richard of St Victor, and the Benedictine St Bernard of Clairvaux, there was a conscious effort to systematise both the theory and practice of mysticism. This effort was considerably helped by the scholastic eagerness to exploit the possibilities of the basic Areopagite tenet of "hierarchy", which reinforced and deepened the Platonic conception of stages in the climb to perfection. And so the mystic's progress through conversion or the awakening of the self, purification, illumination, and union came to be accepted in Western mysticism as the standard description of the mystic way that ends in the unitive life. But within the framework of this standard description "the Benedictine mystics of the twelfth century in their writings

[4] See Dāsgupta, *Hindu Mysticism* (Chicago/London, 1927; New York, 1959).

divide and subdivide the stages of contemplation, the states of the soul, the degrees of Divine Love: and perform terrible *tours de force* in the course of compelling the ever-variable experiences of man's spiritual vitality to fall into orderly and parallel series, conformable to the mystic numbers of Seven, Four, and Three." [5]

The theories of the codifiers stimulated various methods of devotion which became the subject of numerous manuals for the devout life during the later Middle Ages and the Renaissance. One of the most famous, composed in 1521-1541 and printed with Papal approval in 1548, was the *Spiritual Exercises* of St. Ignatius Loyola which had a tremendous influence on English Jesuits during the Counter Reformation. This and other continental manuals were translated into English during the second half of the sixteenth century. And after the opening of the seventeenth century new treatises on meditation began to appear "by the scores and by the hundreds." [6] Henry Vaughan in *The Mount of Olives of Solitary Devotions* (1625) addressing the "pious reader" wrote:

> I know the world abounds with these Manuals, and triumphs over them...
>
> It is for thy good, and for his glory, who in the days of his flesh prayed here himself, and both taught and commanded us to pray, that I have published this." [7]

As much English devotional poetry was influenced both in form and content by these manuals of devotion, it might be useful to bear in mind the main features of these works which can best be illustrated by reference to Loyola's *Spiritual Exercises*. The work is designed as a series of devotions for a period of four weeks corresponding broadly to the four stages in the mystic's progress, but the exercises are capable of being expanded or condensed for longer or shorter periods according to the needs of the persons using them. The meditation is one of the important religious exercises to which St. Ignatius gave a definite pattern which Dr. Helen Gardner describes in the following words:

> A meditation on the Ignatian pattern, employing the 'three powers of the soul', consists of a brief preparatory prayer, two 'preludes', a varying

[5] Underhill, *op. cit.*, p. 459.
[6] Martz, *The Poetry of Meditation*, p. 5.
[7] *The Works of Henry Vaughan*, ed. L. C. Martin (London, 1957), p. 140.

> number of points, and a colloquy. The preparatory prayer is 'to ask God our Lord for grace that all my intentions, actions and operations may be ordered purely to the service and praise of His divine Majesty'. The first prelude is what is called the *compositio loci*: the seeing 'with the eyes of the imagination' either a place 'such as the Temple or the Mountain where Jesus Christ is found', or, if the meditation is of an invisible thing such as sin, a situation: 'that my soul is imprisoned in this corruptible body, and my whole compound self in this vale [of misery] as in exile amongst brute beasts.' The second prelude is a petition 'according to the subject matter'; thus, if the meditation is of the Passion, the petition will be for 'sorrow, tears, and fellowship with Christ in his sufferings'; if the meditation is of sin, the petition will be for 'shame'. The meditation proper follows, divided into points, usually three or five. Lastly, the memory, the storehouse of images, having been engaged in the preludes, and the reason in the points, the third power of the soul, the will, is employed in the colloquy, which is a free outpouring of the devotion aroused.[8]

Turning to India, one finds that there was a similar activity of systematising and codifying of devotional practice and sentiments in the Vaiṣṇava sects of the sixteenth century. The codifiers were obviously influenced and guided by Vedic and Puranic scripture; the exegeses of theistic philosophers like Rāmānuja, Madhva, Nimbārka, and Vallabhācārya; by the devotionalism of the medieval Āḻvārs, the discipline of Buddhist *siddhas*, Nāth *yogīs*; and finally by the fifteenth- and sixteenth-century Vaiṣṇava mystics, especially Caitanya of Bengal (1486-1533) who was a devotee of Kṛṣṇa.

It was in the sixteenth century that the six Goswāmins of the Caitanya sect built up the "modern Vṛndāvana [associated with Kṛṣṇa] as the chief intellectual and religious centre of the sect, where its philosophy, its theology, its ritualism and its Rasa-Śāstra were created. They reclaimed the sacred sites, identified them, and gave to each a distinctive name; they made their wealthy disciples and admirers build the great temples, groves and bathing places, and thus laid the foundations of its modern glory and sanctity."[9] These Goswāmins through their scholarly writings in Sanskrit provided a codification of the sentiment and emotions of bhakti, and thus helped to systematise the theory and practice of Vaiṣṇava devotionalism.

There are five bhakti *bhāvas* or states of emotional experience in the devotional life. The different *bhāvas* result from the specific method of approach adopted by the devotee for achieving his goal of

---

[8] Helen Gardner, *John Donne, The Divine Poems* (Oxford, 1952), pp. l-li.

[9] De, *The Early History of the Vaiṣṇava Faith*, p. 118.

union with the Divine, rather than from a stage reached in his spiritual life. Therefore he may or he may not experience these various states or *bhāvas* as stages in the manner of a spiritual progress, for any one *bhāva* is capable of establishing a union which may satisfy his longings.

Dāsya bhāva is that experienced in a master-servant relationship in which the devotee, though conscious of his own utter unworthiness, dedicates himself in complete self-denial to the service of Hari (Viṣṇu) in the form of Rāma or Kṛṣṇa. *Sākhya bhāva* springs from the establishment of a bond of friendship between the *avatāra* and the devotee. *Vātsalya bhāva* is realised through the tender affection a devotee experiences in a parent-child relationship with the *avatāra* as infant or child. *Mādhurya bhāva* is achieved through love consummated in the lover-beloved union of *avatāra* and devotee, as exemplified in the union of Kṛṣṇa and Rādhā. *Śānta bhāva* is the result of perfect peace experienced in the mystic union, which is not admitted by all commentators as a bhakti *bhāva* if it is interpreted to mean identity with the Absolute and annihilation of the devotee's individuality.

The main tenets of Vaiṣṇava bhakti may be briefly outlined in the following points:

1. Bhakti is not possible without the grace of God.
2. Bhakti, as loving devotion to Rāma or Kṛṣṇa, is the only means of union with God.
3. Bhakti is both the means and the end, that is to say, the human soul experiences the bliss of complete surrender of Self to God without the expectation of God's love in return.
4. Bhakti does not mean identification with the Absolute; so the individuality of the human soul is never lost.
5. Bhakti aims at salvation from re-incarnation, due to *karma*, in order to establish an eternal union with God.[10]

Since Vaiṣṇava bhakti poetry is naturally replete with allusions to incidents and characters of the epics and *Purāṇas*, it is necessary to give an outline of the Rāma and Kṛṣṇa legends before discussing specific English poems with analogies from Hindi. It is also essential to bear in mind that Vaiṣṇavism believes in the necessity for

---

[10] Most of these points have been summarised from Baladeva Upādhyāya, *Bhāgavata Sampradāya* (Banaras, 1953), pp. 618-19.

successive incarnations of the Supreme Being unlike the unique revelation of Himself as man in Jesus Christ. Kṛṣṇa in the *Bhagavad-Gītā* addresses Arjuna (Bhārata) in these words:

> Whenever righteousness declines, O Bhārata,
> and unrighteousness uprises, then I create Myself,
> For the protection of the good and destruction of the wicked, and to confirm the right I am born from age to age.
>
> *Yadā yadā hi dharmasya glānir bhavati bhārata*
> *abhyutthānam adharmasya tadā' tmānam sṛjāmy aham.*
> *Paritrāṇāya sādhūnām vināśāya ca duṣkṛtām,*
> *dharma samsthāpanārthāya sambhavāmi yuge yuge.*
> (*Bhagavad-Gītā* 4: 7-8).

It is not therefore surprising to find that in some lyrics the names of Kṛṣṇa and Rāma are used interchangeably for Hari or Viṣṇu. Rāma and Kṛṣṇa are the seventh and eighth *avatāras* of a series of ten principal incarnations of Viṣṇu. Rāma was born as one of the sons of Daśaratha, King of Ayodhyā, to relieve the distress of the righteous who were being oppressed by the demon Rāvaṇa and others. The Sanskrit *Rāmāyaṇa* inspired several vernacular adaptations and translations. "It is noteworthy," says Professor Wilson, "that the Rāma legends have always retained their purity, and unlike those of Brahmā, Kṛishṇa, Śiva and Durgā, have never been mixed up with indecencies and licentiousness." [11]

The late sixteenth-century Hindi epic of Tulasī Dāsa (? 1532-1623) entitled *Rāma-carita-mānasa*, "The Holy Lake of Rāma's Deeds", has indeed a lofty ethical and philosophical tone. It is at no point erotic like the Kṛṣṇa story, nor does it in any way offend conventional Hindu good taste whether judged from the religious or literary point of view. The Rāma cult of North India was influenced by the philosophy of Rāmānuja and his disciples. It was popularised in Banaras by Rāmānanda and spread into the surrounding country. Tulasī Dāsa was a devotee of Rāma having gained his religious initiation and instruction from his *guru*, or spiritual preceptor, who was a Rāmānandī *sādhū*.

The narrative of the *Rāma-carita-mānasa* deals with Rāma's earthly mission to uphold righteousness and put down wickedness in every shape or form—human or demonic. It traces the history of Rāma's

---

[11] John Dowson, *A Classical Dictionary of Hindu Mythology, etc.*, (London, 1928), p. 260.

childhood, youth, marriage to Sītā or Jānakī (daughter of King Janaka of Mithilā), his fourteen-year exile in the wilds and forests of India when he was accompanied by Sītā and Lakṣmaṇa (one of his three brothers), and the many vicissitudes and adventures they experienced before returning to the royal court at Ayodhyā. During the period of exile, Sītā had been abducted by Rāvaṇa, the demon king of Lankā, and rescued by the forces of Rāma after the final great battle in which Rāvaṇa was slain by Rāma. Hanumān, the monkey-god and faithful servant of Rāma, played an important part alongside Lakṣmaṇa, throughout the final episodes dealing with the invasion and sack of Lankā, the ancient name of the modern Ceylon.

There are in this poem frequent disquisitions on *advaitavāda* (Vedantic monism) and the concept of *neti*, side by side with rapturous adoration of the beauty, love and grace of Rāma, son of Daśaratha. But Tulasī Dāsa's apparent mingling of the streams of *nirguṇa* and *saguṇa* bhakti was probably intended to gain maximum acceptance for his *Rāma-bhakti* among the orthodox, who saw no inconsistency in co-ordinating *smārta* Hinduism with *advaita* philosophy. At the same time, this frequent reminder in *Rāma-bhakti* of the divinity of the *avatāra*, inspiring in his devotees a life of true virtue, may have helped to create a counterweight in North India to the excesses of *Kṛṣṇa-bhakti*.

The earliest mention of Kṛṣṇa is in the *Chandogya Upaniṣad*, but he does not achieve eminence as the incarnation of Viṣṇu until the composition of the *Mahābhārata*. In a famous episode of that epic he instructs Arjuna on the battlefield in the words of the *Bhagavad-Gītā*, ("Song of the Lord") declaring himself to be the Supreme Being who may be approached by many paths:

> As men approach me so do I accept them;
> men on all sides follow my path, O Pārtha [Arjuna].
>
> *ye yathā māṁ prapadyante tāṁs tathai'va bhajāmy aham*
> *mama vartmā 'nuvartante manuṣyāḥ pārtha sarvaśaḥ*
> (*Bhagavad-Gītā* 4:11)
>
> Whatever form any devotee desires with faith to worship,
> I make that very faith of his steady.
>
> *yo-yo yāṁ-yāṁ tanuṁ bhaktaḥ śraddhayā 'ṛcitum icchati*
> *tasya-tasyā 'calām śraddhām tām eva vidadhāmy aham.*
> (*Ibid.*, 7:21)

But the scriptural authority and the inspiration for the popular conception of Kṛṣṇa, the *avatāra*, and the practice of his cult throughout India, is the *Bhāgavata Purāṇa*. It relates in detail the miraculous birth of Kṛṣṇa and his preservation from the wiles of the wicked Kaṃs (who in an attempt to ensure Kṛṣṇa's death massacred the innocents); his being brought up by his foster parents Nanda [12] and Yaśodā among the pastoral folk of Vraja around Vrindābana on the banks of the Jumna river; his loveliness as a child and his exploits from an early age in destroying demons, his youthful escapades and amorous dallyings—all of which endeared him to the rustic folk.

He is represented as the lover of the *gopīs* or milkmaidens, one of his favourite pastimes being the *rāsa-līlā*, or circular dance by moonlight with them, when by his divine illusion he made himself into as many Kṛṣṇas as there were *gopīs*. Kṛṣṇa married numerous *gopīs* but one was his special favourite. She is not mentioned by name in the *Bhāgavata Purāṇa* but later became known as the fair Rādhā, daughter of Nanda.

Kṛṣṇa is usually represented in art as playing upon his flute, the divine music of which charms all hearers. The story of Kṛṣṇa, especially the tenth chapter of the *Bhāgavata Purāṇa* which is most often translated into the vernaculars, is permeated with the erotic emotions of the *gopīs* and Rādhā pining in separation from Kṛṣṇa, rapturously gazing upon his beauty, entranced by his music, or enjoying his favours in the groves and bowers of Vrindābana, the earthly paradise of the Vaiṣṇavas. This is also the subject-matter of a celebrated Sanskrit poem of the twelfth century, Jayadeva's *Gītagovinda*, which has had a great influence on vernacular bhakti poetry. The sensuousness of this work is so marked that it has been difficult to convince the western mind of its mystical quality.[13] A. Berriedale Keith writes:

> Efforts have been made to establish that the poem has a mystical significance and to interpret it in this sense. The desire in part at least has been prompted by the feeling that the loves of Kṛṣṇa and Rādhā are too essentially of the body rather than of the mind, and that to ascribe them to the divinity is unworthy. But this is to misunderstand Indian

---

[12] Hence the frequent use in bhakti poetry of the popular appellation *Nandalāla*, "darling son of Nanda". Some other names of Kṛṣṇa are Kanha (Kanhai), Śyāma, Govinda, Giridhara, Mohana, Mādhava, Keśava.

[13] See, for example, Joseph Campbell, *Masks of Gold* (London, 1962).

> feeling. The classical poets one and all see no harm in the love-adventures of the greatest deities, and what Kālidāsa did in the *Kumārasambhava* was repeated by all his successors in one form or another. But, on the other hand, it must not be forgotten that the religion of Jayadeva was the fervent Kṛṣṇa worship which found in the god the power which is ever concerned with all the wishes, the hopes and fears of men, which, if in essence infinite and ineffable, yet expresses itself in the form of Kṛṣṇa, and which sanctions in his amours the loves of mankind.[14]

Winternitz writes:

> It is a fact that, soon after they were composed Jayadeva's songs were sung as an accompaniment to dances in temples and at religious festivals too. For though we can scarcely agree with those commentators who wish to impute a mystical meaning to some of the erotic verses—the love of the human soul (Rādhā) for God Kṛṣṇa—it is certain, nevertheless, that the poem has a religious character, and that to the poet the whole eroticism of the poem is never more than a part of Bhakti, the religious devotion to the God Kṛṣṇa.[15]

There are striking analogies between English and Hindi religious poetry mainly owing to the fact that the subject matter and sentiments of devotional lyrics and narrative poems are intimately related to the scriptures of Christianity and Hinduism which have certain similarities. English religious verse is chiefly inspired by and derives its material from the Bible, the Apocrypha, and the legends of saints' lives. The subject matter of Hindi bhakti verse is largely related to Vaiṣṇava narratives and legends centring round Rāma and Kṛṣṇa, the seventh and eighth *avatāras* of Viṣṇu. In all these narrative sources, English and Hindi, miracles and other unusual occurences, like trances and visions, figure prominently. Medieval interest and belief in such subjects were common to both the European and Indian temperaments; but whereas the establishment, more or less, of a canon of Holy Scriptures for the Christian Church tended to eliminate many apocryphal accounts from general circulation and acceptance in Europe by the end of the sixteenth century, in India all the extraordinary episodes connected with Rāma and Kṛṣṇa, as related in the Sanskrit epics and *Purāṇas* and reproduced or adapted in Hindi and other vernaculars, continue to be accepted by Vaiṣṇava

---

[14] A. Berriedale Keith, *A History of Sanskrit Literature* (London, 1953), p. 194.

[15] M. Winternitz, *A History of Indian Literature* [trans. from the original German] (Calcutta, 1959), III, 137. In a footnote he adds that as late as Sir William Jones [1746-1794] the *Gītagovinda* was danced and sung at an annual festival.

devotees whether laymen or poet-preachers. Even the most sophisticated believers have no desire to suppress the incredible or highly erotic portions, though they may themselves be inclined to interpret these symbolically rather than accept them as authentic records of historical events.

It is therefore interesting to observe that the apocryphal gospels of the Middle Ages bear many resemblances to Vaiṣṇava literature, especially those portions dealing with the infancy of Kṛṣṇa, the physical charm of his person, and the mystic experiences of Vaiṣṇava saints. The best known of the latter in Hindi are recounted in the prose biographical works on the *Aṣṭachāpa*—eight celebrated Kṛṣṇa devotees of the sixteenth and seventeenth centuries—, and in the descriptive and critical catalogue in verse of Nābhā Dāsa called the *Bhakta Māla* or "The Garland of Saints". The biographies dealing with the *Aṣṭachāpa* recreate the atmosphere of intense devotion in which they experienced the unusual trances and visions common to Eastern and Western mystics. In addition, they contain authentic specimens of the songs composed by some of these poet-saints, Sūra Dāsa (1475-1583) being one of the most distinguished.

The *Aṣṭachāpa* narratives and the *Bhakta Māla* may be regarded as the Hindi counterpart of the Latin *Legenda Aurea* of Jacobus de Voragine (1230-1298) which was the source book for European vernacular works in medieval prose and verse. It is a curious fact that the pseudo gospels, on which Jacobus de Voragine drew, originated mostly in the East, and more specifically in the Syrian Church, during the first six centuries. This was the same period that tradition maintains the Christian Church was established in South-West India. This Church had affiliations with the Eastern Syrian Church and later with the Nestorians in Persia.[16] There has been much debate on the possible influence of Christianity on theistic Hinduism;[17] but it does not seem to have occurred to the critics that Vaiṣṇava legends may have had some share in shaping the Christian apocryphal literature that came into being through the Eastern Syrian Church. However, the significant point in the present context is the fact that both Eastern and Western scholars have been struck by the resemblance between Hindu and Christian devotionalism.

The *Legenda Aurea*, composed about 1260 to 1270, incorporated

---

[16] Bouquet, *Comparative Religion*, pp. 136-137.

[17] Dāsgupta, *A History of Indian Philosophy*, IV, 92-93. Dāsgupta discusses this topic, and disposes of the theory of Christian influence.

most of the pseudo gospels as well as a great collection of legends of Christian saints and martyrs. It was intended to meet a demand for a cycle of pieces to be used during the festivals of the Church Year, and became immediately popular, being regarded by many Christians as authentic although the apocryphal gospels had been objected to by such Church Fathers as St. Jerome and St. Augustine, and condemned in the fifth century by Popes Innocent I and Galasius. However, the *Legenda Aurea*, continued for centuries to provide writers, both in Latin and the vernaculars, with material for religious compositions. J. E. Wells lists among works that made use of the *Legenda*, the Scottish Legendary, Mirk's *Festial*, the smaller Vernon Collection, and Osbern Bokenam's *Lives of Saints*; and he adds that writers of innumerable single pieces of various types drew from it.[18] The *Legenda Aurea* also influenced medieval *drama*, especially the *Ludus Coventriae* which is outside the scope of the present study.

Another well known work incorporating legendary matter is the Middle English *Cursor Mundi* or *Cursor o' the world.* This is a fourteenth-century composition in verse of almost 3,000 lines, consisting of a prologue and seven parts, divided according to the Seven Ages of the World. There are four appendices and further additions. Along with the biblical episodes of the Old and New Testament canonical books, there are numerous apocryphal ones among which are miracles performed by the boy Jesus even as Kṛṣṇa performed wonders while still a child. Another point of similarity is the physical charm of Jesus, not only as a baby, but as a man drawn as though from life, as Hindi *Saguṇa* poets, especially Sūra Dāsa and Tulasī Dāsa, describe the beauty of Kṛṣṇa and Rāma.

The Cotton MSS of the *Cursor Mundi* give the following description:

Of heght he was meteli man,
Efter that the men war than,
Nother to gret, ne right to small,
And wonder semli was wit-al;
His cher was dredful on to loke,
And lufsum als-sua sais the boke;
His hare like to the nute brun,
Quen it for ripnes fals dun,
Apon his sculdres ligand wele,

[18] J. E. Wells, *A Manual of the Writings in Middle English*, (New Haven, 1926), pp. 306-307.

Bi his eres skailand sumdele,
In hefd he had a clift be-forn,
Als nazarens has that thar er born.
His for-hed [fair], wemless to sight,
Wit-vten ani runkel slight,
His vice sumdel wit rede was blend;
On nese and muth was noght at mend,
Forked fair the chin he bare
And tender berd wit mikel hare.
Berd and hefd of a heu ware,
Nute brun als i tald yow are.
Metli har was on his chin,
And als his hefd was scheud in tuin.
Stedfast his lok and simple ai,
His eien clere, and sumdel grai;
Clerli spak he that he wald,
And al his skil wiseli he tald.[19]

It may have been such a description as the one just quoted that Gerard Manley Hopkins had in mind when he wrote in his sermon "for Sunday Evening Nov. 23, 1879 at Bedford Leigh [near Manchester]".

> There met in Jesus Christ all things that can make man lovely and loveable. In his body he was most beautiful. This is known first by the tradition in the Church that it was so and by holy writers agreeing to suit those words to him. Thou art beautiful in mould above the sons of men: we have even accounts of him written in early times. They tell us that he was moderately tall, well built and tender in frame, his features straight and beautiful, his hair inclining to auburn, parted in the midst, curling and clustering about the ears and neck as the leaves of a filbert, so they speak, upon the nut. He wore also a forked beard and this as well as the locks upon his head were never touched by razor or shears; neither, his health being perfect, could a hair ever fall to the ground. The account I have been quoting (it is from memory, for I cannot now lay my hand upon it) we do not indeed for certain know to be correct, but it has been current in the Church and many generations have drawn our Lord accordingly either in their own minds or in his images.[20]

The earthly existence of Viṣṇu incarnated as the *puruṣottama* or "supreme person" in Kṛṣṇa or Rāma is the principal subject of the

[19] R. Morris, ed. *Cursor Mundi* E. E. T. S., o.s. 62 (London, 1876) pt 3, pp. 1078-80, lines 18827-52.

[20] Gerard Manley Hopkins, *The Sermons and Devotional Writings*, ed. C. Devlin (London, 1959), p. 35.

Vaiṣṇava's praise and meditation, just as the life of Jesus is that of Christian worship and devotion. And as the Christian Year evokes in the imagination of believers the entire Gospel story with its associations of persons, places and incidents in the Holy Land of Palestine; so the Kṛṣṇa or Rāma story is recreated for the Vaiṣṇavas by daily rituals, seasonal festivals and yearly pilgrimages to Vrindābana, Mathurā, Ayodhyā and other sacred places and shrines, especially those in North India, associated with the *avatāras.*[21]

The daily rituals of Kṛṣṇa worship at Vrindābana are organised into eight periods, the *aṣṭa-yāma,* [22] which may be considered analogous to the offices of the hours of Christian worship. The purpose of the *aṣṭa-yāma pūjā* (worship) is to bring the Vaiṣṇava devotee into close physical and mental association with the incarnate Viṣṇu or Hari in the form of Kṛṣṇa whose image is the focus of loving attention from dawn to night. The eight periods are generally described as follows:

1. 5 a.m. to 7 a.m. *mangala-āratī*: a solemn and auspicious waving of lights and burning of incense before the image of Kṛṣṇa.
2 7 a.m. to 8 a.m. *śṛngāra*: bathing and decorating the image.
3. 8 a.m. to 10 a.m. *gvāla* or *gopāla*: taking the image into the groves as though Kṛṣṇa, the cowherd (*gopāla*), were out minding the cows in the fields.
4. 10 a.m. to noon, *rāja-bhoga*: offering choicest foods to the image of Kṛṣṇa at his lunch hour; after which there is a general siesta when the ritual activities in the temples and shrines are completely stopped until the next period.
5. 3 p.m. *utthāpana*: waking the image from the siesta.
6. 5 p.m. *bhoga*: offering of refreshment.
7. 6 p.m. *sandhyā-āratī*: the twilight or evening waving of lights.
8. 7 p.m. to 8 p.m. *śayana*: putting the image to bed for the night.

These offices are accompanied by the ringing of bells, blowing of conches, and the singing of hymns in the various moods appropriate to the prevailing atmosphere of the different periods of the *aṣṭa-yāma.* Sūra Dāsa and the other poets of the *Aṣṭachāpa* composed many of their songs especially for these offices, and themselves joined in the worship of songs called *kīrtana.* Sūra Dāsa, because of his saintly

[21] There is still in India a wide-spread belief in the efficacy of pilgrimages.

[22] See Muṃśirāma Śarmā, *Bhakti kā Vikāśa* [The Development of Bhakti] (Banaras, 1958), p. 667.

character and his accomplishment in music and singing, was given the special responsibility of organising the hymns for the *aṣṭa-yāma* worship in the Śrī Nātha temple at Govardhana founded by his *guru* or spiritual master, Vallabhācārya, who was one of the greatest of Vaiṣṇava scholars. Himself a profound philosopher, Vallabhācārya did not advocate among his followers the intellectual approach to the unconditioned Absolute, but rather inculcated in them a devotion to Kṛṣṇa as a child and youth on whom they lavished their love and attention in ritual worship. Hence Vallabhācārya's *puṣṭi mārga*[23] bhakti laid much emphasis upon a vivid recreation of the earthly drama or *līlā* of Kṛṣṇa's existence in Vraja. This is the reason for the *aṣṭa-yāma* worship outlined above, as well as for the religious festivals of the Hindu Year such as the *aṣṭamī* or birthday celebration of Kṛṣṇa, and the *phāga* festival in spring. Just as the festivals of the Christian Year provide the topics and inspiration of many English religious lyrics so do the Hindu festivals inspire most *saguṇa* bhakti poets.

---

[23] Śarmā, *op. cit.*, pp. 660 *et seqq.*

CHAPTER FOUR

MIDDLE ENGLISH LYRICS AND SAGUṆA BHAKTI

In both English and Hindi religious verse there are two main types of poetic expression; one, predominantly emotional in its emphasis, appealing to the senses through vivid images; the other, more intellectual and abstract, springing from a preoccupation with ethical and philosophical concepts. There is, however, more discernible in English than in Hindi a gradual change and development from simplicity and directness of emotional appeal to a complexity and subtlety of poetic ratiocination. At one extreme, there is the simple devotionalism of the M. E. lyrics with their concentration on the basic feelings of hope, joy, pity, love, sorrow, remorse and repentance as these are aroused by religious belief and practice; at the other extreme, is the metaphysical wit of the seventeenth-century religious lyrics of Donne, Traherne, Vaughan, and others whose poetry frequently shows a tension, in greater or lesser degree, between the emotional and the intellectual, or less often an integration of these by a unified sensibility similar to Kabīr's.

In bhakti poetry both are present in parallel streams which are liable to come together in works of one and the same poet, for example, as early as in Kabīr (d. 1518) who is essentially a *nirguṇa* poet and Sūra Dāsa (1478-1583) who is a *saguṇa* poet. However, *saguṇa* bhakti, generally speaking, gave rise in Hindi oral and written verse to devotional lyrics expressing the warm emotions connected with the worship of Vaiṣṇava *avatāras*, especially Kṛṣṇa and (to a lesser extent) Rāma; although it did also inspire poets to write longer episodic and extended narrative works with a symbolic or allegorical import.

An examination of some M. E. lyrics will show that they have in common with *saguṇa* bhakti poetry, a sensuous apprehension of the humanity of the Divine Being incarnate as man. This quality arises from the "imaginative" method of worship or meditation, in which the devotee concentrates upon some particular episode of the biblical or Vaiṣṇava story of the earthly existence of Jesus or the *avatāras*. In the categorisation of Hindu religious sentiments, the tender emotion of *Vātsalya Bhāva* is the Vaiṣṇava analogy of the Christian emotion that arises from meditation on Virgin and Child, as expressed in M. E. and later lyrics written on the subject of the nativity. The theory behind meditating on this aspect of the incarnation is that the emotions generated by a tender loving regard for the baby Jesus, Kṛṣṇa or Rāma, helps to establish a spiritual connexion with the divine love of God. The devotee may imagine himself as witnessing a scene, or identify himself with the mother who fondles and caresses the child; or he may join other characters like the shepherds of Bethlehem or the rustics of Vraja in worshipping the child.

There are numerous examples of such imaginative meditation on the manger scene in the medieval and Renaissance popular treatises on spiritual exercises. Louis Martz quotes such a "composition" or worshipper's visualisation, from the *Meditations* of the early fourteenth century usually, but probably wrongly, attributed to St Bonaventure:

> . . .anone she [the Virgin Mary] devoutly enclynynge with soverayne Joye toke hym in her armes, and swetely clepynge and kyssynge layde hym in her lappe and with a full pappe as she was taught of the holy ghost wasshed hym all aboute with her swete mylke and so wrapped hym in the kerchefe of her head, and layde hym in the cratche, and anone the oxe and asse knelynge downe layde theyr mouthes in the cratche, brethynge at theyr noses upon ye chylde that they knewe by reason that in that colde tyme ye childe so symply covered had nede to be warmed in that maner.[1]

Martz continues, "Not only are we thus to compose the scene but we are to move onto the stage ourselves:"

> Take Him, then, into your arms, keep Him there, earnestly look into His face, reverently kiss Him. [Or, on a visit to Egypt]: I imagine that you will discover Him playing with other children, and that when He sees you, He will run forward to welcome you. Take up, then, the child Jesus in your arms, put Him upon an ass, and carefully lead Him along, and if He wishes at any time to get off, do you joyfully receive Him in your arms and hold Him lovingly there for a while, at least until His Mother reaches you, for at times, she may be tired and walk more slowly.[1]

---

[1] Martz, *The Poetry of Meditation*, pp. 73-74. He quotes the first paragraph from the English adaptation made by Nicholas Love: *The Mirrour of the blessed lyf of Jesus Christ* c. 1400 and printed 1525 as *Vita Christi*. In the second paragraph, he quotes from Sister M. Emmanuel's translation of the complete "Bonaventure" text under the title of *Meditations on the Life of Christ*.

In a sixteenth-century lyric there is a glimpse of just such a scene of the Virgin Mary and Child as that imagined in the first paragraph of the quotation from the "Bonaventure" *Meditations*:

1

In this tyme of Chrystmas,
Bytwyxte an oxe and an asse,
A mayden delyuered was
Of Christ, her dere Son dere.

* * * * * * *

3

When she her deare Sonne se,
She set him on her kne
And song, 'Hydder to me—
Cum basse thy mother, deare.'

4

On her lap she him layde,
And with her pappe he playde,
And euer sang the mayde,
'Come basse thy mother, dere.'

5

With lyppes collyng,
His mouth ofte she dyd kysse
And sayd, 'Sweetehert myne,
I pray you, make good chere.' [2]

But the M. E. lyrics generally pass quickly on from such a scene of unalloyed joy in the mother-child relationship to a foretaste of the experiences of the suffering Redeemer and the sorrows of the Virgin. The fifteenth-century *Thys endris nyghth* expresses the tenderness and immediacy of the human relationship which is uppermost, although the nature of the king and redeemer underlies it.

Thys endris nyghth
I saw a syghth,
A stare as bryght as day,
And euer among
A mayden song,
'Lullay, by, by, lullay.'

---

[2] Richard L. Greene, *The Early English Carols* (Oxford, 1935), pp. 37-38.

1

That lovely lady sat and song,
And to hyr chyld sayd,
'My Sone, my Broder, my Fader der,
Why lyest thou thus in haye?
My swete byrd,
Thus it ys betyde,
Thow thou be kyng veray,
But neuertheles
I wyll not ses
To syng, "By, by, lullay." '

The dialogue in the next three stanzas states that the child is heaven's king whom angels attend, and whom earthly rulers will worship. Then the focus shifts back to the particularities of the human "composition" in the manner recommended by the *Meditations*:

4

'Mary moder, I am thi chyld
Thow I be layd in stall;
Lordes and dukes shal worsshyp me,
And so shall kynges all.
Ye shall well se
That kynges thre
Shall come the Twelfth Day.
For this behest
Yefe me thi brest
And syng, "By, by, lullay."'

5

'Now tell me, swet Son, I the pray,
Thou art me leue and dere,
How shuld I kepe the to thi pay
And mak the glad of chere?
For all thi wyll
I wold fullfyll,
Thou wotyste full well in fay,
And for all this
I wyll the kys
And syng, "By, by, lullay." '

6

'My der moder, whan tym it be,
Thou take me vp on loft,

And set me vpon thi kne,
And handyll me full soft
And in thi arme
Thou hyl me warme,
And kepe nyght and day;
If I wepe
And may not slepe,
Than syng, "By, by, lullay." ' [3]

In the last stanza Mary asks a boon of Jesus, namely, that people may be happy on Christmas Day.

In contrast to the M. E. lyrics, *saguṇa* bhakti poetry dwells on the various stages of infancy and childhood, with the emphasis on the delight afforded to relations and friends of the *avatāras*, and hence vicariously to the Vaiṣṇava devotee. There are numerous hymns of adoration of the infant *avatāras* in which the warmth of the mother-child relationship is expressed in scenes of great charm and tenderness. These hymns bear a striking resemblance to the southern Vaiṣṇava Āḻvār compositions known as "Pillai Tamil" started about the beginning of the eighth century by Peyālvār. He set the fashion of hymning the praises of Kṛṣṇa in a chronological sequence of scenes depicting the utter helplessness of the baby entirely dependent upon the mother's love and protection; his growing awareness of his environment; his smiling, stretching out his arms, and his attempts at clapping; his desire to be kissed, embraced and loved; his growing coordination of movements leading to the stages of crawling and toddling.[4]

Hindi poets do not go into all the minute details of "Pillai Tamil", nor follow the chronological patterns of recital of the charms of the infant *avatāras*; but they nevertheless cover most aspects. Sūra Dāsa's absorption in the joy of *bāla līlā* (the Divine playing the role of a child) and the beauty and happiness of maternal love is reminiscent of those nativity lyrics of M. E. in which the human element is given prominence. In one of his hymns he describes Yaśodā rocking Hari (Kṛṣṇa) to sleep:

Yaśodā Rocks Hari in His Cradle

She rocks, caresses and coaxes him;
She sings him snatches [of lullabies] that come
to her mind:

[3] Greene, *Ibid.*, pp. 107-108.
[4] Malik Mohammad, *Āḻvāra Bhaktoṃ kā Tāmil Prabandham*, pp. 346-347.

Come, O. Sleep, to my precious babe, why don't
    you bring him slumber?
Why don't you come quickly? My Kanha
    is calling you.
Sometimes Hari shuts his eyes,
    sometimes his lower lip twitches.
Just as Yaśodā thinking him asleep and
    with a gesture of her hand enjoins silence,
Hari awakens with a start;
And Yaśodā [once more] sings softly.

O Sūra, the bliss that is difficult
  for immortal sages to obtain,
  The wife of Nanda [Yaśodā] enjoys.

Yaśodā Hari pālane jhulāvai;
halarāvai dularāya malhāvai joi soī kachu gāvai
mere lāla ko āu nidariyā kāhe na āni suvāvai;
tū kāhe na vegi soṃ āvai toke kānha bulāvai
kabahuṃ palaka Hari mūndi leta haiṃ kabahuṃ adhara pharakāvai;
sovata jāni mauna hvai hvai kara kari saina batāvai.
yahi antara akulāi uṭhe Hari Yaśumati madhurai gāvai;
jo sukha Sūra amara muni durlabha so Nanda-bhāmini pāvai.[5]

The above is a *pada* from the lengthy and episodic *Sūra Sāgara* ("The Ocean of Sūra") of over 4,000 *padas* based upon the *Bhāgavata Purāṇa*. In the tenth section, from which this quotation is taken, Sūra describes a long succession of such scenes (associated with Kṛṣṇa's life in Vraja), each complete in itself as a poem and serving the purpose of a "composition" in the devotional manner of the spiritual exercises. He usually states the subject in the opening verse of the *pada* which serves as a refrain when sung, and summarises or comments in the last to which he appends his name in the conventional manner of the bhakti poets. His imagination plays upon the scenes and incidents of Kṛṣṇa's infancy with a lingering, loving devotion backed by a sympathetic understanding of childhood innocence, joy and fancy. He sees the child crawling in the dust of Vraja (*Vraja-raja*), his uncertain gait as a toddler, his crying for the moon to be brought to him, his wish to grow up suddenly,—and through all the scenes Sūra shows the mother's indulgent solicitude and understanding as she humours, coaxes or reproves Kṛṣṇa, but always with a heart full of love. At the end of nearly every *pada* he

[5] *Sūra-sudhā* ed. Miśra-Bandhu (Banaras, 1923), p. 62.

returns to his point of view as commentator on the scene that is but a glimpse of the divine sport or drama which Sūra is privileged to witness. Sometimes the *pada* ends with a personal supplication for grace and forgiveness, or expresses his gratitude for the blessed vision.

Another subject of religious adoration, the theophany, is common to both Hindu and Christian tradition and belief. In several M. E. compositions, for example, the lyrics already quoted above, Jesus even as a baby reveals to his mother his true nature and the reason for the incarnation. The theophanies of Rāma and Kṛṣṇa are of a different kind. Vaiṣṇava devotees are blessed with moments of vision like that of Christ's true identity on the mount of Transfiguration. The classic example, in Sanskrit literature, which doubtless influenced the Hindi bhakti poets is that given in the eleventh chapter of the *Bhagavad-Gītā* where Kṛṣṇa, at Arjuna's request, reveals his Supreme and Divine Form (*paramam rūpam aiśvaram*).

As a new-born babe Rāma gives a fleeting glimpse of this same awful majesty to his mother, Kauśalyā. When the mask of the human infant is removed, he appears like the four-armed Viṣṇu of Hindu iconography bearing the several symbols of his divine attributes,—one in each hand the conch, discus, lotus or bow, and mace:[6]

His mother gazed in rapture upon the
  mystic form that captivates the hearts of sages:
His beautiful eyes, his body dark-hued as
  a cloud, and his four arms with their several weapons;
Adorned with the garland of forest flowers,
  large-eyed ocean of beauty, enemy of the demon Khara.

haraṣita mahatārī muni-mana-hārī
  adbhutarūpa bicārī.
locana-abhirāmam tanughanasyāmam
  nija-āyudha bhuja cārī:
bhūṣana banamālā nayana bisālā
  sobhāsindhu kharārī.[7]

---

[6] See Alain Daniélou, *Hindu Polytheism* (London, 1964), p. 153. "In my [lower right] hand, which represents the revolving or creative tendency, I hold the conch, symbol of the five elements etc."

[7] Tulasī Dāsa, *Rāma-carita-mānasa* ed. Rāma Naresh Tripāṭhi, Bālakāṇḍa, Chand 21. Hill, p. 88. To ensure easy reference my translations correspond in numbering to the *dohas* etc., in Douglas P. Hill's English version of the *Rāma-carita-mānasa*. The Tripāṭhi edition used by Hill is not available to me; therefore my rendering sometimes differs in substance from Hill's. I have indicated this by italicising the English.

On another occasion Tulasī Dāsa describes a theophany in which the mystic vision of the Absolute was revealed by Rāma as comprehending all time, space, existence, ideas, thoughts and emotions:

He displayed the absolute form of his mystic nature to his mother:
In every hair of his she saw myriads of universes—
Numberless suns and moons, Śivas and Brahmās,
Many a mountain, river, ocean, land and forest,
Time, Karma, the three constituents, knowledge, and nature;—
She saw that, too, which *no one has ever heard of.*
Awestruck she stood with palms joined [in worship]
  when she saw that mystic vision.
She saw the all-inscrutable Māyā, the power of illusion,
  and the soul it makes to dance,
And Bhakti [the devotion to God], that sets it free.
Her body thrilled with awe and not a word came from her mouth.
Closing her eyes she bowed her head before his feet.
Seeing that his mother was lost in amazement,
Kharārī [Rāma] once more became a child.

dekharāvā mātahi nija adbhuta rūpa akhanda;
roma roma prati lāge koṭi koṭi brahmanḍa.

aganita rabisasi sivacaturānana,
bahu girisarita sindhumahikānana;
kāla karama guna gyāna subhāū,
sou dekhā jo sunā na kāū.

dekhī māyā saba bidhi gāṛhī,
atisabhita jore kara ṭhāṛhi;
dekhā jīva nacāva'i jāhī,
dekhi bhagati jo chora'i tāhī.

tana pulakita mukhabacana na āvā,
nayana mūndi carananhi siru nāvā;
bisamayavanti dekhi mahatārī,
bhaye bahuri sisurūpa kharārī.[8]

Whereas such insight as Kauśalyā's into the absolute divinity of her son Rāma is only momentary, and impossible for the mind to retain; the Virgin Mary ponders in her heart the implications of the mystery revealed to her (by the angel Gabriel and the baby Jesus) in terms of

[8] *Ibid. Dohā* 202 and *caupāīs* (couplet 201 and quatrains) following. Cf Hill, p. 93.

the redemption of man through the incarnation. Her laments at the thought of her son's future suffering, and her being comforted by him, form the dialogue of a long poem of thirty-seven stanzas with the refrain "Lullay, lullay, la-lullay, Mi dere moder, lullay" (Brown XIVth Cent. No. 56).

Als i lay vp-on a nith,
Alone in my longging,
Me thouthe i sau a wonder sith,
A maiden child rokking.
The maiden wolde with-outen song
Hire child O slepe bringge;. . .

(pp. 70-71, lines 1-6)

but he wishes her to sing to him of his future as mothers usually do.She relates what she knows from the annunciation to the time of the visit of the shepherds. Then the child foretells the main events of his future life up to the crucifixion at which point, seeing his mother's great sorrow, he has to console her:

'Moder,' he seide, 'tak et lithe,
For liuen i sal a-ȝeyne,
& in thi kinde thoru my mith,
for elles i wrouthte in weyne.

To my fader I sal wende
In myn manhed to heuene;
The holi gost sal the sende
With hise sondes seuene.

I sal the taken wan time is
to me at the laste,
to ben with me moder in blis—
Al this than have i caste.

(pp. 74-75; lines 129-140)

His forecast ends with the final Judgement Day, and the composer rounds up his song with a variation on the first stanza:

Serteynly, this sithte i say,
This song i herde singge,
Als i lay this ȝolis-day
Alone in my longingge.

(p. 75, lines 145-148)

By virtue of the immaculate conception and the Virgin's intimate experience of the nature and purpose of the incarnation, her participation in the passion and agony of the suffering saviour, her joy at his resurrection and ascension, and her own assumption to heaven (according to tradition), the Blessed Virgin occupies a place in Christian religious poetry which has no parallel in Hindi bhakti poetry. In Vaiṣṇava poetry the consorts of Kṛṣṇa and Rāma share in the reflected glory of the *avatāras* (and they are themselves regarded as *avatāras* of Śakti, the creative power of the divine Viṣṇu); but in terms of the human narrative they do not acquire the divine or almost divine status accorded to the Blessed Virgin. However much they may, as Śakti, be integrated in the metaphysical concept of the Viṣṇu-Lakṣmi identity, in their human forms they remain subordinate to the *avatāras*. Sītā, the paragon of wifely virtue, is certainly adored by Vaiṣṇavas, but more as an exemplar of perfect devotion to Rāma than as Lakṣmi. The same may be said of Rādhā in connexion with Kṛṣṇa, although in the Rādhā cult there is more emphasis upon her worship than on Sītā in the Rāmavat sect.

This difference in the positions occupied by the Blessed Virgin on the one hand and Rādhā on the other, accounts for the difference in tone between the English and the Hindi lyrics as regards the feelings of reverence and love which are evoked. In Vaiṣṇava worship, the *mādhurya bhāva* of bhakti is realised in an identification of the devotee with Rādhā as the beloved of Kṛṣṇa; but, generally speaking, the Christian's prayer to the Blessed Virgin for her grace and pity, or her help as intercessor, is due to his veneration for her as the "Mother of God". Yet, in spite of great reverence for her, there are some hymns, especially of the thirteenth, fourteenth and early fifteenth centuries, in which the ardour of the devotee has recourse to images, not unlike those found in the courtly love lyrics of medieval secular poetry, which bear a close resemblance to the concrete particularities of *saguṇa* bhakti poetry with its sensuous expressions of female beauty.

In *A Salutacion to Ure Lady*, a poem of 408 lines, are enumerated in the conventional manner of the *nakha-sikha* (toe to head) description of *saguṇa* bhakti verse, the different parts of the Virgin Mary's body, but the emphasis is on the purity and holiness of her person rather than on the sensuous qualities. Her head is worthy of the crown of heaven, her ears to hear the angel's message or man's prayers, etc. The nearest approach to a sensuous evocation of the human warmth of her person is the clinging affection demonstrated in this mother-child picture:

Blessed beo, ladi, thi white sweere:
Ihesu, that thou louest deere,
    Clupped hit ofte-a-boute.
Whose wol his synne forsake
And of that cluppyng Ioye make,
    Hym thar no develes doute. Aue.[9]

A close reading of this poem shows that it is intended for the devotee engaged in a spiritual exercise making use of the visual imagination supported by recital of over sixty *aves*, as the mind dwells principally upon the events of the gospel story associated with the Virgin's joys and sorrows. It therefore ends appropriately with a summing up of her blessed life, soul and body as worthy of adoration:

Blessed ladi, Blesse I schal
Thy Lyf, thi Soule, thi Bodi al
    That eeuene to heuene went.[10]

Another of the Vernon MS poems, *Off alle floures feirest fall on,/And that is Marie Moder, fre,*[11] has the unmistakable quality of courtly love both in diction and sentiment. The devotee, like the medieval lover, adores his lady from a distance; is faithful to her and will do nothing unworthy of her love in which he is absorbed to the exclusion of everything else. The poem is a song of love to the Blessed Virgin written in the form of a lover's complaint:

Ladi, to the my mone I mene!

The devotee imagines himself in his *degree* as serving the queen of bliss better and better as the days go by. And as pagan lovers appeal to the god of love, Cupid, so he prays to the *king of love*—an ambiguous phrase with both pagan and Christian associations.

The loue that I have ȝeorned ȝore,
  The king of love graunt hit me!

He describes the Virgin's beauty with the conventional epithets and images of the courtly love lyric:

[9] E.E.T.S. o.s. 98. *The Minor Poems of the Vernon MS*, Pt. I ed. Carl Horstmann (London, 1892), p. 127.
[10] *Ibid.*, p. 131.
[11] Brown, *Religious Lyrics of the XIVth Century*, no. 111.

A louely lyf to loken vp-on,
  So is my ladi, that Emperys;
Mi lyf I dar leye ther-vppon,
  That princesse is peerles of prys;

So feir, so clene, so good, so wys
  And therto trewe as eny steel,
There nis no such to my deuys—
  Lor God, that I loue hire wel!

I likne that ladi to the Rose—
I-blessed beo that buirde briht!
* * * * * * *

That ladi lofsum most of lere.
* * * * * * *

Heo is of colour and beute
  As fresch as is the Rose In May.

He longs for a sight of the beatific vision of the Blessed Virgin after this earthly existence, and therefore addresses this prayer to her:

In heuene help me a boure to bylde,
  Ladi, ȝif thi wille be.

This unmistakable note of courtly love is continued in the fifteenth-century devotional lyrics like—*I Have now Set my Heart so High, A Love Message to My Lady, I will Serve my Lady until Death*, and *I Will Have No Other Spouse*. (Brown: XVth Century, Nos. 45-48). But there is not the same spontaneity and intimacy of feeling in spite of the phrases of the secular love lyric. The accent of a spontaneous tender affection is more pronounced in the thirteenth and fourteenth centuries. The famous *Quia Amore Langueo* [12] shows this clearly in a lyric with an unusual emphasis upon the humanity of the Blessed Virgin.

The devotee has a vision by moonlight of the Virgin Mary languishing in love for man's soul even as her devotees in many a love-song pine for her:

In a tabernacle of a toure,
As I stode musyng on the mone,
A crouned quene, most of honoure,

[12] Brown, *XIVth Century*, no. 132.

Apered in gostly syght ful sone.
She made compleynt thus by hyr one,
For mannes soule was wrapped in wo:
'I may nat leue mankynde allone,
Quia amore langueo.

As mother and sister she appeals to man, her child and brother, to forsake sin and turn to her who will give him a loving welcome:

Thys hundreth yere yef thow were (me) fro;
I take the ful fayne, I clyppe, I kysse,
Quia amore langueo.

And in the last stanza she becomes a lover:

'Nowe man, have mynde on me for-euer,
loke on thy loue thus languysshyng;
late vs neuer fro other disseuere,
Myne helpe ys thyne oune, crepe vnder my wynge;
Thy syster ys a quene, thy brother [ys] a kynge,
Thys heritage ys tayled, sone come ther-to,
Take me for thy wyfe and lerne to synge,
Quia amore langueo.'

The ambiguity of *sone* in line 6 meaning either "soon" or "son", allows for a variant reading of line 7 where the MS. Douce 78 has *for thi modure* instead of *for thy wyfe*, as noted by Brown who makes use of Douce 322 for his text. He also observes: "It is singular that this, justly one of the most admired lyrics in Middle English, should have been printed hitherto only from Lambeth MS. 853, p. 4 (*Pol. Rel. and Love Poems*, EETS., pp. 177-9), especially as this MS. gives an inferior and much altered text." [13]

The Lambeth MS. omits, among others, the last stanza quoted above and that in which occurs the line

"I take the ful fayne, I clippe, I kysse."

It is possible that editors before Brown used this particular MS. to avoid hurting the sensibilities of pious readers, who might think the imagery of the omitted stanzas too earthly for the divine status of the Blessed Virgin; although Brown has remarked that "nothing is more characteristic of medieval mysticism than the note, 'Take me for thy wife', with which this poem concludes." [14] If one is to enter into the

[13] Brown, *op. cit.*, p. 286.
[14] *Ibid.*, p. xxi.

spirit of the M.E. religious lyric, one must accept the conventions of the devotional tradition of the Middle Ages even as Hindus continue to worship Viṣṇu in the form of Rāma or Kṛṣṇa with the intention of experiencing the emotional states of the various bhakti *bhāvas*. It must therefore be admitted that the Virgin in the role of lover, is the result of a convention of meditation which utilises the *mādhurya bhāva* of the lover-beloved relationship. There is nevertheless an ambivalence in the *Quia Amore Langueo* lyric which combines the roles of mother, sister and lover. It is an ambivalence partly due to the paradox of the mother-maid dialectic which constantly excited the theological wonder of the medieval mind.

Although there are other M.E. lyrics which centre round the lover-beloved analogy to describe the close communion between the Blessed Virgin and man's soul, such imagery is more commonly used for the love between Christ and his Bride—the individual soul or the corporate Christian Church—a symbolism sanctioned by the Church. "Quia amore langueo", is of course, a quotation from the Vulgate version of the *Song of Solomon*. A verse from the Authorised Version reads: "I charge you, O daughter of Jerusalem, if ye find my beloved, that ye tell him, I am sick of love." (Chapter 5:8).

There is a second *Quia Amore Langueo* or *Christ's Complaint for his Sister, Man's Soul* in the Lambeth MS. which follows the Virgin's Complaint seemingly as a continuation.[15] In this the erotic imagery is obviously derived from the *Song of Solomon* where *sister* and *spouse* are synonymous. The Lambeth MS. has the following lines:

I am true love, that fals was nevere
    Mi sistyr, mannis soule, y loued hir thus;
(lines 17-18)

* * * * * * * *

My fair spouse, & my loue briȝt.
(line 25)

But since Jesus as lover of the human soul is a commonplace of M.E. religious poetry there is no inhibition in this *Quia Amore Langueo* which gives in some instances almost direct transcripts from the *Canticles* as in stanza eleven:

Fair loue, lete us go pleye!
    Applis ben ripe in my gardayne,

[15] F. J. Furnivall, ed., *Political, Religious and Love Poems*, E.E.T.S. o.s. 15, (1st ed. London, 1866; re-edited London, 1903), pp. 180-189.

I schal thee clothe in a newe aray,
Thi mete schal be mylk, hony, & wiyn.
Fair loue, lete us go digne,
Thi sustynaunce is in my crippe, lo!
Tarie thou not, my faire spouse myne,
Quia amore langueo.

And in stanza fourteen:

My loue is in hir chaumbir: holde ȝoure pees,
Make ȝe no noise, but lete hir slepe.

The tone of these two Complaints of the Virgin and Jesus is similar in their tender yearning for the love of man, and the symbolism of the human relationship employed in the expression of it has a directness and immediacy of experience which later M.E. lyrics do not possess, but which continue to be a commonplace of Hindi *saguṇa* bhakti lyrics as will be seen in the chapters that follow.

CHAPTER FIVE

THE BAROQUE IN ENGLISH AND HINDI RELIGIOUS POETRY

Robert Southwell's Poetry

The shifting emphasis of fourteenth-century religious lyrics from the more purely emotional response of Christian devotion, to the more obviously ethical and theological commentary of the fifteenth-century lyrics, points the way to a new development best exemplified in the poetry of Robert Southwell (1561-1595). "His work sometimes recalls the past, sometimes anticipates the future which he was unconsciously helping to create, and often seems to belong to no period at all . . . But it is as an early 'Metaphysical' that Southwell is of most historical interest and also, perhaps, at his best." [1]

Southwell seems to have written in two modes; one is that of the meditator and moraliser in a simple and relatively unadorned style; the other that of the Roman Catholic mystic whose poetry has a warmth of passion with a richness of expression. This latter style is full of alliteration, hyperboles, reiterations, paradoxes, and a concatenation of images reminiscent of the sensuousness of Hindi *saguṇa* poetry. The content of his poems is always religious, and the form is usually influenced by the meditative exercises of spiritual life, as may be seen by a comparison with some of the M.E. lyrics discussed above. His shorter poems have as the focus of meditation such scenes and episodes from the New Testament as are the constant topics of M.E. poetry. Some of the titles are *The Virgin's Conception, The Visitation, The Nativity of Christ, His Circumcision, The Epiphany, The Presentation, The Flight into Egypt, Christ's Childhood, Christ's Bloody Sweat, Christ's Sleeping Friends, The Virgin Mary to Christ on the Cross, St. Peter's Afflicted Mind, etc.* It is noticeable that they follow the chronological progression of events in the Church's Year, obviously inspired by an organised system of worship.

---

[1] C. S. Lewis, *English Literature in the Sixteenth Century* (Oxford, 1954), pp. 544-45.

Most of these poems show how close Southwell was in spirit to the devotee employing the *compositio loci* as setting the mood for his meditation. For example, in *New Prince, New Pompe*, he pictures a simple scene of the nativity:

Behould a sely tender Babe,
   In freesing winter nighte,
In homely manger trembling lies;
   Alas, a pitious sighte! [2]

With this may be compared the opening verses of the fourteenth-century *Christ Child Shivering with Cold* (Brown, XIV Cent., no. 75)

Ler to Louen as y loue the;
On al my limes thu mith i-se
Hou sore thei quaken for colde;
For the i suffre michil wo.

But Southwell usually employs the manger scene as an emblem in which the imaginative reconstruction is reinforced by a moral or allegorical explication as in *New Heaven, new Warre* (He addresses the "heavenly quires"):

The same yow sawe in heavenly seate,
Is He that now suckes Marye's teate;
Agnize your Kinge a mortall wighte,
His borowed weede letts not your sight;
Come, kysse the maunger where He lies;
That is your blisse aboue the skyes.

This little babe so fewe daies olde,
Is come to rifle Satan's foulde;
All hell doth at His presence quake,
Though He Him self for cold do shake;
For in this weake unarmèd wise
The gates of hell He will surprise.

With teares He fightes and wynnes the feild,
His naked breste standes for a sheilde,
His battering shott are babishe cryes,
His arrowes, lookes of weepinge eyes,
His martiall ensignes, colde and neede,
And feeble fleshe His warrier's steede.

---

[2] *The Complete Poems of Robert Southwell, S. J.* ed. A. B. Grosart (London, 1872), p. 107.

His campe is pitchèd in a stall,
His bulwarke but a broken wall,
The cribb His trench, hay-stalkes His stakes,
Of shepeherdes He His muster makes;
And thus, as sure His foe to wounde,
The angells' trumpes alarum sounde.

My soule, with Christ joyne thow in fighte;
Sticke to the tents that He hath pight;
Within His cribb is sureste warde,
This little babe will be thy garde;
If thow wilt foyle thy foes with joye,
Then flitt not from this heavenly boye.[3]

A more concentrated example of the emblematic quality of an imaginative instance is to be found in *The Burning Babe*. This short lyric of only sixteen lines falls into two parts. In the first is an "epiphany" of the Christ Child to the poet on a winter's night as he stood shivering in the snow. Feeling a sudden heat that made his heart glow, he looked up:

A prety Babe all burninge bright, did in the ayre appeare,
Who scorchèd with excessive heate, such floodes of teares did shedd,
As though His floodes should quench His flames which with His teares were fedd...

The second part is the colloquy in a concise theological exposition of the scene as a series of sacred emblems expressing Christ's passion and the power of his redeeming love. The abundance of equivalents between the physical and mental following in such quick succession gives the impression of a consuming intensity of passion which burns and purifies and vanishes, leaving a peaceful conviction of God's love as manifested in the incarnation:

Alas! quoth He, but newly borne, in fiery heates I frye,
Yet none approch to warme their hartes or feele my fire but I!
My faultles brest the fornace is, the fuell woundinge thornes,
Love is the fire, and sighes the smoke, the ashes shame and scornes;
The fuell Justice layeth on, and Mercy blowes the coales,
The mettall in this fornace wrought are men's defilèd soules,
For which, as nowe on fire I am, to worke them to their good,
So will I melt into a bath to washe them in My bloode:

---

[3] *Ibid.*, pp. 111-112.

With this He vanisht out of sight, and swiftly shroncke awaye,
And straight I callèd unto mynde that it was Christmas-daye.[4]

The meditative method of Southwell transforms the *compositio loci* into emblems charged with intense feelings of repentance, hope and joy in such lyrics as *New Heaven, New War* and *The Burning Babe*. He exploits these feelings through a proliferation of images and the use of hyperbole and paradox to heighten a devotionalism which is essentially an integration of the emotional and intellectual response of the human being seeking a union with the Divine. *St. Peter's Complaint* shows an elaboration of the method employed in his shorter lyrics and the prose *Mary Magdalene's Funeral Tears*.

In this long poem, employing the verse pattern of Shakespeare's *Venus and Adonis*, the subject matter is the entire life and ministry of Jesus (with Old Testament allusions and echoes), relived in a series of dramatic scenes in which the changing moods of the repentant Peter are identified with those of the devotee.

The turbulent emotions of the repentant soul are at the very beginning of the poem the focus of meditation. The poet launches directly into the explication of emblems based on the sustained image of the soul tossed about in a sea of grief as Peter recalls his betrayal:

Launch forth, my soule, into a maine of teares,
  Full fraught with griefe, the trafficke of thy mind;
Torn sailes will serue, thoughts rent with guilty feares:
  Giue Care the sterne, vse sighs in lieu of wind:
Remorse, thy pilot; thy misdeede thy card;
Torment thy hauen, shipwrack thy best reward.

Shun not the shelfe of most deseruèd shame;
  Sticke in the sands of agonizing dread;
Content thee to be stormes' and billowes' game;
  Diuorct from grace, thy soule to pennance wed;
Fly not from forraine euils, fly from thy hart;
Worse than the worst of euils is that thou art.[5]

In the following verses Peter recalls the period of his discipleship, his protestations of love and service, and his final betrayal in the hour of weakness and fear. The numerous references to the Gospel episodes

[4] *Ibid.*, pp. 109-110.
[5] *Ibid.*, p. 11.

are interspersed with Old Testament allusions to such characters as David, Solomon, Samson and Adam—all victims of women's wiles, but none as blameworthy as Peter himself, because he betrayed his Lord out of fear of a women's inquiries. Then he speaks of the look that Jesus cast on him after the third denial, and the poem becomes a rhapsodic description of those heavenly eyes which epitomise for the mystic the ideas of beauty, holiness, and love:

O sacred eyes! the springs of liuing light,
The earthly heauens where angels ioy to dwell,
* * * * * * *

Sweet volumes, stoard with learning fit for saints,
Where blissfull quires imparadize their minds;
Wherein eternall studie neuer faints,
Still finding all, yet seeking all it finds:
How endlesse is your labyrinth of blisse,
Where to be lost the sweetest finding is! [6]

He goes on to apostrophise the eyes of Jesus in such phrases as "cabinets of grace", "blazing comets", "living mirrors", "pools of Hesebon", "the baths of grace", "O suns", "Bethlem cisterns", "turtle twins all bathed in virgin's milk"; and ends on a paean of love, a love that creates, controls and "invites devotion":

O gratious spheres! where loue the center is,
A natiue place for our selfe-loaden soules;
The compasse, loue,—a cope that none can mis,
The motion, loue,—that round about vs rowles:
O spheres of loue, whose center, cope, and motion,
Is loue of us, loue that inuites deuotion!

O little worlds! the summes of all the best,
Where glorie, heauen; God, sunne; all vertues, stars;
Where fire,—a loue that next to heauen doth rest;
Ayre,—light of life that no distemper marres;
The water,—grace, whose seas, whose springs, whose showers,
Cloth Nature's earth with euerlasting flowers.[7]

Thus all creation in its fourfold elements of fire, water, air and earth is permeated with the love revealed in the eyes turned upon Peter, even as it turns upon the poet himself as devotee. The extravagance

[6] *Ibid.*, p. 25.
[7] *Ibid.*, p. 28.

of this catalogue of correspondences between the eyes of Jesus and all phenomena, as well as grace, beauty, wisdom and love, reads, at first glance, merely like Baroque indulgence; but in reality, to the mystic vision the images are at one and the same time the means and the end of a spiritual apprehension of the unity behind all appearances. Having once had a glimpse of "the love that moves the sun and the other stars", the poet returns to it at the end of the poem, no matter by what devious means and through stretches of monotony, in the certainty that in being itself, love will forgive and redeem:

> With mildnes, Iesu, measure mine offence;
> Let true remorse Thy due reuenge abate;
> Let teares appease when trespasse doth incense;
> Let pittie temper Thy deseruèd hate;
> Let grace forgiue, let loue forget my fall:
> With feare I craue, with hope I humblie call.
>
> Redeeme my lapse with raunsome of Thy loue,
> Trauerse th'inditement, rigor's doome suspend;
> Let frailtie fauour, sorrowes succour moue,
> Be Thou Thyselfe, though changeling I offend.
> Tender my sute, cleanse this defilèd denne,
> Cancell my debts, sweet Iesu, say Amen! [8]

In writing on the quality of *the Burning Babe*, Professor Mario Praz has said that in this poem "the alexandrianism of the emblems of sacred love melts into a mystical rapture, and the flames and tears of the artificial school of Petrarch revive at the heat of a Baroque imagination." [9] Other critics, too, have commented on the Baroque in Southwell's poetry; and they nearly all seem to have in mind his power of analysing and exaggerating feeling, his generous excess and his rhapsodic quality. These are brought out by a technique employing loosely associated image clusters, startling conceits, paradoxes and word play woven on a verse texture that is strongly alliterative, repetitive, and in parts liturgical in effect. All this is amply demonstrated in *St. Peter's Complaint* in spite of its uneven quality. In its best passages, (for example, the one quoted on the glance of Jesus,) the sensuous may be said to be subsumed in the spiritual when the medieval convention of meditating on scriptural

[8] *Ibid.*, pp. 43-44.

[9] Mario Praz, "Baroque in England", *Modern Philology*, LXI (February, 1964), p. 177.

episodes is directed towards the heightening of feeling into a passion that rises near to the ecstasy of a mystical experience. It is a passion deliberately and skilfully exploited by the Baroque imagination of Southwell.

Hindi Saguṇa Bhakti Poetry

The examination of Hindi *saguṇa* bhakti poetry shows a similar imagination at work. For example, the emblematic, emotional quality of Peter tossed upon the sea of remorse may be compared with the following from Sūra Dāsa:

> Who can save me now, O Lord?
> O Murāri [Kṛṣṇa] ocean of mercy, I am sinking
> In this sea of existence:
> The waters are very deep, the colours of Māyā and covetousness are surging.
> I am seized by invisible monsters which are dragging me down into the fathomless deep.
> The fishes of the [five] senses are biting fiercely; and on my head is the heavy burden of sin.
> My feet, entangled in the seaweeds of worldly infatuation, find no foothold anywhere.
> The tempests of lust, anger and desire are extremely violent;
> * * * * * * * *
> I am weary, bewildered and confused in the midst [of the sea].
> O, root of mercy, hear me!
> O Śyāma [Kṛṣṇa] grasp Sūra and the people of Vraja by the arm and draw us to thyself.

> *aba ko nātha mohiṃ udhāri.*
> *magana hauṃ bhava-ambunidhi meṃ kṛpā-sindhu murāri.*
> *nīra ati gambhīra māyā lobha laharati ranga;*
> *laye jāta agādha jala meṃ gahe grāha ananga.*
> *mīna indriya atihi kāṭati, moṭa agha sira bhāra;*
> *paga na ita uta dharana pāvata urajhi moha-sivāra.*
> *kāma krodha sameta tṛṣṇā pavana ati jhakajhora;*
> * * * * * * * *
> *thakyo bīca bihāla bihvala suno karuṇāmūla;*
> *śyāma bhuja gahi kāṛhi lījai sūra braja ke kūla.*[10]

Although the Hindu theology of Māyā underlying the sensuousness of Sūra Dāsa is different from the Christian theology of Southwell, it

---

[10] Sūra Dāṣa, *op. cit.*, p. 8.

is nevertheless evident that both poets are putting the senses to the service of a spiritual aspiration, namely, union with the Supreme; and that in many points of imagery and verse structure their poetry is similar.[11] Another instance of the elaboration of an initial image into a number of associated emblems is this of man's earthly existence as a dark and dangerous forest from which the poet, Tulasī Dāsa, prays to be delivered, like Sūra Dāsa, by the mercy of God:

> This forest of human existence [or the world] is terrifying, dense, impenetrable,—
> Thick, O Murārī, with the trees of thronging [human] actions:
> Desires are the creepers, and restlessness [of unfulfilled desires] the many sharp thorns;. . .
> The various mental activities are the flocks of hawks, owls, cranes, vultures and other devourers of flesh;
> Absolutely wicked and skilled in deceits, they are ever on the look-out for an opening to bring suffering into the life of the human wayfarer.
> Anger is the enraged elephant, lust the lion, drunken passion the wolf, pride the bear—all fierce in action;
> * * * * * * * * *
> Ever worried by the thought of all these mean creatures gathered together, Tulasī [Thy] servant, is caught in this dreadful dense forest;
> O Jewel of Raghu's race [Rāma], Thou mine of compassion, protect my terrified soul in these cruel times of the age of dire conflicts.

saṃsāra-kāṃtāra ati ghora, gambhīra, ghana,
gahana tarukarma-saṃkula, murārī;
vāsanā balli khara-kaṃṭakākula vipula,
nibiṛa viṭapāṭavī kaṭhina bhārī.

vividha citavṛtti-khaga-nikara syenolūka,
kāka baka gṛdhra āmiṣa-ahārī;
akhila khala, nipuna chala, chidra nirakhata sadā,
jivajana pathika mana-khedakārī.

krodha karimatta, mṛgarāja kandarpa, mada-darpa
vṛka-bhālu ati ugrakarmā;
* * * * * * * *

sakala saṃghaṭa poca socavasa sarvadā,
dāsa tulasī viṣama gahana-grastam;
trāhi raghubaṃsa-bhūṣana kṛpākara, kaṭhina
kāla bikarāla-kalitrāsa-trastam.[12]

---

[11] Compare the use of rhyme, alliteration and assonance (As shown in the transliteration) of Sūra Dāsa's Hindi with Southwell's verses.

[12] Tulasī Dāsa, *Vinaya Patrikā* ed. Devanārāyaṇa Dvivedī (Banaras, 1962). No. 59, pp. 125-126.

Yet another example of the amplification of an idea by an elaborate concatenation of associated images, may be cited from Tulasī Dāsa in a passage which shows more virtuosity and a lighter surface play of the Baroque imagination than in Sūra Dāsa: Rāma addressing Lakṣmaṇa, his brother, after Sītā has been abducted by Rāvaṇa says—

See, brother, how beautiful is the spring,
but bereft of my beloved, I look on it with dread.

Finding me distressed by my loss and thinking me powerless and quite alone,
Kāmadeva [Cupid] has sped to the assault with the aid of the woods, the bees and the birds.
But hearing from his spy who has seen that I am with my brother,
The god of love has seemed to check his army and pitch his camp:

The tangled creepers in the spreading trees seem like so many tents that he has pitched;
The plantains and palms are his flags and standards, amazing all but the boldest;
And all the flowering trees are his archers, arrayed in different uniforms;
On this side and on that stand trees of wondrous beauty looking like the several encampments of fighting men.
The koels' voices are as the trumpeting of maddened elephants,
the cranes and cuckoos are his camels and mules;
The peacocks, partridges and parrots are his mettlesome horses,
the pigeons and swans his Arab horses;
The sand-grouse and quails are his squadrons of foot, no tongue can describe Kāmadeva's hosts;
The mountain crags are his chariots, the waterfalls his drums,
the pied cuckoos the bards that chant his praises;
The buzzing bees are his bugles and hautboys,
The winds—soft, cool, and fragrant—are his spies.
Thus with his army of horses, elephants, chariots and foot
he goes about inciting all to battle.[13]

dekhahu tāta basanta sohāvā,
priyāhīna mohi bhaya uppajāvā.

biraha-bikala balahīna mohi jānesi nipaṭa akela,
sahita bipina madhukara khaga madana kīnhi bagamela,
dekhi gayeu bhrātā sahita tāsu dūta suni bāta,
ḍerā kīnheu manahuṃ taba kaṭaku haṭaki manajāta.

[13] Hill, *op. cit.*, pp. 319-320. Hill's translation has been slightly adapted and set out to correspond with the arrangement of the couplets and quatrains of the Hindi for quick reference and comparison.

biṭapa bisāla latā arujhānī,
bibidha bitānu diye janu tānī;
kadali tālabara dhvajā patākā,
dekhi na moha dhīra manu jākā;
bibidha bhāṃti phūle taru nānā,
janu bānaita bane bahu bānā;
kahuṃ kahuṃ sundara biṭapa suhāye,
janu bhaṭa bilaga bilaga hoi chāye;
kūjata pika mānahuṃ gaja māte,
dheka mahokha ūṃṭa bisarāte;
mora cakora kīra bara bājī,
pārāvata marāla saba tājī;
tītara lāvaka pada-cara jūthā,
barani na jāi manoja-barūthā;
ratha girisilā dundubhī jharanā,
cātaka bandī gunagana baranā;
madhukara-mukhara bheri sahanāī,
tribidha bayāri basīṭhi āī;
caturanginī sena sanga līnhe,
bicarata sabahiṃ cunautī dīnhe.

Though the Baroque has usually been associated with the Counter-Reformation in Europe, the essence of the Baroque is not uniquely European, as Hindi *saguṇa* bhakti poetry shows. Psychological factors common to human nature, and historical circumstances combined to produce a religious poetry informed by the same kind of spirit both in the West and the East. The historical explanation of the Baroque as a manifestation of religious ardour in the face of persecution has much to commend it, when one considers that the development of Hindi bhakti poetry was due partly, as most Indian critics think, to the Hindu devotee's turning to Viṣṇu for refuge from Muslim persecution, about the same time that the Counter-Reformation was in progress in Europe. There was, of course, another important factor contributing to the vogue of the Baroque in Europe, namely, the desire of Christian poets to combat the new paganism that had arisen with the humanistic tendencies of the Renaissance.[14] In many cases, therefore, religious poets consciously exploited the techniques more obviously associated with secular love poetry of the period. But the religious ardour, both Western and Eastern, operated in sensibilities combining habits, of allegorising and spiritualising the concrete, inherited from the Middle Ages, with a new search for ways of expressing the eternal verities of spiritual experience.

---

[14] See p. 38 above.

That the sensibility can be the means of arriving at the supreme verity of the spiritual unity behind all appearances is the conviction of the *saguṇa* bhakti poets. But their conception of the world of the senses is basically different from that of their Western counterparts, the European Baroque poets like Robert Southwell. The Hindu poets aim at a direct apprehension of the spiritual reality immanent in the phenomenal world, while at the same time transcending it. Therefore, to them, sense data like the images in Southwell's poems, are not merely correspondences of divine ideas but manifestations of the conditioned Absolute. Sūra Dāsa writes:

> My eyes have seen the form of Śyāma [Kṛṣṇa].
> He who pervades every single body, he is of light the form incomparable.
> He whose feet are the seventh hell, his head is the sky;
> Sun, moon, planets and fire—all are his light.
>
> *nainani nirakhi śyāmasvarūpa.*
> *rahayo ghaṭa ghaṭa vyāpi soī jyotirūpa anūpa.*
> *caraṇa sapta patāla jā ke śīśa hai ākāśa;*
> *sūra candra nachatra pāvaka sarva tāsu prakāśa.*[15]

But this conception of the Absolute as Brahman, or immensity, is very difficult, if not impossible, for the mind of most devotees to grasp. So the *saguṇa* poets seek to realise it in the human form of an *avatāra*, like Kṛṣṇa or Rāma, and in his *līlā* or earthly sport:

> The mind unsupported by some association [of the Absolute] with form, symbol, constituent element, or species, runs about bewildered;
> Therefore considering the Absolute from every point of view, Sūra sings in verse about the conditioned Absolute's *saguṇa līlā* [its manifestation as the play of the universe exemplified in the earthly life of Kṛṣṇa].
>
> *rūpa rekha guṇa jāti jugati binu*
> *nirālamba mana cakṛta dhāvai;*
> *saba vidhi agama vicārahiṃ*
> *tāte Sūra saguna līlā pada gāvai.*[16]

Tulasī Dāsa expresses the same idea in the following passage from the *Rāma-carita-mānasa*:

---

[15] Sūra Dāsa, *op. cit.*, p. 38.
[16] *Ibid.*, p. 1.

Let those who contemplate the Absolute, from everlasting and without a second, attainable only by intuition, beyond intellectual reach, speak of It and know It; we O Lord, hymn unceasingly thy glory as personal! [*saguṇa*]

je brahma ajam advaita mana-bhava-gamya mana para dhyāvahīṃ;
te kahahu jānahu nātha hama tava saguna jasa nita gāvahīṃ.[17]

In their approach to the conditioned Absolute, the *saguṇa* poets desire to realise the presence of Kṛṣṇa or Rāma in an actual experience of the flesh. Although their ultimate goal is salvation from rebirth in order to establish a lasting, ever-conscious spiritual union, they still implicitly believe that it is possible, by the grace of Hari, to be blessed with a vision of the historical *avatāra*. Therefore in the history of the Vaiṣṇava faith from the Middle Ages to the present time, there are records of numerous instances of trances and visions in which the Supreme Being has been realised in the form of Kṛṣṇa or Rāma. There are such records of the experiences of Sūra Dāsa and Tulasī Dāsa in the *Bhakta Māla*. But even the ecstasy of the mystic, in which Kṛṣṇa or Rāma is realised as human, for all its desirability, may still hold the devotee's mind captive to the senses. As he was about to die Sūra Dāsa is said to have sung the following verses describing Kṛṣṇa's eyes:

Wagtail eyes intoxicating with beauty and bliss,
Exceedingly lovely, lively and piercing,
not for an instant still in the nest,
[With a shake of the head] turning again and again
towards the ears,
they ensnare the earrings in disarray;
And Sūra is caught in the matter of the
Conditioned Absolute as though in the beauty
salve of Kṛṣṇa's eyes,[18]
Or he would this moment depart [from this life].

Khanjana naina rūpa rasa māta;
atisaya cāru capala aniyāre,
pala pinjara na samāta.
cali-cali jāta nikata sravanana ke,
Sūradāsa anjana guṇa aṭaka,
nataru abahiṃ uṛi jāta.[19]

---

[17] Hill, *op. cit.*, p. 439. The translation is Hill's.
[18] *anjana guṇa aṭaka*, literally; "in the salve-element stuck".
[19] Quoted by P. Mitala in *Sūradāsa—Ek Viśleṣaṇa*, All India Radio, Publications Division, (Delhi, 1960), p. 10.

Much of *saguṇa* bhakti poetry is an expression of this divine infatuation with the beauty and love of the *avatāras*; especially is this true of the Kṛṣṇa bhakti poetry of the Aṣṭachāpa poets. Carried to its extreme the sensuousness of religious poetry results in an unhealthy indulgence of the physical senses as in the case of the Gauḍīya school of Kṛṣṇa-bhakti in Bengal. S. K. De in his *Early History of the Vaiṣṇava Faith and Movement in Bengal* makes the following observations:

> It is not always true that religious rapture, however erotically inclined, leads to moral default; it is also admitted that in a mystic attitude of emotional exaltation, even of the erotic type, the senses and the spirit can meet; but there can be little doubt that eroticism as a devotional principle is perilously liable to religious and moral excess. The erotic apotheosis of the legendary Kṛṣṇa and Radha in a background of highly sensuous charm is given a mystic, and even an austere, significance; and however much the mentality of such erotic emotionalists be criticised, the devout saints of Vaiṣṇavism have been, in actual life, morally irreproachable. Caitanya himself was susceptible to such emotional rapture, but personally he held to an ascetic type of morality and expressed strict views regarding sexual relationship. All this is freely admitted; but it should also be admitted that the danger comes not so much from erotic portrayal of the divine sport, which may be (but is not) symbolically understood, as from the excess of exclusive emotional strain involved in the imaginative experience of the erotic sentiment, and from actual practice of erotic situations as a religious rite. The Bengal school of Caitanya, no doubt condemns direct erotic practice, but it encourages vicarious erotic contemplation. It emphasises the inward realisation of the divine sports in all their erotic implications as the ultimate felicitous state, and thereby promotes the abnormal satisfaction of a highly refined erotico-religious sensibility.[20]

This is reminiscent of Miss Odette de Mourgues' indictment of Baroque sensibility as giving expression to a "carnal mysticism" in religious art and poetry. Writing on "The European Background to Baroque Sensibility",[21] she maintains that this sensibility reacted so violently to the problems posed by the political, economic and religious conflicts of the late Renaissance, that intelligence was not always able to control it; hence there was a destruction of the balance between feeling and intellect. She continues:

---

[20] S. K. De, *op. cit.*, p. 551.

[21] Odette de Mourgues, "The European Background to Baroque Sensibility" in *From Donne to Marvell* (Penguin Books, Harmondsworth, 1956).

> The conflict between the spirit and the senses was not a new one... Renaissance humanism had proposed the *mens sana in corpore sano*, but that was too obviously an enticing pagan tag. The solution of the Jesuits and of devout humanism was to enlist the senses in the service of God. This was one of the most impressive attempts towards preserving at least part of the unity of a threatened universe. It gave birth to the stern *Spiritual Exercises* of Ignatius Loyola, the art of the Counter-Reformation, the Emblem-books of the Jesuits, and an enormous bulk of religious poetry (poetry like that of Crashaw). In its excess this appeal to the senses *ad majorem Dei gloriam* leads to a distorted vision of life in which religious themes, such as the repentant Magdalene, the ecstatic Teresa, the Sacred Heart, the crucified Saviour, the Holy Innocents, are translated into undulating marble raptures in sculpture or pictorial symbolic metaphors in poetry. They compose a decorative pageant based on an emotion which is of doubtful quality: a strange mixture of crude pathos and sensuous pleasure. It leaves us with the impression that senses and imagination have been indulged out of all proportion to the needs of religion. This carnal mysticism leads us to suspect that something has gone wrong in this interpenetration of spirituality and materiality, and that one thing has been substituted for another: the roses, pearls, flaming hearts, and doves for some kind of escapism into fairy-land; the voluptuous tears of sinners for the bitter-sweet delights of masochism, and the raptures and swoons of saints for erotic experiences.[22]

These remarks are in some degree applicable to the divine infatuation of some of the Hindi *saguṇa* bhakti poets; and possibly to Crashaw in whose poetry the balance between sensuous details and spiritual significance certainly appears precarious to English Protestant readers. But Southwell's Baroque sensibility never degenerates into the "carnal mysticism" which Miss Mourgues implies is the unhealthy, obsessive sublimation of unsatisfied eroticism. However, there is no denying that Southwell's poetry is often flabby with an abundance of sensuous images loosely connected; and that he seldom achieves the nicely balanced precision of passion and wit, as in *The Burning Babe* and the best passages of *St. Peter's Complaint*, which entitles him to be called "an early Metaphysical".

[22] Odette de Mourgues, *Ibid.*, pp. 90-91.

CHAPTER SIX

DIVINE INFATUATION

Crashaw and Mīrāṃ Bāī

The spiritual ardour of the Counter-Reformation and the literary influence of the Italian Baroque, which merged in the writings of Robert Southwell, are more marked in the poetry of Richard Crashaw. Both poets were as much influenced by the Christian meditative tradition, which gave rise to the M.E. devotional lyrics, as they were by the themes and techniques of Tansillo and Marino. It has been shown how Southwell combined the warm humanity of the M. E. lyrics with theological concern in his treatment of the Nativity. The same thing may be observed in Crashaw's *A Hymne of the Nativity, Sung by the Shepherds* (1646), in which the focus is the Virgin and her "fair-ey'd Boy" worshipped by the shepherds. There is present in this earlier version of 1646 the medieval concreteness of the *compositio loci* with a reference to the conventional lullaby and motherly solicitude and tenderness:

> The Babe no sooner 'gan to seeke,
> Where to lay his lovely head,
> But streight his eyes advis'd his Cheeke,
> 'Twixt Mothers Brests to goe to bed.
> Sweet choise (said I) no way but so,
> Not to lye cold, yet sleepe in snow.
>
> * * * * * * *
>
> Shee sings thy Teares asleepe, and dips
> Her Kisses in thy weeping Eye,
> Shee spreads the red leaves of thy Lips,
> That in their Buds yet blushing lye.[1]

But the last four lines quoted above are omitted in the 1648 edition and the poem has been revised with the aim of expressing the theological fact of the Virgin birth, as a divine mystery and paradox, in words which do not appear in the earlier version:

---

[1] Richard Crashaw, *The Poems English Latin and Greek of Richard Crashaw*, ed. L. C. Martin (Oxford, 1927), pp. 107-8.

The Phaenix builds the Phaenix' nest.
  Love's architecture is his own.
The BABE whose birth embraues this morn,
Made his own bed e're he was born.[2]

Although modified or permeated by a spiritual dialectic the sensuous is indispensable to Crashaw's passionate approach to the Divine; and nowhere in English poetry is the lover-beloved mood, akin to the *mādhurya-bhāva* of bhakti, so clearly expressed as in Crashaw. The physical and spiritual beauty of Jesus and the Blessed Virgin; the warmth of their love and tenderness; and the sacred associations of the gospel narrative, legendary and historical episodes and characters—all these form the subject of his poems which have the surging emotions that are also characteristic of Mīrāṃ Bāī's poetic effusions in Kṛṣṇa bhakti verse.

The affinity between her poetry and Crashaw's is no less remarkable than the similarity in their lives as devotees of the Supreme Lover, the "Absolute sole Lord" of St. Teresa whom also Mīrāṃ Bāī resembles in her raptures and trances. Through all his chequered career as a Laudian in the face of protestant criticism, his associations with the religious community at Little Gidding, his suffering at the vandalism of the Cromwellian attack on Cambridge and his exile from it, his hardships after he became a Roman Catholic, and his final brief but peaceful period at *Santa Casa* in Loreto, Crashaw's was a life dedicated to God. Though he may not have taken a vow of celibacy, he had expressed his desire to live a single life, and did in fact never marry.

I would be married, but I'de have no Wife,
I would be married to a single Life.[3]

His joyous surrender to the love of God was made in a sensuous atmosphere rich in symbols and rites of ceremonial worship. Not for him the puritan austerity that would discard the sumptuous accoutrements of devotion:

Rise then, immortall maid! *Religion* rise!
Put on thy selfe in thine own looks: t' our eyes
Be what thy beauties, not our blots, have made thee,

[2] *Ibid.*, p. 249.
[3] *Ibid.*, p. 183.

Such as (e're our dark sinnes to dust betray'd thee)
 Heav'n set thee down new drest; when thy bright birth
Shot thee like lightning, to th'astonisht earth.
From th' dawn of thy faire eye-lids wipe away
Dull mists and melancholy clouds: take day
And thine owne beames about thee: bring the best
Of whatsoe're perfum'd thy *Eastern nest.*[4]

Crashaw's experience at Little Gidding strengthened his natural inclination to make the fullest use of traditional forms of worship engaging the senses through the use of icons and other appurtenances of devotion in the set offices of corporate Christian worship and private contemplation. This accounts for his *The Office of the Holy Crosse* [5] translated from the medieval Latin as well as his free renderings of Latin hymns like *Vexilla Regis, Stabat Mater, Adoro Devote, Lauda Sion Salvatorem*, and *Dies Irae*. These are all associated with feasts or sacraments of the Church's Year, and serve a functional purpose in corporate worship or provide points of concentration for private contemplation. A consideration of their purpose shows how similar is Crashaw's inspiration to that of the Hindi *Aṣṭachāpa* poets who dedicated their poetic gifts to the service of Kṛṣṇa in the Vaiṣṇava temple at Govardhana in Vraja.

The Prayer Book is, for Crashaw, "love's great Artillery" against the "ghostly foe" and "fortifies the hold of the chaste heart" against the assault of sin. It is the vademecum of the devout soul preparing herself by prayer and praise for the coming of her divine Bridegroom with

Amorous languishments; luminous trances;
Sights which are not seen with eyes;
Spiritual & soul-piercing glances
Whose pure & subtil lightning flyes
Home to the heart, & setts the house on fire
And melts it down in sweet desire
   Yet does not stay
To ask the windows leave to passe that way;
Delicious Deaths; soft exaltations
Of soul; dear and diuine annihilations;
   A thousand vnknown rites
Of ioyes and rarefy'd delights;

[4] *Ibid.*, pp. 137-138.
[5] See Brittain, *The Penguin Bk. of Latin Verse* for originals.

A hundred thousand goods, glories, & graces,
  and many a mystick thing
  Which the diuine embraces
Of the deare spouse of spirits with them will bring
  For which is no shame
That dull mortality must not know a name.[6]

Thus the influence of the Prayer Book, together with the symbols of ritual worship, inspires Chashaw's sacred verse with the intense love-longing of *mādhurya bhāva* which is the predominant mood of his poetry. It is in a rapturous passage of Baroque sensuousness that he rises to a climax of love's consummation in the concluding verses of his poem on the Prayer Book:

O fair, o fortunate! O riche, o dear!
O happy & thrice happy she
    Selected doue
    Who ere she be,
    Whose early loue
    With winged vowes
Makes hast to meet her morning spouse
And close with his immortall kisses.
Happy indeed, who neuer misses
To improue that pretious hour,
    And euery day
    Seize her sweet prey
All fresh & fragrant as he rises
Dropping with a baulmy Showr
A delicious dew of spices;
O let the blissfull heart hold fast
Her heaunly arm-full, she shall tast
At once ten thousand paradises;
    She shall haue power
    To rifle & deflour
The rich & roseall spring of those rare sweets
Which with a swelling bosome there she meets
    Boundless & infinite
    Bottomles treasures
Of pure inebriating pleasures.
Happy proof! she shal discouer
    What ioy, what blisse,
How many Heau'ns at once it is
To haue her God become her Lover.[7]

[6] Richard Crashaw, *op. cit.*, p. 330.
[7] *Ibid.*, pp. 330-331.

As the Baroque sensuousness of the poet plays upon the profound faith of the Catholic devotee, undisturbed by doubts or fears, the morning fragrance and dew of the *Song of Solomon* melt into the "rich and roseall spring" of spiritual rapture when God becomes the Lover.

The human-divine union is effected by the "wound of love" and the mystical experience is the commingling of pain and joy. Therefore, as Austin Warren has pointed out, St. Teresa is chiefly celebrated in Crashaw's poem as "Love's Martyr".[8] She would go to a physical martyrdom among the Moors as a child of six, but is called upon by divine Love, her "Absolute sole lord", to live a life of martyrdom in devotion and service to him through contemplation and social duties combining the roles of Mary and Martha. Instead, therefore, of "bleeding on a barbarous knife" she becomes "love's victim" and daily dies.

> THOV art love's victime; & must dy
> A death more mysticall & high.
> Into loue's armes thou shalt let fall
> A still-suruiuing funerall.
> His is the DART must make the DEATH
> Whose stroke shall tast thy hallow'd breath;
> * * * * * * *
> O how oft shalt thou complain
> Of a sweet & subtle PAIN.
> Of intolerable IOYES;
> Of a DEATH, in which who dyes
> Loues his death, and dyes again.
> And would for euer so be slain.[9]

This paradox of the exquisite pain of love, this dying into an eternity of heavenly bliss, is expressed in Crashaw's poem with all the splendour and passion of the Baroque imagination in which the concrete melts into the abstract under the heat of a spiritual ardour, only to be poured into the ethereal mould of maiden stars, and crowned souls:

> . . . Sons of thy vowes
> The virgin-births with which thy soueraign spouse
> Made fruitfull thy fair soul, goe now

[8] Austin Warren, *Richard Crashaw, A Study in Baroque Sensibility* (London, 1939), p. 143.

[9] Crashaw, *Poetical Works*, p. 319.

And with them all about thee bow
To Him, put on (hee'l say) put on
(My rosy loue) That thy rich zone
Sparkling with the sacred flames
Of thousand soules, whose happy names
Heau'n keeps vpon thy score. (Thy bright
Life brought them first to kisse the light
That kindled them to starrs.) [10]

Mīrāṃ Bāī is in her religious ecstasies like an Indian St Teresa, and in her poems like Crashaw a poet of divine love. In time she antedates them both, though the tone of her love-longing fluctuates between the sensuous apprehension of Crashaw's unwavering faith with little if any real inner conflict, and the intellectual-emotional tension of George Herbert's varying moods. The dates of Mīrāṃ Bāī's life are most uncertain. Paraśurāma Caturvedī supports the case for ?1498-1546. Rāmakumāra Varmā suggests 1573 as the latest possible date of her death.[11] So they agree that she was a contemporary of the other great Kṛṣṇa bhakti poet, Sūra Dāsa (1478-1583). Though she was not one of the *Aṣṭachāpa* poets, like them she spent much of her life in the Kṛṣṇa country of Vraja completely engrossed in the various offices of the Vaiṣṇava devotional life of ritual, hymn singing and dancing before the image of Kṛṣṇa.

Born a princess of Rajasthan, even as a little girl she regarded herself as the bride of Lord Kṛṣṇa. Later her divine infatuation became the cause of much misunderstanding and even of persecution. About 1516 she was married to a Rajput prince of Mewar who died a few years later. From then on Mīrāṃ Bāī became absorbed in her devotion to Kṛṣṇa and in ministering to the needs of *sādhūs*, holy men, in whose company she was often to be found. She began to frequent the neighbouring temples where she used to sing and dance before the image of Kṛṣṇa. Her fame as a Vaiṣṇava saint spread far and wide with the result that people came long distances to get a glimpse of her. There is a legend that even the great Mogul Emperor Akbar (1562-1605) putting his life in jeopardy came incognito with his celebrated court singer, Tān Sen, into the Hindu stronghold of Chitor just to see and hear the saintly singer and

---

[10] *Ibid.*, p. 321.

[11] See Caturvedī, *Mīrāṃ Bāī kī Padāvalī* [Collected Poems of Mīrāṃ Bāī] 11th ed. (Allahabad, 1962); and R. Varmā, *Hindī Sāhitya kā Alocanātmaka Itihāsa* [A Critical History of Hindi Literature] (Allahabad, 1958).

poetess. But according to Paraśurāma Caturvedī [12] this has no historical basis, although it is a fact that there was at this period much hostility between the Muslim invaders and the Rajput princes. The latter had their own dissensions and wranglings which involved Mewar and the neighbouring Hindu princedoms in sporadic fighting.

The relations of Mīrāṃ Bāī's deceased husband frowned upon her temple activities and her association with mendicant ascetics and saints. Having tried in vain to dissuade her from her ways, they resorted to persecuting her, and it is said that they even sought to bring about her death. There appears to be internal evidence for this in some of the lyrics ascribed to her. Mīrāṃ Bāī, after a number of pilgrimages, finally settled in Vraja where she is said to have met one of the Caitanya Goswāmins [13] of Vrindābana who refused at first to give audience to a woman. Mīrāṃ Bāī sent her reply to his refusal in words to the effect that she had always been under the impression that Kṛṣṇa was the only man in Vrindābana, and that all devotees were women since like the *gopīs* they were all the beloved of the Divine Lover. This so moved the Goswāmin that he hastened to meet her. Mīrāṃ Bāī spent her last years in Vraja as a devotee in the temple of Raṇachoṛa at Dvārkā where, legend has it, she was absorbed into the image of Kṛṣṇa and so disappeared from this earthly existence.

Educated by tutors in the court of her grandfather, the pious Rāo Dūdājī, Mīrāṃ Bāī had a good knowledge of music and literature which inevitably included a history of the Hindu search for the Absolute through *karma, jñāna* and *bhakti.* Although her poetry shows traces of the concepts of *advaitavāda* and *māyā* her natural inclination was towards the emotional approach of bhakti and especially through devotion to Kṛṣṇa.

The corpus of her works may have included a commentary on Jayadeva's *Gītagovinda,* but the mass of her lyrical compositions was in the nature of songs to Kṛṣṇa transmitted through the centuries by oral tradition. It has therefore been impossible so far to produce a definite authentic text of her poems. Several attempts have, however been made to collate existing MSS. (by copyists and possibly imitators), printed texts of the last hundred years, and the songs of the oral tradition still extant among Vaiṣṇava sects. Such an attempt

---

[12] See Caturvedī, *op. cit.*, pp. 19-20.

[13] See above, Chapter 3.

is Caturvedī's *Mīrāṃ Bāī kī Padāvalī* which is the basis of the present study.

Mīrāṃ Bāī's bhakti occasionally takes the form of the *dāsya bhāva* in which she is the penitent sinner seeking to enter the service of Lord Kṛṣṇa as his maidservant or slave; but more often (some commentators say, always) she assumes the role of a *gopī* or one of the beloved milkmaidens of Kṛṣṇa in Vrindābana. In this way she becomes absorbed in the *mādhurya bhāva* in which she realises a lover-beloved relationship with Kṛṣṇa. Her songs in form and matter have been influenced by such distinguished precursors as Jayadeva, Vidyāpati, and Candidāsa,—all of whom wrote as *saguṇa* bhakti poets on the Kṛṣṇa theme; as well as by the santa *nirguṇa* bhakti poets, like Kabīr, whose vocabulary of *advaita* ideas is echoed in some of her verses. She is never tired of repeating herself with slight variations on the subject of Kṛṣṇa's name, beauty, and earthly *līlā* especially his amorous dallyings with Rādhā and the *gopīs* in Vrindābana. Her poems, usually with refrains, are in fact mostly petitions to Kṛṣṇa whose glory she sings in the conventional terms of *saguṇa* bhakti poetry; but the feminine sensibility of her poetic genius gives her poems a yearning tenderness more convincingly realised as a devotee of Kṛṣṇa than that of the poets who assume a woman's role to evoke the *mādhurya bhāva*. She vows eternal faithfulness and service to her divine lover; and her songs reproduce the experiences and moods of her physical and spiritual autobiography. In her meditation she forgets the needs of the body, and is indifferent to the opposition of her relations and the persecution she suffers at their hands.

Her entire life is a renunciation of the world and a concentration on devotion to her Lord Kṛṣṇa. She prays to him for salvation from rebirth in order to be united with him forever. She speaks occasionally in the manner of the *nirguṇa* poets of this world as an illusion, and of the distinction of the human soul from the divine Absolute as merely apparent. But her poems are generally permeated with the sensuous apprehension of a personal God incarnate as Kṛṣṇa, and distinct from the human soul which is always aching for union with the divine. This ache of love-longing is like St. Teresa's "wound of love", a commingling of pain and joy expressed in Hindi by the word *viraha*. This is the paradox of bhakti like the joy of Christian martyrdom in dying daily, and of the "wound of love" of Christian mysticism. *Viraha* is usually translated as "the pain of separation", but "love-longing" gives a clearer idea of its connotation for it implies both the pain of separation and the anticipation of joy realised in the consummation of love. In Hindi bhakti poetry *viraha* is the essence of love. The sixteenth-century Hindi Ṣūfī poet, Jāyasī says:

> In love itself dwells the savour of *viraha*,
> As in the honeycomb the elixir-like honey.
>
> *premahiṃ māṃha biraha rasa rasā,*
> *maina ke ghara madhu amṛta basā.*[14]

Commenting on this verse of Jāyasī's, Pandit Caturvedī writes: "*Viraha* must be understood as always being inherent in true love; for if love exists it is indeed because of *viraha*; the essence of love is *viraha* itself."[15] It is this *viraha* that forms the core of Mīrāṃ Bāī's poetry.

> Without a vision of thee not a moment is pleasing to me.
> Home delights me not, sleep comes not to me, and the love-pain of separation (*viraha*) torments me.
> Wounded I wander about, and no one knows my pain.
> My life wastes away in pining and my eyes in weeping.
> I expectantly gaze and gaze standing upon the path which I have swept clean for thy approach.
> O Lord of Mīrāṃ, when wilt thou come? Only union with thee will bring me happiness.
>
> *ghaṛī ceṇa ṇā āvarāṃ, theṃ darasaṇa viṇa moya.*
> *dhāma ṇa bhāvāṃ nīnda ṇa āvāṃ, viraha satāvāṃ moya.*
> *ghāyala ri ghūmā phirā mhāro darada ṇa jāṇyā koya.*
> *prāṇa gumāyāṃ jhūratāṃ re, naiṇa gumāyāṃ roya.*
> *pantha nihārāṃ ḍagara majhārā, ūbhī māraga joya.*
> *Mīrāṃ re prabhu kaba re milogāṃ, theṃ milyāṃ sukha hoya.*[16]

> Beloved, come and show thyself to me, for without thee I cannot rest.
> Life without thee is like the lotus without water and the night without the moon.
> Bewildered and afflicted I spend the night with *viraha* devouring my heart.
>
> I have no hunger by day, no sleep at night; I cannot express [my feelings] in words.

---

[14] Quoted in Caturvedī, *op. cit.*, p. 48.

[15] *loc. cit.*, "*viraha ko sadā sacce prema kā bhītara nihita samajhanā cahie, kyoṃki prema kā astitva yadi hai to vaha viraha ke hī kāraṇa hai—viraha hī prema kā sāra hai.*"

[16] *op. cit.*, p. 132. *pada* 102.

Who will listen to me, to whom shall I relate [my condition]? Union with my Beloved will extinguish the fire [of my anguish].
O thou who knowest my innermost secret,[17] why dost thou prolong my unfulfilled desire? With thy coming to me my pain will go.
Mīrāṃ, who has been thy slave from existence to existence [i.e. in previous existences], now falls at thy feet.

pyare darsaṇa dīyo āya theṃ viṇa rahyā ṇa jāya.
jala viṇa kaṃvala canda viṇa rajanī, theṃ viṇa jīvaṇa jāya.
ākula vyākula raiṇa bihāvā, viraha kalejo khāya.
divasa ṇā bhūkha ṇa nidarā raiṇo, mukha sūṃ kahyā ṇa jāya.
koṇa suṇe kāsūṃ kahiyārī, mila piva tapaṇa bujhāya.
kyūṃ tarasāvāṃ antarajāmī,[17] *āya milo dukha jāya.*
Mīrāṃ dāsī jaṇama jaṇama rī, parī tumhāre pāya.[18]

Grounded in *saguṇa* bhakti, the devotion of Mīrāṃ Bāī is often expressed, as in the above songs, with a prevailing melancholy in a love-longing that employs the conventional phrases of the medieval lover's complaint. Yet though her poetry is full of tears, sighs and heartaches, it avoids the sheer eroticism associated with Kṛṣṇa and the *gopīs* as described in Jayadeva's Sanskrit *Gītagovinda* and many of the *padas* in the *Sūra Sāgara*. The difference between Sūra Dāsa and Mīrāṃ Bāī in the treatment of the erotic element of the Kṛṣṇa legend is important in any discussion of the allegorical import of their poetry.

Sūra Dāsa writing on Kṛṣṇa's *prema-līlā* ("love-play") is pre-eminently the poet of *śṛngāra rasa* which is, according to Indian poetics, the erotic sentiment of sexual love realised when the mind is absorbed in the charms, allurements and dallyings of lovers. Sūra Dāsa rings the changes upon the love between Kṛṣṇa and the *gopīs* according to the varying moods in the changing circumstances of the world of Vraja. In doing so he is following an artistic tradition of medieval Sanskrit dramaturgy and rhetoric transmitted to vernacular poetry. According to this tradition there is an elaborate classification of heroes and heroines (*nāyaka nāyikā bheda*) in which they are described with set physical and mental characteristics and conventional patterns of behaviour.

In the *prema-līla* padas of the *Sūra Sāgara*, therefore, Kṛṣṇa plays various roles by turns: the impartial lover giving his attentions equally to all the *gopīs*, or the faithful lover of his one beloved, the fair

[17] *antarajāmī* also means "dwelling within"; so the alternative translation of this verse is, "Thou who dwellest within my heart."
[18] *op. cit.*, pp. 131-3. *pada* 101.

Rādhā; the indulgent acquiescent lover, or the tantalising philanderer. Similarly, the *gopīs* are either his paramours with whom he philanders; or his true loves thrilled by the music of his flute, pining away in his absence, or united with him in blissful enjoyment of the *rāsa līla* or circular dance by moonlight. In some of his *padas* Sūra Dāsa gives all the sensuous details of the physical beauty of Kṛṣṇa's dress and person, as well as those of the *gopīs*; and he describes vividly their amorous abandon in physical embraces with a voluptuousness that has not failed to elicit the censure, however mild, of even his most ardent admires among discriminating Indian critics like Ayodhyā Siṃha Upādhyāya, himself a distinguished modern Kṛṣṇa poet. Commenting on Sūra Dāsa's poetry this critic writes:

> He has achieved supreme excellence in his description of the sentiment of love [*śṛngāra*]. No where else in Hindi literature is to be found such natural descriptions of real gusto; but I will say that it would have been as well if some of his erotic descriptions had taken a different form. However, from the point of view of art they are of considerable value.[19]

In contrast to Sūra Dāsa, Mīrāṃ Bāī is a poet of *mādhurya rasa*, the sentiment that transcends or aims at transcending the sensuous in a spiritualising of sex. The elements of erotic imagery are very much the same in both *śṛngāra rasa* and *mādhurya rasa* but differently exploited by the sensibility with the result that the tone of the poetry is basically different in the two *rasas*. The emphasis in *mādhurya rása*, unlike that in *śṛngāra rasa*, is not on the concreteness of erotic details but upon a generalised description aiming at inducing a pervasive hypnotic mood[20] rather than at the exciting of physical passion. Crashaw similarly employs the imagery of the *Song of Songs* in *The Assumption* to heighten the mood of joyous adoration to the music of the Blessed Virgin's coronation as Queen of Heaven:

> She's calld. Hark, how the dear immortall doue
> Sighes to his syluer mate rise vp, my loue!
> Rise vp, my fair, my spottlesse one!

---

[19] Ayodhyā Siṃha Upādhyāya, *Hindī Bhāṣa aura uske Sāhitya kā Vikāśa* (Patna, 1934), p. 251.

[20] Warren, *op. cit.*, p. 175, draws attention to a similar quality in Crashaw's poetry: "The hypnotic intent of Crashaw's poetry has been little observed because most English readers have, in preoccupation and attitude, been too alien to him for the establishment of initial confidence".

The winter's past, the rain is gone.
    The spring is come, the flowrs appear
No sweets, but thou, are wanting here.
        Come away, my loue!
        Come away, my doue! cast off delay,
        The court of heau'n is come
        To wait vpon thee home; Come come away!
        The flowrs appear.
Or quickly would, wert thou once here.[21]

But while Crashaw's is a vicarious experience through poetic identification with pious prototypes or sacred personifications, Mīrāṃ Bāī's is her own as a Kṛṣṇa devotee making a personal confession. Aware of the Upanishadic concept of the Absolute Brahman in its immensity as embracing all existence, she found the idea of the conditioned Brahman not only more conducive to her meditation, but she seems also to have believed herself to be a reincarnation of one of the *gopīs*. So the eternal Hari (Viṣṇu the theistic Brahman) may be said literally to be her true love Kṛṣṇa, whose beauty stabs her into delirious raptures. In the conventional manner of the *nāyaka nāyikā bheda* she confesses her love to her confidante, one of the other *gopīs*:

O my friend, the glances of my dark lover [Kṛṣṇa] are like daggers of love.
Becoming delirious with their stroke I forget body and mind.
My body is pervaded with the pain [of love] and my mind with intoxication.
Some of our companions, too, have been completely demented [with his love].

Well do I know him; he is Vihārī the wanderer of the groves, [or he who sports in the groves.]
As the cakora bird longs for the moon, and the moth to be consumed by the lamp,
As the fishes die without water, so is my lover dear to me.
How can I exist away from his sight; my heart knows no rest.
Go and say to him, "Mīrāṃ is yours."

ālī sāṃvaro kī dṛṣṭi, mānūṃ prema rī kaṭārī heṃ.
lagana behāla bhaī tana kī suddhi buddhi gaī.
tanaha meṃ vyāpī pīra, maṇa matavārī heṃ.
sakhiyāṃ mili doya cyārī, bāvarī bhaī heṃ sārī.

---

[21] Crashaw, *op. cit.*, p. 304.

haurṃ to vāko nīko jāṇo, kuṃja ko vihārī heṃ.
canda ko cakora cāhai, dīpaka patanga dāheṃ.
jala binā marai mīna aisī prīta pyārī heṃ.
bina deṣyāṃ kaise jīveṃ kala ṇa parata hīyeṃ.
jāya vākūṃ aise kahiyau mīrāṃ to tihārī heṃ.[22]

Although Mīrāṃ Bāī's love-longing is central to her devotion and often colours even some of her happier songs, she nevertheless expresses many changes of mood with the different offices of daily ritual worship, as well as with the variety of seasonal occupations and festivals in the Kṛṣṇa country. Her songs therefore present a wide gamut of moods associated with her spiritual biography. In this respect she resembles George Herbert more than Crashaw whose emotional range is more limited.

George Herbert and Mīrāṃ Bāī

Herbert's poetry is more personal in tone as it is in diction than Mīrāṃ Bāī's. The latter is content to set down her feelings in the conventional framework of Kṛṣṇa verse employing stock images of love poetry inherited from Sanskrit and Prakrit literature and the Āḻvār hymns. Herbert is determined to give a wide berth to "enchanted groves", "sudden arbours", and the other clichés of Renaissance secular poetry:

I envie no mans nightingale or spring;
Nor let them punish me with losse of rime,
    Who plainly say, My God, My King.[23]

(*Jordan I*)

Though Herbert chose to write "plainly" eschewing the vocabulary of pastoral and secular love poetry, his poems are in fact often complex both in the experience communicated and the manner of its communication. There is in his poetry an intellectual quality absent from Mīrāṃ Bāī. His poems are, like hers, often direct petitions, or songs of praise, love-longing or love realised, but they nearly always have a groundwork of self communing that reveals a highly analytical turn of mind. Further, whereas Mīrāṃ Bāī's life from childhood was one of utter surrender to Kṛṣṇa, her Lord; Herbert's had been one of

[22] Caturvedī, *op. cit.*, p. 152. *pada* 174.

[23] *The Works of George Herbert* ed. F. E. Hutchinson (Oxford 1945), p. 57. Hereafter all page references after quotations will apply to this edition.

wrestling between his soul and God before his acceptance of the service of his Master in which he finally realised the "perfect freedom" of full devotion.

In spite of these differences between the two poets in poetic technique and submission to the divine will, there is an amazing resemblance in their yearning for union with the Lord of their devotion. Compare, for example, Mīrāṃ Bāī's longing in the poems already quoted with this opening stanza of a Herbert lyric:

Come Lord, my head doth burn, my heart is sick,
While thou dost ever, ever stay:
Thy long deferrings wound me to the quick,
My spirit gaspeth night and day.
O show thy self to me,
Or take me up to thee!

(*Home* p. 107)

The last two verses serve as the refrain at the end of each of the following twelve stanzas and recall the ache of separation; but Herbert does not yield himself to a soporific enjoyment of the love-sick mood. Immediately after the first stanza, he moves on to a meditation on the theological conception of the grace of God that hastes down to man in the incarnation of Jesus; from this he turns to a consideration of the vanity and spiritual barrenness of the world—in itself a trite religious theme, but expressed by Herbert in a strikingly novel manner. He then expresses a desire for release from earthly existence, and rounds off the poem with a variation on the opening stanza:

Come dearest Lord, passe not this holy season,
My flesh and bones and joynts do pray:
And ev'n my verse, when by the ryme and reason
The word is, *Stay*, sayes ever, *Come*.
O show thy, &c.

(*Ibid.*, p. 109)

Herbert's emotion is disciplined by an intellect that is not submerged in the love pain of separation, like Mīrāṃ Bāī's *viraha*, but continually breaking out in unexpected comparisons and sudden turns of thought as in

What is this weary world; this meat and drink,
That chains us by the teeth so fast?

What is this woman-kinde, which I can wink
    Into a blacknesse and distaste?
        O show thy, &c.

* * * * * *

We talk of harvests; there are no such things,
    But when we leave our corn and hay:
There is no fruitfull yeare, but that which brings
    The last and lov'd, though dreadfull day.
        O show thy, &c.

(*Ibid.*, p. 108)

Another of Herbert's poems which begins with a love plaint like Mirāṃ Bāī's *viraha* is *The Search*:

Whither, O whither art thou fled,
    My Lord, my Love?
My searches are my daily bread;
    Yet never prove.

My knees pierce th' earth, mine eies the skie;
    And yet the sphere
And centre both to me denie
    That thou art there.

(*The Search*, p. 162)

The rest of the stanzas explores the idea of the soul's estrangement from God, the distance from whom can be annihilated by His will so that "East and West touch, the poles do kisse,/ And parallels meet". The evidence of God's love in herb and star, the devotee's search with sighs and groans,—these are the more conventional elements in this poem which blends the concrete with the abstract through a sensibility that is constantly transmuting the imagistic into the apprehension of a spiritual experience.

Where is my God? what hidden place
    Conceals thee still?
What covert dare eclipse thy face?
    Is it thy will?

(*Ibid.*, p. 163)

This same "will" that apparently may erect fences and bars, can so integrate the devotee with God that "no edge so keen or point so piercing can appear to come between them". In making this point Herbert maintains a tension between his emotional longing yet uncertainty and his theological belief (in the efficacy of the Almighty Will) that gives a vibration and resonance to the poem. This kind of tension is absent from the songs of Mīrāṃ Bāī read singly; they are essentially what they were intended to be—short snatches of song that sob and sigh or praise and rejoice; and they never profoundly disturb the devotional mood of submission with doubts or psychological probings.

Yet her songs, like Herbert's poems, express a variety of moods changing with the daily and seasonal round of religious offices, or with the ebb and flow of the solitary contemplative's spiritual musings. For example, the first office of the Vaiṣṇava *aṣṭa-yāma* [24] is celebrated by Mīrāṃ Bāī in this *aubade*:

> Awake, my darling flute-player, awake my Beloved.
> The night is past, the dawn has come, every house opens its doors.
> The *gopīs* churning milk make a jangling sound with their bangles.
> Awake, my Darling, the dawn is here: gods and men stand at thy door.
> The cowherd boys are noisy with shouts of greeting, *etc.*
>
> *jāgo bansīvāre lalanā, jāgo more pyāre.*
> *rajanī bītī bhora bhayo hai, ghara ghara khule kiṃvāre*
> *gopi dahi mathata suniyata hai, kanganā ke jhaṇakāre.*
> *uṭho lāla jī bhora bhayo hai, sura nara thāṛhe dvāre.*
> *gvāla bāla saba karata kulāhala, jaya jaya sabada ucāre.*[25]

She sings, too, of the meeting of Rādhā and Kṛṣṇa in the flowery groves and alleys of Vrindābana; and of the merry spring festival of *Phāga* when Kṛṣṇa drenches the *gopīs* in the dyes and perfumes of a riotous carnival of the senses. As the heat of summer increases, her songs take on a mood of weary desolation in harmony with the parched and thirsting earth; then the huge dark clouds pile up in July heralding with thunder and lighting the cooling rainstorms; and the refreshing of her withered spirit is realised in the return of her Lord Kṛṣṇa.

> O the rainclouds of Sāvana (July-August), the soul-delighting Sāvana.
> My heart leaps up in Sāvana as I hear the unfolding news (from the clouds) of Hari's approach.
> The dense clouds come gathering and piling up with lighting flashes that bring the showers.

---

[24] For *aṣṭa-yāma* see end of Chapter 3.
[25] Caturvedī, *op. cit.*, p. 150, *pada* 165.

The seed-drops of rain have come, of the rain with the cooling refreshing breezes.
O Lord of Mīrāṃ, Giridhara Nāgara, this is the hour of blissful song.

barasāṃ rī badariyā sāvana rī, sāvana rī maṇa bhāvaṇa rī.
sāvana māṃ umangyo mhāro maṇarī, bhaṇaka
suṇyā hari āvana rī.
umaṛa ghumaṛa ghaṇa meghāṃ āyāṃ, damaṇa
ghaṇa jhara lāvaṇa rī.
bījāṃ būndāṃ mehāṃ āyāṃ barasāṃ sitala
pavaṇa suhāvaṇa rī.
mīrāṃ ke prabhu giradhara nāgara, belā
mangala gāvaṇa rī.[26]

This tumultous upsurge of pure joy so unlike Mīrāṃ Bāī's usual *viraha* is more in the passionate vein of Southwell or Crashaw and quite in contrast to the quieter manner of Herbert. This poem and the *aubade* are characteristic of Mīrāṃ Bāī's absorption in a prevailing mood without any moral implication; and in this respect she is markedly different from Herbert. As already stated, like her he expresses a variety of moods in accordance with the daily and seasonal duties of devotional life, but these are generally starting points or a basis for religious analysis and didactics. Whereas Mīrāṃ Bāī is absorbed in her emotional experience of which the rainclouds and showers of Sāvana are the physical correlatives, Herbert uses his similar experience of a spiritual regeneration for the purposes of an explicit personal analysis and a wider moral application. This point is well illustrated in his poem, *The Flower*:

How fresh, O Lord, how sweet and clean
Are thy returns! ev'n as the flowers in spring;
To which, besides their own demean,
The late-past frosts tributes of pleasure bring.
Grief melts away
Like snow in May,
As if there were no such cold thing.
* * * * * *
And now in age I bud again,
After so many deaths I live and write;
I once more smell the dew and rain,
And relish versing: O my onely light,
It cannot be

[26] *Ibid.*, p. 144, *pada* 146.

That I am he
On whom thy tempests fell all night.

These are thy wonders, Lord of love,
To make us see we are but flowers that glide:
Which when we once can finde and prove,
Thou hast a garden for us, where to bide.
Who would be more,
Swelling through store,
Forfeit their Paradise by their pride.

(*The Flower*, pp. 165-67)

The Flower is moreover a statement of Herbert's final submission and the resulting peace at the end of his spiritual conflicts in which there were frequent alternations of joy and grief, rather than the evocation of a passing exhilaration like Mīrāṃ Bāī's at the approach of the rains in July. Taken altogether the poems of Herbert and the songs of Mīrāṃ Bāī represent many aspects of religious experience (both communal and private) related to the natural seasons and the festivals of the religious year, Hindu and Christian. But *the Temple* of Herbert has a consciously organised structural unity such as cannot be claimed for Mīrāṃ Bāī's spontaneous hymns, many of which were probably composed extemporaneously.

The Temple is seen by Martz as structured to correspond to the stages of meditation laid out in the manuals of spiritual exercises.[27] Elizabeth Stambler maintains that it is more like a cycle of courtly love lyrics:

> The Temple, like the best volumes of courtly love lyrics, is unified in its protagonist. His role of courtier, soldier, and poet resembles Dante's, Petrarch's, and Sidney's protagonists. There can be no doubt, I think, of the consistent character of Herbert's *persona*: he is one throughout the volume ... Herbert's God appears in *The Temple* very much as the beloved woman appears in courtly lyrics, characterised indirectly, via the reactions of the protagonist.[28]

Joseph Summers thinks that *The Temple* was conceived by Herbert as "a hieroglyph for the body, particularly the human body

---

[27] Martz, *op. cit.*, pp. 288-320.

[28] Elizabeth Stambler, "The Unity of Herbert's 'Temple'", *Cross Currents*, Vol. X, No. 3, 1960, p. 252.

in the service of God and the divine body of Christ".[29] According to Hutchinson in his preface to Herbert's works:

> These intimate poems exactly correspond to the description which he [Herbert] gave to them in his last message to Ferrar, that he would find there 'a picture of the many spiritual Conflicts that have past betwixt God and my Soul, before I could subject mine to the will of Jesus my Master, in whose service I have now found perfect freedom'.

It is possible, more or less, to reconcile all the above views if it is agreed that Herbert adopted and modified to his own purpose certain medieval and Renaissance conventions. His poetry combines the affective devotionalism of the M.E. religious lyrics and the medieval habit of allegorisation with a searching analysis of his own mental processes. The analogies from Hindi bhakti poetry can serve a useful purpose in directing the reader's attention to the nature of the "persona" adopted in the various lyrics by noting its similarity to the corresponding *bhāva*, or sentiment experienced according to the particular relationship assumed by the devotee towards the God of his devotion. For example, in *The Odour*, it might be said that Herbert realises the *dāsya-bhāva*, or the sentiment resulting from the Master-servant relationship, with a true "orientall fragrancie":

The Odour. 2. Cor. 2. 15

How sweetly doth *My Master* sound! *My Master!*
As Amber-greese leaves a rich sent
Unto the taster:
So do these words a sweet content,
An orientall fragrancie, *My Master.*

Anyone who can "relish the flavour" (to use an expression of Indian poetics) of the mood of sweet submission in Herbert's poem can appreciate the true connotation, in the context of bhakti poetry, of these two words: *master, servant*, and their synonyms *lord, maid-servant, slave,*— so often used in the songs already quoted from Mīrāṃ Bāī.

In both Herbert and Mīrāṃ Bāī this *dāsya-bhāva* flows into the *mādhurya-bhāva* of the lover-beloved relationship expressed in its

[29] Joseph Summers, *George Herbert: His Religion and Art* (Cambridge, Mass., 1954), p. 85.

extremes as the intense love-longing of *viraha* or the ecstasy of love consummated; it is also expressed in uncertainties and hesitancies in the direction of fulfilment as in

Love bade me welcome: yet my soul drew back,
Guiltie of dust and sinne.
(*Love III*, p. 188)

It has already been pointed out that Herbert does not abandon himself to the love-lorn mood; but he comes very near to despair in *Longing* which ends on the typical *viraha* noted of Mīrāṃ Bāī:

My love, my sweetnesse, heare!
By these thy feet, at which my heart
Lies all the yeare,
Pluck out thy dart,
And heal my troubled breast which cryes.
Which dyes.
(*Longing*, p. 150)

For all his masculine control of emotion, Herbert makes this feminine surrender of himself to God, the divine lover. This surrender is made not vicariously, as in Crashaw through the living martyrdom of St. Teresa, but in his own person as Herbert, the devotee who transcends the institutionalism symbolised in a priest in the singing robes of Aaron. Yet he uses the ritualism of the Church as steps to ascend to a union with God; and *The Temple* therefore comprises poems that voice the general spirit of Christian worship, as well as those that reveal the more intimate and more personal experiences of Herbert. It is in the latter, which covers the intimacy, longing, and 'lover' aspect of his religious experience, that Herbert shows affinities with Mīrāṃ Bāī.

CHAPTER SEVEN

THE METAPHYSICAL VISION

Kabīr, Traherne and Vaughan

Common to both seventeenth-century English religious poetry and Hindi *nirguṇa* bhakti poetry is a certain metaphysical element due to the poets' philosophical consciousness of an intimate relationship between the individual self and the universe, between the human spirit and the cosmic Absolute Being. The religious sensibility that explores this relationship is manifested in a poetry marked by a constant tension, conflict, or fusion of thought and feeling.

English religious lyrics from the fourteenth to the seventeenth centuries varied, from time to time, in their emotional and intellectual quality with the shifting emphasis on different aspects of the spiritual life. It has been shown above that the more obviously affective devotion of the fourteenth- and fifteenth-century lyrics gradually admitted more of a reflective quality; and that by the end of the sixteenth century, Southwell's poetry passionately striving towards a human-divine communion, has a clearly metaphysical and didactic element.

The late sixteenth and seventeenth centuries combined the emotional and speculative in longer poems of an allegorical or explicitly didactic type most clearly seen in the poetry of Spenser and his imitators. There was also in this period, a more restless curiosity about the psychology of the human mind, which placed greater emphasis upon the analysis of mental and emotional processes. The "well-made" poems of Herbert show how the intellectual tone and the logical progression of thought are combined with the devotional warmth of his poetry. Nearer to Donne than to the rhapsodic Crashaw, in his control of the logical development of a theme, he is nevertheless not quite so philosophical as Vaughan and Traherne.

Literary criticism, since World War II, has tended to qualify the importance and range of the term "metaphysical" as applied to the seventeenth-century English poets of the school of Donne, and to emphasise the devotional aspect in their more obviously religious lyrics.[1] It is true that the theory and practice of Christian meditation, deriving from the Middle Ages, play a large part in seventeenth-century religious poetry, as can be seen in the works of Herbert and Crashaw; but the term "metaphysical" in preference to "devotional", is useful in describing those religious poems of Vaughan and Traherne that were "inspired by a philosophical conception of the universe and of the role assigned to the human spirit in the great drama of existence."[2] Commenting on this conception as characteristic of seventeenth-century English Metaphysical poetry, Miss White observed more than thirty years ago that "metaphysical poetry is no isolated phenomenon peculiar to the seventeenth century, but a recurrent aspect of universal poetry".[3] She had in mind, of course, Sir Herbert Grierson's reference to the metaphysical quality in Dante and Goethe; and her application of "universal" was probably restricted to Europe. But an examination of Hindi bhakti poetry shows that the sphere of metaphysical poetry extends beyond the literatures that are derived from the European literary and religious traditions.

Hindi *saguṇa* bhakti poets like Sūra Dāsa and Mīraṃ Bāī make the conditioned Brahman, manifested in the lives of the *avatāras*, the focus, of their worship, devotion and poetry. In contrast to them, *nirguṇa* bhakti poets aim at identification with the unconditioned Absolute, and their poetry generally expresses the search for an all-inclusive unity through the philosophical ideas of Vedānta, Buddhism and suggestions of Ṣūfīsm. But these two schools of *saguṇa* and *nirguṇa* poetry, representing the two main aspects of bhakti, cannot be contained in water-tight compartments. It has already been pointed out that in the poetry of *saguṇa* bhakti poets like Sūra Dāsa and Tulasī Dāsa, metaphysical ideas are expressed in works that are predominantly emotional and centred on the sectarian worship of Kṛṣṇa and Rāma. So, too, in *nirguṇa* bhakti poetry there are strong traces of the influence of theism; for even though their belief is generally monistic the *nirguṇa* poets have recourse in some of their verses to the more sensuous imagery of Vaiṣṇava bhakti. In Western terms, the two schools of *saguṇa* and *nirguṇa* poetry may be said to follow broadly, in the one case, the path of affective devotion; and, in

---

[1] See, Mario Praz, "Baroque in England", *Modern Philology*, LXI, Feb., 1964.

[2] H. J. C. Grierson, *The Background of English Literature and Other Collected Essays and Addresses* (London, 1925), p. 115.

[3] Helen C. White, *The Metaphysical Poets: A Study in Religious Experience* (New York, 1st ed., 1936, repr. 1956), p. 72.

the other, the way of speculative mysticism in which the intellect plays the leading part; and reaches its peak in the concept of the *via negativa* as in the *Cloud of Unknowing*, which is akin to the *neti* of Vedānta *advaita*.

It has already been shown that Herbert's poetry has both the emotional and intellectual strands of Christian devotion; and that he resembles the *saguṇa* bhakti poets in his approach to a personal loving God manifested in the incarnation. *Nirguṇa* bhakti basically differs from *saguṇa* bhakti and Herbert's devotionalism, in that it does not believe in a conditioned Godhead revealed as an incarnation. Although the *nirguṇa* poets often use the names Hari (Viṣṇu) and Rāma, they generally intend these to signify the unconditioned Absolute. Sometimes they also employ the symbolism associated with the various *bhāvas* of *saguṇa* bhakti, as is the case with Kabīr, the *santa* poet.

Santa is the name given to a holy person whose life is dedicated by precept and example, to helping his fellow-men towards union with the Absolute, which he himself has wholly or partly achieved. The medieval *santas* were not necessarily ascetics or anchorites who had withdrawn from the occupations of everyday life; but they cultivated the ability of retreating at will into their inner being by a self-control of body and mind. Thus, through spiritual discipline, they were led to self-realisation and union with the supreme Self, the unconditioned Absolute. The *santas* came into prominence in North India towards the end of the fourteenth and the beginning of the fifteenth century. During the next hundred years, they counted among their number the three great poet-preachers—Kabīr, Guru Nānak and Dādū Dayāl. The practical side of their teaching aimed at social reform, for example, the eradication of caste distinctions, and the idolatry of polytheistic worship. On the metaphysical level, they gave wide circulation to the ancient Vedantic concept of non-dualism or monism; but instead of the Sanskrit language, they employed the popular vernaculars of the uneducated. Indeed, many of the *santa* poets were themselves unlearned men. Kabīr himself has said that he never touched pen, ink or paper; and from this, it has been generally inferred that he was illiterate. Yet it must be remembered that, especially in India when the disciple used to get his instruction entirely by word of mouth from his *guru*, or spiritual preceptor, to have been illiterate did not mean the same thing as being ignorant. However, much of *santa* poetry violates the rules of Hindi prosody, partly because of the poets' ignorance, but chiefly because they are preoccupied with the moral and didactic. Even so accomplished a poet as Sundara Dāsa, a disciple of Dādū, while advocating the observance of poetic rules, maintains that the praise of God is the soul of poetry:

> Says Sundara, the praise of Hari is life,
> And [poetry] without the praise of Hari is like a corpse.
>
> *kahi sundara hari-jasa jīva hai,*
> *hari-jasa bina mṛta kahi tathā!*[4]

The work of the *santa* poets did not generally receive serious literary consideration from Hindi critics until between the two World Wars, although poets like Kabīr and Nānak were long held in high esteem by devout Indians. In the West, Kabīr's name has become better known than that of any other Hindi poet since the appearance in 1915 of Rabindranath Tagore's translation, *One Hundred Poems of Kabir*. There was no definitive edition of Kabīr's work when the distinguished Bengali poet made his selection from Kshiti Mohan Sen's collection, largely drawn from oral tradition.[5] Several of the translations in *One Hundred Poems of Kabir* are consequently based on Hindi originals of doubtful authenticity or corrupt texts. They are, nevertheless, essentially characteristic of the philosophy of Kabīr, though in some cases coloured by the personality of the translator.

The seminal work in Kabīr studies is Pitāmbara Datta Baṛathvāla's *The Nirguṇa School of Hindi Poetry*, a thesis submitted for a higher degree of the Banaras Hindu University, and originally published in English in 1936. During the course of his researches, Baṛathvāla realised the great importance of a study of the *santa* poets generally, and of their precursors, the Buddhist *siddhācāryas* and the Nātha *yogīs*, in a just appreciation of *nirguṇa* poetry, especially that of Kabīr. Just as English Metaphysical poetry of the seventeenth century is illuminated by a knowledge of scholasticism and the meditative tradition of the Middle Ages, so *nirguṇa* poetry is made clearer by a

---

[4] Ganeśa Prasāda Dvivedī, *Hindī Santa-Kāvya Sangraha* (A Collection of Santa Poetry) 1st ed., 1939. Revised by P. Caturvedī (Allahabad, 1952), p. 9.

[5] Pārasanātha Tivārī, *Kabīra Granthāvali* (Allahabad, 1961), is the most scholarly edition to date, and is likely to become the definitive text as far as it goes; but a canon of the entire corpus of Kabīr's works has yet to be established. See bibliography for other useful editions.

study of the metaphysical ideas and the religious practices of medieval Buddhism and the Nātha sect.

The *santa* poets, and especially Kabīr, employ a number of stock cryptic terms from the language of the esoteric cults that had resulted from a syncretism of decadent Buddhism and Tantrism. Originally, Buddhism was chiefly ethical in its teaching, virtuous living being its main concern. But the popularisation in India of *Mahāyāna*, one of the two branches of classical Buddhism, led during the Middle Ages to the accretion of ideas and practices which grew into a religion of outward forms and rituals. The *mantras*, for example, of *Mahāyāna*, which served the purpose of stating principles and doctrines of Buddhism in brief *sūtras* serving as concise mnemonics, through association with the Tantric *mantras* became debased and invested with an allegedly supernatural potency. Similarly, the *yantras*, or geometric diagrams, which were the visual equivalents of the *mantras*, became more than symbolic to the superstitious mind.[6] So there gradually developed a number of esoteric cults of Tantric Buddhism in which the emphasis was upon the physical and concrete aspects of worship; and the most sensual of these cults went so far as to incorporate sexual rites.

Sahajayāna, one of the sects of medieval Buddhism, condemned the sensual practices of the Tantric cults, as well as all other forms of ritual worship connected with polytheistic or monotheistic beliefs. The adherents of *Sahajayāna* followed the way of *jñāna-yoga*, for they maintained that pure intellectual concentration, achieved through physical and mental discipline, was the only means of gaining salvation from rebirth and thus merging the individual self in the universal void, (*śūnya*). The Buddhist ascetics of the *Sahajayāna* sect were variously known as *yogī*, *siddha* and *avadhūta*. Kabīr often addresses the *yogī* in a slightly disparaging tone because he is sceptical of the *yogī's* mechanical reliance, at least in the initial stages of his novitiate, on physical and mental austerity for sounding the depths of the Absolute. He has more respect for the *avadhūta* or *siddha*, that is, the "arrived" *yogī* who has achieved *siddhi* or spiritual perfection, and is fit to be a *guru* or *sata-guru* (true spiritual preceptor).

The Buddhist *siddhācāryas* (masters perfected in spirituality) wrote *cāryapadas* (songs) and *dohās* (couplets) in a language akin to Old

---

6 See, Daniélou, *op. cit.*, pp. 334-361 for an account of *mantras* and *yantras*.

Hindi and Old Bengali. "No definite date can be assigned to the songs [and couplets]. The lower limit, however, is 1200 and the upper limit cannot be much later than 1050." [7] These compositions were only discovered in this century among Buddhist manuscripts in Tibet. But their influence had been transmitted to the *santa* poets through the intervening Nātha *yogīs* who practised the extreme physical austerity and mental concentration of the *haṭha-yoga* taught by Gorakha Natha, the founder of their sect.

Though never a *yogī* himself, Kabīr absorbed a great deal of knowledge about *haṭha-yoga* along with other religious and philosophical ideas current in his time, from which he shaped an eclectic philosophy of his own and gave expression to it in his *nirguṇa* bhakti poetry. There is, nevertheless, in Kabīr's poetry a definite influence of the *prema-bhakti* (the devotion of love) preached by Rāmānanda in propagating the *Rāma-bhakti* cult in Banaras where Kabīr lived most of his life. But like other *nirguṇa* poets, Kabīr identifies Rāma and Hari (Viṣṇu) with the Absolute, and not with the theistic Viṣṇu or his *avatāras*. However, there is no denying the fact that in many of the verses attributed to Kabīr, the names Rāma and Hari are clearly associated with the *bhakti bhāvas* of *saguṇa* poetry. For example, he employs the *mādhurya bhāva* of conjugal love and speaks of the human soul as the bride of Rāma in the following verses:

O my wedded companions, sing the auspicious nuptial songs:
The Lord Rāma, my husband, has come to my house.

The five elements shall witness my wedding,
as I dedicate to him body and soul.
Rāma, my God, has come as my guest,
and my youthfulness is intoxicated [with love for him].
While Brahmā himself recites the Vedas [during the marriage ceremony],
I shall make an offering of my body at the altar;
With my God, Rāma, I shall walk around the sacrificial fire.
Great indeed is my good fortune!

Innumerable gods and multitudes of great sages have come to our wedding;
Says Kabīr, I am going to marry the Immortal Being.

---

[7] Sukumāra Sen, *The History of Bengali Literature* (Delhi, 1960), p. 27.

dulahinīṃ gāvahu mangalacāra,
haṃma ghari ā'e rājā Rāṃma bharatāra.

taha rata kari maiṃ mana rati karihauṃ,
pāṃca'u tatta barātī.
Rāṃma deva morai pāhunaiṃ ā'e
maiṃ jobana maiṃmātī.

sarīra sarobara bedī karihauṃ,
Brahmā beda ucārā;
Rāṃma deva sangi bhāṃvari lehahauṃ,
dhaṃni dhaṃni bhāga hamārā.

sura taiṃtīsauṃ kautiga ā'e,
munivara sahasa aṭhāsī;
kahai Kabīra haṃma byāhi cale haiṃ,
purikha eka abināṃsī.[8]

The love-longing of *viraha*, too, is expressed in a *pada* that might well be attributed to Mīrāṃ Bāī:[9]

O my Beloved, come to my house,
Without thee, my body is aching.

Everyone calls me thy wife, and this disturbs me with doubt;
Until we are united as one and sleep together,
How can there be love? (or. . . what kind of love can that be?)

I have no taste for food, and sleep does not come to me;
I am restless indoors and outside.
Dear as the beloved to her lover, and as water to the thirsty [Art thou to me].
Is there any such benefactor as will take my news to Hari:
"Kabīr is delirious: he will die if he does not see thee."

Bālama ā'u hamṃrai greha re;
tumha bina dukhiyā deha re.

saba koi kahai tumhārī nārī, mokauṃ yaha andeha re;
ekameka hvai seja na sovai, taba lagi kaisā neha re.

anna na bhāvai nīnda na āvai, griha bana dharai na dhīra re;
jyauṃ kāṃmīṃ kau kāṃmini pyārī, jyauṃ pyāse kau nīra re.

---

[8] Tivārī, *op. cit.*, text of the poems, p. 5, no. 5.
[9] Cf. Chapter 6 above, p. 97.

hai koī aisā para upagārī, Hari saum̩ kahai sunāi re;
aba tau behāla Kabīra bha'e haim̩, binu dekham̩ jiu jāi re.[10]

The imagery and general tone of passionate yearning in the above *pada* are in striking contrast to the following succinct expression of Kabīr's *viraha* in one of his other verse forms known as *sākhī*:

> *Viraha*, like a serpent, sits in this body,
> and cannot be cast out by any spell;
> He who is separated from Rāma cannot exist,
> and if he does, he goes mad.
>
> *biraha bhuvangama tana basai,*
> *mantra na mām̩naim̩ koi;*
> *Rām̩ma biyogī nām̩ jiai,*
> *jiai ta ba'urā hoi.*[11]

Kabīr has two styles: the *padas* usually more lyrical and impassioned; the *sākhīs* colloquially terse and pithy. The former are devotional songs and the latter statements of sententiousness and moral insight. Whichever form his poetic expression takes from the inspiration or demand of the occasion, Kabīr's imagination exploits a wide range of experiences for his images. In addition to the erotic figures of the *bhāvas* of *saguṇa* bhakti, he draws analogies from the commonplace objects and occupations of the home and the market place. He compares, for example, the life of materialism to his own preoccupation with his craft as a weaver. As such, he is attached to *māyā* or unreality like a son to his mother. When freed by dispassion from the illusion of the world, he realises the Absolute as the fulfilment of all his spiritual longings.

> Having abandoned the warp and the woof,
> Kabīr has written the name of Rāma in his own body.
>
> Inwardly weeping, Kabīr's mother says:
> "Son, how can the world continue without me?"
>
> As long as the weaver is occupied with his loom,
> So long will the love of Rāma be forgotten.

---

[10] Tivārī, *op. cit.*, text of poems, p. 9, no. 13.
[11] *Ibid.*, p. 140.

Says Kabīr, "Listen, O mother,
the Lord of the three-fold universe supplies all my wants." [12]

tananāṃ bunanāṃ tajyau Kabīra,
Rāṃma nāṃma likhi liyau sarīra.

musi musi rovai Kabīra kī māī,
e bārika kaise jīvahiṃ khudāī.

jaba lagi tāgā bāhauṃ behī,
taba lagi bisarai Rāṃma sanehī.

kahata Kabīra sunahu merī māī,
pūranahārā tribhuvana-rāī.[12]

Some commentators interpret these verses to mean that Kabīr, becoming absorbed in the spiritual quest, neglected his means of livelihood and thus caused grief to his family. Pandit Paraśurāma Cuturvedī, while admitting that the verses may be taken literally, thinks that the metaphysical meaning is in keeping with Kabīr's love of the symbolic.[13]

Kabır's diction is on the whole simple, but his poetry is certainly resonant with symbolic significance because of the varied elements that have been introduced into his work. For an understanding of the deeper import of much of his verse, it is essential to have some acquaintance with the vocabulary of *haṭha-yoga* which is based on the theory of the human body as a microcosm containing the immensity of the Brahman or Absolute. According to the pseudo-scientific theory of *haṭha-yoga*, there are in the spinal column three channels: *iṛa, pingalā* and *suṣumnā*. These are symbolically referred to as the three sacred rivers of North India, namely, the Ganges, Jumna and Sarasvati whose confluence is the Triveṇī. The three channels ascend through six centres (*cakras*—literally, "wheels"). Each centre has a lotus blossom and a presiding deity together with his female countenpart or *śakti* (energy), and is associated with its particular colour and *mantra* (mystic phrase or formula). These centres are situated at the base of the spine, the genitals, near the navel, the heart, the throat, and between the eyebrows. There is in addition to these a special seventh centre with a thousand-petalled

[12] Tivārī, *op. cit.*, text p. 9, no. 12.

[13] See P. Caturvedī, *Uttarī Bhārata kī Santa-Paramparā* (Allahabad, 1964), pp. 152-153.

lotus situated at the top of the brain. Kabīr refers to the lotuses of *haṭha-yoga* in the following couplet:

Do not go to the garden of flowers!
O Friend! go not there;
In your body is the garden of flowers.
Take your seat on the thousand petals of
the lotus, and there gaze on the Infinite Beauty.[14]

bāgoṃ nā jā re nā jā, terī kāyā meṃ gulajāra;
sahasa-kaṃvala para baiṭhake tū dekhe rūpa apāra.[15]

The aim of the practitioners of *haṭha-yoga* is to bring these lotus centres under the control of the will by a rigid discipline of body and mind in order to arrive at spiritual perfection (*siddhi*), and so realise the Absolute within themselves. According to them, at the base of the spine is supposed to lie coiled and dormant a serpent, *kuṇḍalinī*, the symbol of vital force and sexual energy.[16] By the means of *haṭha-yoga* exercises, this *kuṇḍalinī* is supposed to be roused into motion, and made to ascend through the central channel of the *suṣumnā* past three "gates" and the six *cakras*. In doing so, it activates the various lotuses and deities until it reaches the top of the brain. The *siddha* or *avadhūta*, that is, the "arrived" *yogī*, is the ascetic whose spiritual discipline has been perfected in the *kuṇḍalinī's* union with its Beloved, Śiva, on the thousand-petalled lotus which is the source of the immortal nectar with which the mystic in his ecstasy becomes inebriated.

Arthur Koestler has observed that "the process of awakening and moving the *kuṇḍalinī* serpent has a physiological and a symbolical aspect—the former grotesquely unappetising, the latter beautiful and profound. Both are derived from the archetypal erotic imagery which permeates Hindu religious art and ayurvedic medicine." He further remarks that "Kuṇḍalinī's painful journey ... is one of the most ancient symbols for the sublimation of the libido." [17]

During the *kuṇḍalinī's* upward progress in stages through the various centres, the *yogī* is said to be aware of a number of inner

---

[14] *One Hundred Poems of Kabir*, p. 3.
[15] Hazārī-Prasāda Dvivedī, *Kabīra* (7th ed. Bombay, 1964), P. 233.
[16] Cf. Alain Daniélou, *Hindu Polytheism*, p. 217: "... The main meaning attached to the serpent is to represent the basic dormant energy, akin to the sexual power, etc."
[17] Arthur Koestler, *The Lotus and the Robot*, (London, 1960), pp. 97-8.

sounds (*anahadanāda*), musical in effect, as well as of spiritual lights or illuminations similar to those described by western mystics. The sounds are like the waves of the sea, thunder, drums, waterfalls, conches, bells, the flute, bumble-bees and the lute. But these mystic sounds and sights cease when the final consummation has been realised between Śiva and his spouse, *Kuṇḍalinī*,[18] in the centre of the thousand-petalled lotus, and the *yogī* in a state of ecstatic trance, *samādhi*, is lost in the infinite void of the Absolute.

The esoteric symbolism of *haṭha-yoga*, music and wine as emblems of the Ṣūfī's communion with the divine, and the Vedic conception of the ineffable Brahman as the ground of all being—these are all integrated in the following expression of Kabīr's spiritual happiness:

1

The light of the sun, the moon, and the stars shines bright:
The melody of love swells forth, and the rhythm of love's detachment beats time.
Day and night, the chorus of music fills the heavens; and Kabir says,
'My Beloved One gleams like the lightning flash in the sky.'

2

Do you know how the moments perform their adoration?
Waving its row of lamps, the universe sings in worship day and night,
There are the hidden banner and the secret canopy:
There the sound of the unseen bells is heard.
Kabir says: 'There adoration never ceases;
there the Lord of the Universe sitteth on His throne.'

3

The whole world does its works and commits its errors:
but few are the lovers who know the Beloved.
The devout seeker is he who mingles in his heart the double currents of love and detachment, like the
mingling of the streams of the Ganges and Jumna;
In his heart the sacred water flows day and night; and thus the round of births and deaths is brought to an end.

4

Behold what wonderful rest is in the Supreme Spirit!
and he enjoys it, who makes himself meet for it.

---

[18] Daniélou, *op. cit.*, p. 254 quotes from the *Linga-arcana Tantra*: "This primordial goddess [Pārvatī, Śiva's spouse] is known as 'the coiled', Kuṇḍalinī... Only because he is united with Energy is the eternal lord of sleep [Śiva] a doer of actions."

Held by the cords of love, the swing of the Ocean of Joy sways to and fro; and a mighty sound breaks forth in song.
See what a lotus blooms there without water!
and Kabir says, 'My heart's bee drinks its nectar.'

5

What a wonderful lotus it is, that blooms at the heart of the spinning wheel of the universe!
Only a few pure souls know of its true delight.
Music is all around it, and there the heart partakes of the joy of the Infinite Sea.
Kabir says: 'Dive thou into that Ocean of sweetness:
thus let all errors of life and death flee away.'

* * * * * * * *

9

I have had my Seat on the Self-poised one[19]
I have drunk of the Cup of the Ineffable
I have found the Key of the Mystery,
I have reached the Root of Union.
Travelling by no track, I have come to the Sorrowless
Land: very easily has the mercy of the great Lord come upon me.[20]
They have sung of Him as infinite and unattainable:
but I in my meditations have seen Him without sight.
That is indeed the sorrowless land,
and none know the path that leads there:
Only he who is on that path has surely transcended all sorrow.
Wonderful is that land of rest, to which no merit can win;
It is the wise who has seen it, it is the wise who has sung of it.

* * * * * * * * * *

13

What a frenzy of ecstasy there is in every hour!
and the worshipper is pressing out and drinking the essence of the hours;
he lives in the life of Brahma.

* * * * * * * * * *

16

Joy for ever, no sorrow, no struggle!

---

[19] The Hindi text in Dvivedī reads *adhara āsana kiyā*, which he translates as "seated in the void [of the Infinite]" meaning the moment of the mystic union with the Absolute.

[20] Dvivedī suggests that Kabīr means he is not the follower of any sect; and that his mystic experience has come to him *simply* (*sahaja*) through the mercy of the Lord of the Universe.

There have I seen joy filled to the brim,
perfection of joy;
No place for error is there.
Kabir says: 'There have I witnessed the sport of One Bliss.

17

I have known in my body the sport of the universe:
I have escaped from the error of this world.
The inward and the outward are become as one sky,
the Infinite and the finite are united.

18

I am drunken with the sight of this All!
This light of Thine fulfils the universe:
the lamp that burns on the salver of knowledge.
[My tent is pitched in the abode of the Infinite].[21]
Kabir says: 'There error cannot enter, and the conflict of life and death
is felt no more.'[22]

1

graha candra tapana jota barata hai,
surata rāga nirata tāra bājai;
naubatiyā ghurata hai raina dina sunna meṃ,
kahaiṃ kabīra piu gagana gājai.

2

kṣaṇa aura palaka kī āratī kaunasī,
raina-dina āratī visva gāvai;
ghurata nissāna tahaṃ gaiba ki jhālarā,
gaiba kī ghanṭaka nāda āvai.

3

kaheṃ kabīra tahaṃ raina-dina āratī,
jagata ke takhta para jagata sāṃīṃ.[23]
karma au bharma saṃsāra saba karata hai,
pīva ki parakha koī premi jānai;
surata au' nirata dhāra mana meṃ pakaṛakara,
ganga aura jamana ke ghāṭa ānai.
nīra nirmala tahāṃ raina-dina jharata hai,
janama au' marana taba anta pāī.

---

[21] This line occurs in the Hindi text only.
[22] *One Hundred Poems of Kabir*, pp. 17-25.
[23] According to the meaning, these two lines should conclude stanza 2 as in Tagore's translation.

4

dekha vojūda meṃ ajaba bisarāma hai,
hoya maujūda to sahī pāvai; [24]
surata kī ḍora sukha-sindha ke jhūlanā,
ghora kī sora tahaṃ nāda gāvai.
nīra-bina kaṃvala tahaṃ dekha ati phūliyā,
kahaiṃ kabīra mana bhaṃvara chāvai.

5

cakra ke bīca meṃ kaṃvala ati phūliyā,
tāsu kā sukkha koi santa jānai;
śabda kī ghora cahuṃ ora tahaṃ hota hai,
asīma samundara kī sukkha mānai.
kahaiṃ kabīra yoṃ ḍūba sukha-sindha meṃ,
janma aura marana kā bharma bhānai . . .

9

adhara āsana kiyā agama pyālā piyā,
joga kī mūla jaga juguti pāī;
pantha bina jāya cala sahara begamapurā,
dayā jagadeva kī sahaja āī.
dhyāna dhara dekhiyā naina-bina pekhiyā,
agama agādha saba kahata gāī;
sahara begamapurā gamma ko nā lahai,
hoya begamma jo gamma pāvai.
gunā kī gamma nā ajaba bisarāma hai,
saina jo lakhai soī saina gāvai . . .

13

āṭhahū pahara matavāla lāgī rahai,
āṭhahū pahara kī chāka pīvai;
āṭhahū pahara mastāna mātā rahai,
brahma ke deha meṃ bhakta jīvai . . .

16

sadā ānanda duga-danda vyāpai nahīṃ
puranānanda bharapūra dekhā;
bharma aura bhrānti tahaṃ neka nahiṃ pā'iye,
kahaiṃ kabīra rasa eka pekhā.

17

khela brahmāṇḍakā piṇḍa meṃ dekhiyā,
jagata kī bharamana dūra bhāgī;

---

[24] Dvivedī observes that *vojūda* and *maujūda* are Ṣūfī terms.

bāharā-bhītarā eka ākāsavata,
dhariyā meṃ adhara bharapūra lāgī.

18

dekha dīdāra mastāna maiṃ hoya rahyā,
sakala bharapūra hai nūra terā;
jñāna kā thāla aura prema dīpaka ahai,
adhara āsana kiyā agama ḍerā.
kahaiṃ kabīra tahaṃ bharma bhāse nahīṃ,
janama aura marana kā miṭā pherā.[25]

Although his mystic vision expressed in these rhapsodic verses has certain imagistic associations with *saguṇa* bhakti poetry,—for example, the Beloved radiant on high adored like Kṛṣṇa with a waving of lights (*āratī*)—the recurring note of the identity of the finite with the Infinite is unmistakable. In the main, the poetry of Kabīr is that of a *bhakta*, or saint, who tries to give an intimation of the ineffable Absolute that cannot strictly be said to be either conditioned or unconditioned.

O how may I ever express that secret word?
O how can I say He is not like this, and He is like that?
If I say that He is within me, the Universe is ashamed:
He makes the inner and the outer worlds to be indivisibly one;
The conscious and the unconscious, both are His footstools.
He is neither manifest nor hidden.
He is neither revealed nor unrevealed:
There are no words to tell that which He is.[26]

aisā lo nahiṃ taisā lo,
maiṃ kehi bidhi kathauṃ gambhīrā lo.
bhītara kahūṃ to jagamaya lājai,
bāhara kahūṃ to jhūṭhā lo.
bāhara-bhītara sakala nirantara,
cita-acita do'u pīṭhā lo,
dṛṣṭi na muṣṭi paragata agocara,
bātana kahā na jāī lo.' [27]

Thomas Traherne

The English Metaphysical poet who, in the apprehension of the unity underlying all existence, comes nearest to Kabir's ecstatic

[25] Dvivedī, *op. cit.*, pp. 243-250.
[26] *One Hundred Poems of Kabir*, p. 9.
[27] Dvivedī, *op. cit.*, p. 238.

spiritual happiness is Thomas Traherne (1637-1674). In his poetry and in his prose meditations, the *Centuries*, he writes of the *felicity* experienced through his love for God, His creatures and all phenomena. K. W. Salter, in a recent study, says of him:

> What Traherne writes in the *Centuries* must be taken to complete or enlarge what is written in the poetry. One conclusion we may draw is this. Christian thinkers have always hesitated to identify the innermost self with God. Yet the actual experience of the mystics impels them to this very conclusion which the conscious doctrinal mind is reluctant to make, that this secret self, this 'sphere of light' is also God. (Incidentally ... this identification is one that other mystical traditions, outside Christianity, for instance that of the *Vedanta*, did not flinch from making.) Traherne feels this identity to be a fact of experience. . . .[28]

The following verses clearly express Traherne's sense of the Infinite in the finite:

> A vast and Infinit Capacitie,
> Did make my Bosom like the Deitie,
> In Whose Mysterious and Celestial Mind
> All Ages and all Worlds together shind.
> Who tho he nothing said did always reign,
> And in Himself Eternitie contain.
> The World was more in me, than I in it.
> The King of Glory in my Soul did sit.
> And to Himself in me he always gave,
> All that he takes Delight to see me have.
> For so my Spirit was an Endless Sphere,
> Like God himself, and Heaven and Earth was there.
>
> (*Silence*, lines 75-86) [29]

As an Anglican clergyman, Traherne is faced with the problem of reconciling the truth of his mystic experience with the doctrines of orthodox Christianity; of identifying the Creator God of Herbert with his own intuition of an immanent and transcendent Absolute as pure Being. *My Spirit* states Traherne's belief that his real self is simple being akin to the Absolute Being: and awareness of this as a fact is the supreme *felicity*.

---

[28] K. W. Salter, *Thomas Traherne, Mystic and Poet* (London, 1964), p. 69.

[29] Thomas Traherne, *Centuries, Poems and Thanksgivings*, ed. H. M. Margoliouth (Oxford, 1958), 2 Vols. II, 48, 50.

My Spirit

1

My Naked Simple Life was I.
That Act so Strongly Shind
Upon the Earth, the Sea, the Skie,
That was the Substance of My Mind.
The Sence it self was I.
I felt no Dross nor Matter in my Soul,
No Brims nor Borders, such as in a Bowl
We see, My Essence was Capacitie.
That felt all Things,
The Thought that Springs
Therfrom's it self. It hath no other Wings
To Spread abroad, nor Eys to see,
Nor Hands Distinct to feel,
Nor Knees to Kneel:
But being Simple like the Deitie
In its own Centre is a Sphere
Not shut up here, but evry Where.

2

It Acts not from a Centre to
Its Object as remote,
But present is, when it doth view,
Being with the Being it doth note.
Whatever it doth do,
It doth not by another Engine work,
But by it self; which in the Act doth lurk.
Its Essence is Transformd into a true
And perfect Act.
And so Exact
Hath God appeard in this Mysterious Fact,
That tis all Ey, all Act, all Sight,
And what it pleas can be,
Not only see,
Or do; for tis more Voluble then Light:
Which can put on ten thousand Forms,
Being clothd with what it self adorns.

In the next two sections Traherne dilates upon the fact that his being is identified with all natural phenomena, however remote. They seem to be at one and the same time outside and within him by virtue of his Spirit:

The Act was Immanent, yet there,
The Thing remote, yet felt even here.

He seems to vacillate between monism and a qualified dualism, which is essentially Christian theism. And in this respect he is unlike Kabir the monist. But the experience, however it may be accounted for in metaphysical and theological terms, doubtless brings the poet unqualified happiness:

5

O Joy! O Wonder, and Delight!
O Sacred Mysterie!
My Soul a Spirit infinit!
An Image of the Deitie!
A pure Substantiall Light!
That Being Greatest which doth Nothing seem!
Why twas my All, I nothing did esteem
But that alone. A Strange Mysterious Sphere!
A Deep Abyss
That sees and is
The only Proper Place or Bower of Bliss.
To its Creator tis so near
In Lov and Excellence
In Life and Sence,
In Greatness Worth and Nature; And so Dear;
In it, without Hyperbole,
The Son and friend of God we see.

7

O Wondrous Self! O Sphere of Light,
O Sphere of Joy most fair;
O Act, O Power infinit;
O Subtile, and unbounded Air!
O Living Orb of Sight!
Thou which within me art, yet Me! Thou Ey,
And Temple of his Whole Infinitie!
O what a World art Thou! a World within!
All Things appear,
All Objects are
Alive in thee! Supersubstancial, Rare,
Abov them selvs, and nigh of Kin
To those pure Things we find
In his Great Mind
Who made the World! tho now Ecclypsd by Sin.
There they are Usefull and Divine,
Exalted there they ought to Shine.

This poem is Traherne's most comprehensive expression of his spiritual life and its culminating mystic experience[30]. "It contains the experience of the Infant Eye reflected on in maturity, the mature experience of the Infant Eye regained, the mature man's mystical inner experience, and all three united in an act of the understanding which is itself a further experience." [31] The "Infant Eye" refers to Traherne's vision in childhood as pure *felicity* recorded in such poems as The *Salutation, Wonder, Eden* and *Innocence* in which the child is "A little Adam in a Sphere of Joy". Salter speaks of Traherne's feelings in these poems as being of "childhood *as he remembers it*".[32] Miss Wade suggests that the poems, though professedly autobiographical, are more valuable as symbolic of the poet's awareness of the childlike intuition of the mystic. "Thus for Traherne the child is a living parable, an embodiment of truth; but he is not the truth itself, as some would have us believe. And there can be no doubt that the poems of childhood wherever they occur in Traherne are the richer when we understand their symbolism." [33] Whether it is recollection or the search for symbols that motivates the poetry of Traherne, he resembles Vaughan in his nostalgia for childhood. Yet his own emphasis is on the child as "A Naked Simple Pure Intelligence" that intuitively grasps the unity underlying all appearances, and thereby attains the *felicity* of simple, pure being:

2

Then was my Soul my only All to me,
A Living Endless Ey,
Far wider then the Skie
Whose Power, whose Act, whose Essence was to see.
I was an Inward *Sphere of Light*,
Or an Interminable Orb of *Sight*,
An Endless and a Living Day,
A vital Sun that round about did *ray*
All Life and Sence,
A Naked Simple Pure *Intelligence*.

4

For *Sight* inherits Beauty, *Hearing* Sounds,
The *Nostril* Sweet Perfumes,
All *Tastes* have hidden Rooms

---

30 *Thomas Traherne*, ed., Margoliouth, II, 50-56.
31 *Ibid.*, p. 349.
32 Salter, *op. cit.*, p. 34.
33 G. I. Wade, *Thomas Traherne* (New Jersey/London, 1946), p. 170.

Within the *Tongue*; and *Feeling Feeling* Wounds
with Pleasure and Delight: but I
Forgot the rest, and was all Sight, or Ey.
Unbodied and Devoid of Care,
Just as in Heavn the Holy Angels are.
For Simple Sence
Is Lord of all Created Excellence.

5

Be'ing thus prepard for all Felicity,
Not prepossest with Dross,
Nor stifly glued to gross
And dull Materials that might ruine me,
Not fetterd by an Iron Fate
With vain Affections in my Earthy State
To any thing that might Seduce
My Sence, or misemploy it from its use
I was as free
As if there were nor Sin, nor Miserie.

(*The Preparative*) [34]

But this "Simple Pure Intelligence" is for a period obscured by the adult experience of Traherne; and a re-illumination of his spirit is only to be achieved by a return to the inner condition of his pristine innocence:

An Antepast of Heaven sure!
I on the Earth did reign.
Within, without me, all was pure.
I must becom a Child again.

(*Innocence*, lines 57-60) [35]

This return is not, however, possible without the co-operation of the highest reason and faith. Traherne's *Centuries*, impassioned and lyrical, attempts to reconcile his intuition of the immanent and transcendent Absolute as pure Intelligence and Being with the Christian doctrine of redemptive love as the instrument of union between creature and Creator. But Traherne, unlike Kabīr to whom the world is unreal, looks upon the world as a manifestation of God, rather than His creation existing as a separate entity outside Himself:

---

[34] *Thomas Traherne*, ed. Margoliouth, II, 20, 22.
[35] *Ibid.*, II, 18.

> ..... how do we know, but the World is that Body, which the Diety hath assumed to manifest His Beauty and by which He maketh Himself as visible, as it is Possible He should? [36]

From this speculation he goes on to assert that

> ..... ancient Philosophers hav thought GOD to be the *Soul of the World.* Since therfore this visible World is the Body of GOD, not his Natural Body, but which He hath assumed; let us see how Glorious His Wisdom is, in Manifesting Himself therby. It hath not only represented His infinity and Eternity which we thought impossible to be represented by a Body, but His Beauty also, His Wisdom, Goodness, Power, Life and Glory, His Righteousness, Lov, and Blessedness: all which as out of a plentifull Treasurie, may be taken and collected out of this World. (*The Centuries,* II, 21) [37]

From this point Traherne elaborates on the nature and structure of the universe as a demonstration of God's Infinity, Eternity and Beauty. He continues in the next section of the *Second Century* with the observation that man reveals most fully the Glory of God:

> Abov all, Man Discovereth the Glory of GOD: who being Himself Immortal, is the Divinest Creature. He hath a Dominion over all the rest and GOD over Him. By Him, the Fountain of all these Things is the End of them: for He can return to their Author deserved Praises. Sences cannot resemble that which they cannot apprehend; nor express that which they cannot resemble, but in a shady maner. But Man is made in the Image of GOD, and therfore is a Mirror and Representativ of Him. And therfore in Himself He may see GOD, which is His Glory and Felicitie. His Thoughts and Desires can run out to Everlasting. His Lov can extend to all Objects, His Understanding is an endless Light, and can infinitly be present in all Places, and see and Examine all Beings, survey the reasons, surmount the Greatness, exceed the Strength, contemplat the Beauty, Enjoy the Benefit, and reign over all it sees and Enjoys like the Eternal GODhead. Here is an Invisible Power, an Indivisible Omnipresence, a Spiritual Supremacy, an Inward, Hidden, unknown Being Greater then all. A Sublime and Soveraign Creature meet to live in Communion with GOD in the fruition of them. (*The Centuries,* II, 23) [38]

It is evident that Traherne is grateful for the joyous senses of the physical man. In his liturgical *Thanksgivings for the Body* he writes:

---

[36] *Ibid.,* I, 66.
[37] *Ibid.,* I, 66.
[38] *Ibid.,* I, 68-69.

> For our Bodies therefore, O Lord, for our earthly Bodies, hast thou made the World: Which thou so lovest, that thou hast supremely magnified them by the works of thy hands: . . .
>
> O Miracle
> Of divine Goodness!
> O Fire! O Flame of Zeal, and Love, and Joy!
> Even for our earthly bodies, hast thou created all things.[39]

He goes on to say that by "all things" he means both the visible and the invisible, even

> The holy Angels minister unto us.
> Architects and Masons build us Temples.
> The Sons of Harmony fill thy Quires.
> Where even our sensible bodies are entertained by thee with great magnificence; and solaced with Joys.
> Jesus Christ hath washed our feet.
> He ministred to us by dying for us.
> And now in our humane body, sitteth at thy right hand, in the throne of Glory.[40]

But the resurrected body of Jesus is the physical body transformed even as he "shall change our vile body, that it may be fashioned like unto his glorious body; according to the working whereby he is able to subdue all things to himself." [41] It appears from this that Traherne is not content with his physical body and looks forward to its spiritualisation in the hereafter:

> *Then shall each Limb a spring of Joy be found,*
> *And ev'ry Member with its Glory crown'd:*
> *While all the Senses, fill'd with all the Good*
> *That ever Ages in them understood,*
> *Transported are: Containing Worlds of Treasure,*
> *At one Delight with all their Joy and Pleasure.*
> *From whence, like Rivers, Joy shall overflow,*
> *Affect the Soul, though in the Body grow.*
> *Return again, and make the Body shine*
> *Like Jesus Christ, while both in one combine,. . .*[42]

---

[39] *Ibid.*, II, 220.
[40] *Thomas Traherne*, ed., Margoliouth, II, 223-224.
[41] *Ibid.*, p. 225.
[42] *Ibid.*, pp. 225—226.

Although this poem occurs in a context which clearly relates the regeneration of man to the redemption by Christ, it is nevertheless suffused with the light of Traherne's *felicity* experienced in the microcosm of the individual human soul when the body is transcended. This *felicity* of his faded childhood, he now hopes, will ultimately be recaptured by the redemptive spiritualisation of the physical body. The spiritualising of the earthly is similar in conception to *siddhi*, the perfection to which the *siddha* or *avadhūta* attains through *haṭha yoga* so that his body, no longer subject to the laws of time and space, becomes immortal. The body so transformed is the *bhāva-deha* of pure being and the "Naked Simple Pure Intelligence". Thus it appears that, in spite of doctrinal differences, Traherne's spiritual insight comes quite close to Kabīr's apprehension of the unity that underlies all being, but he remains essentially a Christian theist.

Henry Vaughan

The tone of Henry Vaughan's poetry is chiefly devotional and quietistic with only occasional traces of the mystical rapture so evident in Kabīr and Traherne. His attitude to the universe is certainly different from Kabīr's, since to him nature is the extraneous quickening agent of his insight into his own destiny as a creature of God; and in this respect he appears to be somewhat different from Traherne, too, whose all-comprehensive vision (in spite of his theistic beliefs) often seems to identify all things animate and inanimate with God.

The world provides Vaughan with numerous emblems of the spiritual into which he hopes to be perfected by God's love to mankind. Natural phenomena, the passage of time, day and night, and the seasons of the year,—all suggest correspondences between the physical, transitory aspects of human experience and the spiritual realities of the Christian faith. The emblematic in the phenomenal world is intended by God to be read by man created in His own image. The percipient observer of nature is therefore able, as it were, to interpret the hieroglyphics of God seen in the objects of the world, and to realise that they speak to him of what is essentially true of his own nature. This is clearly stated in *The Tempest*:

How is man parcell'd out? how ev'ry hour
    Shows him himself, or somthing he should see?

This late, long heat may his Instruction be,
And tempests have more in them than a showr.

He must learn from the tempest to make a period of "long heat" the preparation for fertilizing showers. Sighs of an apparently barren period spiritually, can result in new growth watered by the tears of genuine repentance, if man would but learn the lesson of nature:

O that man could do so! that he would hear
The world read to him! all the vast expence
In the Creation shed, and slav'd to sence
Makes up but lectures for his eie, and ear.

Sure, mighty love foreseeing the discent
Of this poor Creature, by a gracious art
Hid in these low things snares to gain his heart,
And layd surprises in each Element.[43]

Another poem, *The Showre*, is similarly an emblematic expression of the course of true repentance leading from sighs and tears to the grace of God's sunshine on a refreshed soul:

Yet, if as thou doest melt, and with thy traine
Of drops make soft the Earth, my eyes could weep
O're my hard heart, that's bound up, and asleep,
Perhaps at last
(Some such showres past,)
My God would give a sun-shine after raine [44]

Vaughan's emblems generally show a vigour of exploration in which the progression of thought matches the dynamism of the images as the correspondences increase in number and significance. In this respect Vaughan is unlike both Traherne and Kabīr, for their images tend to be static and to make their impression by reduplication of ideas. *The Water-fall* is a good example of how Vaughan's creative sensibility operates. The poem starting off with the cataract as the emblem of fall or death, immediately after leads on to a new movement of the fallen drops in the running stream below, the symbol of continued and fuller life:

---

[43] Henry Vaughan, *The Works*, ed., L. C. Martin, (Oxford, 1957), p. 461.
[44] *Ibid*., p. 413.

. . .All must descend
Not to an end:
But quickend by this deep and rocky grave,
Rise to a longer course more bright and brave.[45]

The stream as a perpetual current of drops that come and go now becomes the emblem of men's souls returning to God. There should, therefore, be no fear of falling into the power of death in the grave, of shade or night, since all souls have come from a sea of light to which God will reunite them. But to be restored to the sea of life there must be redemption through cleansing. So the thought returns to the "useful Element and clear", to the "Fountains of Life, where the Lamb goes." To discern all this significance in the emblem of the stream, the mind must be quickened by the Spirit,

Which first upon thy face did move,
And hatch'd all with his quickning love.[46]

This allusion to the Spirit of God moving upon the face of the waters at creation suggests the immensity and calm of eternity for which the poet longs in the tumult of this life, which is like the movement and sound of the waterfall. So the thought has come full circle back to the fall of waters which is but the preliminary to the final calm of union with God, the source of movement and life.

In his most perceptive moments nature is, for Vaughan, the shadow of eternity and a partial manifestation of the divine spirit. In such moments he has intimations of God's all-pervasive presence and of a possible kinship between man and nature. In the following stanzas from the poem beginning "I walkt the other day (to spend my hour)", he expresses an awareness of God's immanence in natural phenomena:

7

O thou! whose spirit did at first inflame
And warm the dead,
And by a sacred Incubation fed
With life this frame
Which once had neither being, forme, nor name,

---

[45] *Ibid.*, p. 537.
[46] *Ibid.*, p. 538.

Grant I may so
Thy steps track here below
That in these Masques and shadows I may see
Thy sacred way,
And by those hid ascents climb to that day
Which breaks from thee
Who art in all things, though invisibly;
Show me thy peace,
Thy mercy, love, and ease. . .[47]

And "meditating on a verse in the Epistle to the Romans [vii, 19] which declares that inanimate objects await the revelation of the Sons of God, he realises that this transcends the Aristotelian categories": [48]

And do they so? have they a Sense
Of ought but Influence?
Can they their heads lift, and expect,
And grone too?. . .[49]

Yet Vaughan remains very conscious of the existence of human beings as separate from that of the lower creatures which he refers to in the poem entitled *Man* as "mean things which here below reside". At the same time he has noticed in them a strict adherence to the law of their being:

. . . . all things that subsist and be,
Have their Commissions from Divinitie,
And teach us duty. . . .[50]

They never deviate from their proper duty as bird, plant, stone or star; while man, because of his perverse will, violates the divine law of God by sinning, and thus mars the beauty of God's creation. He therefore prays for God's love to restore him to constancy of devotion which is man's duty towards the divine.

3

I would I were some *Bird*, or Star,
Flutt'ring in woods, or lifted far

[47] *Ibid.*, p. 479.
[48] Geoffrey Bullough, *Mirror of Minds*, (London, 1962), pp. 43-44.
[49] Vaughan, *op. cit.*, p. 432.
[50] *Ibid.*, p. 489.

Above this Inne
And Rode of sin!
Then either Star, or *Bird*, should be
Shining, or singing still to thee.

(*Christs Nativity*) [51]

2

I would I were a stone, or tree,
Or flowre by pedigree,
Or some poor high-way herb, or Spring
To flow, or bird to sing!
Then should I (tyed to one sure state,)
All day expect my date;
But I am sadly loose, and stray
A giddy blast each way;
O let me not thus range!
Thou canst not change.

3

Sometimes I sit with thee, and tarry
An hour, or so, then vary.
Thy other Creatures in this Scene
Thee only aym, and mean;
Some rise to seek thee, and with heads
Erect peep from their beds;
Others, whose birth is in the tomb,
And cannot quit the womb,
Sigh there, and grone for thee,
Their liberty.

4

O let me not do lesse! shall they
Watch, while I sleep, or play?
Shall I thy mercies still abuse
With fancies, friends, or newes?
O brook it not! thy bloud is mine,
And my soul should be thine;
O brook it not! why wilt thou stop
After whole showres one drop?
Sure, thou wilt joy to see
Thy sheep with thee.[52]

Though Vaughan feels the urgent need for union with God who is in

---

[51] *Ibid.*, p. 442.
[52] *Ibid.*, pp. 432-433.

all things though invisibly, he nevertheless steers clear of both non-dualism and pantheism. To him the world, space and time are realities. Only after death will man find his true centre and permanent home, when he is finally admitted into the "great Ring of pure and endless light" that is Eternity. There is for Vaughan a clear division between the present existence and life after death:

> Two *Lifes* I hold from thee, my gracious Lord,
> Both cost thee dear,
> For one, I am thy Tenant here;
> The other, the true life, in the next world
> And endless is. . .
>
> (*The Match,* ii, 7-11) [53]

But there are suggestions in his poetry that it is possible to catch glimpses of Eternity behind the veil of the flesh, and to have some brief experience of the *felicity* which such visions bring to mystics like Kabīr and Traherne. This was the kind of happiness he had in his "Angell-infancy" when he

> . . . . . felt through all this fleshly dresse
> Bright *shootes* of everlastingnesse.
>
> (*The Retreate,* lines 19-20) [54]

Vaughan's philosophy like Traherne's is therefore seen to be different from Kabīr's in that it is basically derived from his Christian belief in a Creator God who is only partially manifested in this world; and with whom full communion will only be restored in the life to come. But in *The Night* Vaughan beautifully integrates the neo-Platonic doctrine of the pseudo-Dionysius concerning the nature of the unconditioned Absolute with biblical associations worked into the manner of a spiritual exercise. The result is a powerfully symbolic poem reflecting a near mystic intuition of God as the all-embracing unconditioned Absolute:

> There is in God (some say)
> A deep, but dazling darkness; As men here
> Say it is late and dusky, because they
> See not all clear;

[53] *Ibid.*, p. 435.
[54] *Ibid.*, p. 419.

O for that night! where I in him
Might live invisible and dim.

(*The Night*, lines 49-54)

The New Testament episode of Nicodemus' visit to Jesus by night blends with the lover-beloved intimacy of the Canticles to express the communion of the human with the divine:

Gods silent, searching flight:
When my Lords head is fill'd with dew, and all
His locks are wet with the clear drops of night;
His still, soft call;
His knocking time; The souls dumb watch,
When Spirits their fair kinred catch.

(*The Night*, lines 31-36) [55]

Thus in *The Night* Vaughan combines a warm personal emotion with his fleeting apprehension of the unconditioned Absolute as "a deep, but dazling darkness". And in doing so, he shares in the metaphysical vision of Kabīr and Traherne. However, his poetry considered as a whole seems to support Miss Jennings' conclusion:

> In the modern sense of metaphysics as the study of *being*, Vaughan is not a Metaphysical at all; he does not study being but embraces it. His poetry appears at that point where inquiry ends and affirmation begins. He stands passive before the transcendent and makes it immanent through the medium of poetry.[56]

In the process of attempting to make the transcendent immanent through the medium of poetry, Vaughan's sensibility responds to a wide range of experience and knowledge. And as Kabīr's eclecticism absorbs various aspects of *haṭha-yoga, Rāma-bhakti,* Vedānta and Ṣūfīsm, so Vaughan's Christianity assimilates ideas and concepts from neo-Platonism, seventeenth-century science and hermeticism into his poetic interpretation of nature, God and the human spirit. This is evident in the complex undercurrents of meaning in the commonplace images of light, ray, star, veil, etc., as Professor Mahood has shown in her study of Vaughan's imagery. [57]

The wholly, or partially, successful assimilation of neo-Platonic and

[55] *Ibid.*, pp. 522-523.
[56] Elizabeth Jennings, *Every Changing Shape*, (London, 1961), p. 82.
[57] M. M. Mahood, *Poetry and Humanism*, (London, 1950), pp. 252-295.

hermetic ideas and terminology into the description of Christian religious experience in the case of Vaughan, or of *haṭha-yoga* in the expression of the *santa's nirguṇa* bhakti in the case of Kabīr, shows how skilfully esoteric philosophy of the sixteenth and seventeenth centuries is put to the service of a genuine religious quest. Kabīr is not, however, as successful as Vaughan in making the esoteric as readily available to the uninitiated in terms of their everyday experiences. Though Vaughan's thought may, for example, in *Cock-crowing*, partly derive its impetus from his acquaintance with the hermetic theory of the "Ray" of God's divine light implanted in all creatures like a "Sunnie seed", the poem is, nevertheless, comprehensible to all those who associate cock-crowing with dawn.

> Father of lights! what Sunnie seed,
> What glance of day hast thou confin'd
> Into this bird? To all the breed
> This busie Ray thou hast assign'd;
>   Their magnetisme works all night,
>   And dreams of Paradise and light. . . .[58]

The analogy between birds awaiting the morning light and the human soul's longing to be united with God, the divine light, is easy to grasp. The poem has its own logic and does not depend upon any extraneous aid for its deciphering. Further, the emotional and intellectual satisfaction derives from Vaughan's characteristic exploration of the image by an extension of its meaning into the related images of sleep and death, resurrection and eternal life:

> If joyes, and hopes, and earnest throws,
> And hearts, whose Pulse beats still for light
> Are given to birds; who, but thee, knows
> A love-sick souls exalted flight?
>   Can souls be track'd by any eye
>   But his, who gave them wings to flie?
>
> Onely this Veyle which thou hast broke,
> And must be broken yet in me,
> This veyle, I say, is all the cloke
> And cloud which shadows thee from me.
>   This veyle thy full-ey'd love denies,
>   And onely gleams and fractions spies.

---

[58] Vaughan, *op. cit.*, p. 488.

O take it off! make no delay,
But brush me with thy light, that I
May shine unto a perfect day,
And warme me at thy glorious Eye!
O take it off! or till it flee,
Though with no Lilie, stay with me! [59]

Kabīr's *haṭha-yoga* imagery is dependent on its metaphysical signification for the initial movement towards communication between poet and reader; and some of his obscurer verses, such as the *ulaṭavāṃsī* which employs paradox and riddle, are almost meaningless without a gloss. For example:

O avadhūta, consider such wisdom as this:
Those who enter the boats are drowned in the sea,
While those without any support go across. . . .

Those who go into the temple are drenched through,
but those who remain outside are entirely dry.

avadhū aisā gyāna bicāreṃ
bherai caṛhe su adhadhara ḍūbe, nirādhāra bhaye pāraṃ. . .
mandira paisi cahūṃ disi bhīge, bāhari rahe to sūkā.[60]

Commentators taking their clue from the address to the *avadhūta* (the *yogī* perfected in spirituality) explain these verses to mean that devotees who rely upon the worship of gods fail to gain release from the ocean of existence, while those not dependent upon gods achieve salvation. These who enter the temple of the universal void (the *śūnya* of *haṭha-yoga*) are soaked in the ecstasy that comes from achieving identity with the Absolute. Since Kabīr addresses himself to the hearts and intelligences of the ordinary masses, his intention is certainly not to be cryptic merely for the sake of being obscure, or for concealing the truth from them so that they might hear and yet not understand. The explanation lies in the very nature of Kabīr's vision which sees truth as essentially having a logic contrary to that of ordinary reason. To him the apparently real is unreal, the world is illusion and the values of conventional life meaningless. Paradoxes and contrarieties are therefore his natural mode of thinking, and one of the means of intimating to others his spiritual vision.

---

[59] *Ibid.*, p. 489.
[60] Kabīr, *Kabīra Granthāvalī*, ed. Śyāmasundara Dāsa (Banaras, 1964), p. 110, *pada* 175.

To Kabīr the phenomenal world is *māyā* with the seductiveness of a woman who woos the soul from that dispassion on which is dependent its sense of identity with the Absolute. Therefore his affirmation of his belief in the Absolute results in a negation of the world of the senses. In contrast to this, Traherne's and Vaughan's conception of the spiritual is a fulfilment of their joy in the phenomenal world and human existence. This difference in attitude accounts for the distinctive use of nature imagery in the works of these poets. Kabīr is motivated by his ethical or philosophical intention to use the images as illustrations. In Traherne and Vaughan the imagery itself is part of the experience to be conveyed for its own sake, since they enter into the life of the world as a foretaste of the eternal happiness to come. But in the final analysis, the metaphysical poetry of East and West, like that of Kabīr, Traherne and Vaughan, suggests that the successful quest transcends the limits both of the physical senses and the human intellect.

CHAPTER EIGHT

ENGLISH METRICAL PSALMS, DONNE'S HOLY SONNETS AND TULASĪ DĀSA'S *VINAYA PATRIKĀ*

Many English Renaissance poets, from the song and sonnet writers of the sixteenth century to the Metaphysicals of the seventeenth, were drawn to the Old Testament Psalms for comfort in times of personal sorrow, or by a desire to hymn the greater glory of God in preference to composing secular love lyrics; (although according to Professor Hallett Smith the versification of the Psalms to compete with profane lyrics was perhaps the least important of the motives that impelled the translators).[1] Among the best known of these who produced metrical versions of just a few or all the Psalms were Wyatt, Surrey, Thomas Sternhold, John Hopkins, Thomas Norton, Archbishop Parker, Sir Philip Sidney and the Countess of Pembroke, Spenser (whose Penitential Psalms are no longer extant), George Wither, Herbert, Vaughan, Crashaw and Milton.

Henry Howard, Early of Surrey, who was executed in 1547, translated during his final imprisonment, three Psalms—numbers 55, 73 and 88—in which he expresses his grief at the oppression he suffered at the hands of his enemies, his contrition because of his sinfulness, his fear of death, and finally his trust in God in the hour of his extremity. In all three of the Psalms he allows himself the utmost latitude in translation thus imbuing them with the passionate invective or overwhelming anguish of his personal experience. In Psalm 55 written in unrhymed hexameters (the other two are in fourteeners, derisively labelled Poulter's Measure), his touching laments alternating with expressions of vindictiveness against his enemies and the desire for retaliation, finally end on the note of trust in God's grace. The following excerpt will give some idea of the long-drawn-out movement of the verse and the concreteness of the images employed in Surrey's version of Psalm 55:

Giue eare to my suit, Lord! fromward hide not thy face.
Beholde, herking in grief, lamenting how I praye.
My fooes they bray so lowde, and eke threpe on so fast,

[1] See Hallett Smith, "English Metrical Psalms in the Sixteenth Century and their Literary Significance", *Huntington Library Quarterly* 9 (1945-46) pp. 249-271.

Buckeled to do me scathe, so is their malice bent.
Care perceth my entrayles, and traueyleth my spryte;
The greslye feare of death enuyroneth my brest;
A tremblynge cold of dred clene ouerwhelmeth my hert.
"O!" thinke I, "hadd I wings like to the symple doue,
This peryll myght I flye, and seke some place of rest
In wylder woods, where I might dwell farr from these cares."
What speady way of wing my playnts shold thei lay on,
To skape the stormye blast that threatned is to me?

The final verses are:

But in the thother Psalme of David fynd I ease:
Iacta curam tuam super dominum et ipse te enutriet.[2]

The personal note in Surrey's versions is further emphasised by the prologues that he wrote to Psalms 73 and 88 which are different in temper from Psalm 55 probably written, according to Padelford, before Surrey's trial on the charge of treason.

> Most significant are the prologues of these two Psalms, one of which was addressed to George Blage, with whom Surrey had had the quarrel which precipitated his trial, and the other to Sir Antony Denny, one of the secretaries of the King, who must have had a hand in Surrey's downfall. Never more courageous than in the presence of death, Surrey would have his enemies understand that he no longer feared what they could do.[3]

But the calm assurance of Surrey's final poetic statement was only achieved after the agony of self-communing through these two Psalms 88 and 73, translated in that order by him. They reveal his spirit struggling through the tempests of doubts, fears, and physical suffering to a peaceful refuge in God. Psalm 73 and its prologue are closely associated in tone by the image of the storm-tossed soul.

---

[2] *The Poems of Henry Howard, Earl of Surrey* ed. F. M. Padelford (Seattle, 1928), pp. 110-111. Padelford comments on the last two lines: 'By "thother Psalm" I think that Surrey meant not another Psalm, but the untranslated verse (23) of the present Psalm: *Jacta super Dominum curam tuam. . . .*' It is possible that he has overlooked the fact that "more than once an attempt has been made [in Biblical exegesis] to divide up the lament into two originally independent Psalms." Artur Weiser, *The Psalms: A Commentary* (London, 1965), p. 419. For such an attempt see Elmer A. Leslie, *The Psalms* (New York, 1944), pp. 332-336.

[3] *Ibid.*, p. 43.

PROLOG TO PSALM 73

The soudden stormes that heaue me to and froo
Had welneare pierced faith, my guyding saile,
For I, that on the noble voyage goo
To succhor treuthe and falshed to assaile,
Constrayned am to beare my sayles ful loo
And neuer could attayne some pleasaunt gaile,
For vnto such the prosperous winds doe bloo
As ronne from porte to porte to seke availe.
This bred dispayre, whereof such doubts did groo
That I gan faint and all my courage faile.
But, my Blage, myne errour well I see;
Such goodlye light King David giueth me.[4]

This is an elaboration which anticipates the Baroque of Robert Southwell and was suggested by Psalm 88:17 rendered in Surrey's version as

Like to the roring waues the sunken shipp surrounde,
Great heaps of care did swallow me and I no succour found.[5]

It is further carried over into lines 54 and 55 of Surrey's Psalm 73 where the Hebrew original and translations like Coverdale's make no mention of a ship or voyage.

But when I stode in drede to drenche, thy hands still did me stay.
And in eache voyage that I toke to conquer synne,
Thow wert my guyd, and gaue me grace to comfort me therin.
And when my withered skyn vnto my bones did cleue,
And fleshe did wast, thy grace did then my simple sprits releue.
In other succour then, Oh Lord, why should I trust,
But onely thyn, whom I haue found in thy behight so iust.[6]

However, in the face of the suffering of the innocent and the prosperity of the wicked, the justice of God will only be finally realised by a faith born of spiritual ordeal since man's wisdom cannot fathom the ways of God.

In terrour of the iust thus raignes iniquitye,
Armed with power, laden with gold, and dred for crueltye.

[4] *Ibid.*, p. 91.
[5] *Ibid.*, p. 112.
[6] *Ibid.*, p. 114.

Then vayne the warre might seme that I by fayth mayntayne
Against the fleshe, whose false effects my pure hert wold distayne.
For I am scourged still, that no offence have doon,
By wrathes children; and from my byrth my chastesing begoon.
When I behelde their pryde and slacknes of thy hand,
I gan bewaile the woful state wherin thy chosen stand.
And as I sought whereof thy sufferaunce, Lord, shold groo,
I found no witt cold pierce so farr, thy hollye domes to knoo,
And that no mysteryes nor dought could be distrust
Till I com to the holly place, the mansion of the iust,
Where I shall se what end thy iustice shall prepare
for such as buyld on worldly welth, and dye ther colours faire.[7]

A fourth Psalm, number 8, in praise of God's glory and majesty as Creator, was probably translated by Surrey before the period of his trial and desertion by his friends. This particular "translation is free, very spirited, full of colour, and worshipful in tone";[8] but, by the very nature of its subject matter, it does not have the emotional intensity of the other three, which provided the vehicle for Surrey's personal laments during the period of his greatest suffering.

Wyatt, similarly, in time of adversity wrote his version of the seven Penitential Psalms, posthumously published in 1549. Many others were also translating the Psalms in prose and verse, but the most popular versions were metrical psalms intended for singing. Professor Hallett Smith has suggested that the most familiar verse to English ears in the second half of the sixteenth century was the "Common Meter" of the rhyming Psalter known as Sternhold and Hopkins' Old Version.[9] This was begun by the courtier Thomas Sternhold during the forties in the reign of Henry VIII, continued and completed by the parson John Hopkins, Thomas Norton and other collaborators including some of the Puritan exiles in Geneva. *The Whole Booke of the Psalms*[10] was finally completed in 1562, the same year in which the poetically superior French Marot-Bèze version was completed.

In spite of the great popularity of the Old Version of Sternhold and Hopkins there was much dissatisfaction among people of

[7] *Ibid.*, p. 113.

[8] *Ibid.*, p. 231.

[9] Hallett Smith, "English Metrical Psalms in the Sixteenth Century and their Literary Influence", *Hutington Library Quarterly* 9 (1945-46), p. 251.

[10] "The first to publish the whole *Psalter of David translated into Englysh metre* was Robert Crowley. . . 1549" (Campbell, *Divine Poetry and Drama* p. 44.)

discriminating literary taste at the fact that nothing had been composed in English as good as the continental versions of the Marot-Bèze Psalter and the Lutheran hymns, although Thomas Wyatt's handful of Psalms had some genuine poetical qualities. He had employed the *terza rima* for his version of the seven Penitential Psalms,[11] and *ottava rima* for the links which helped to give the whole the appearance and, to some extent, effect of a unified work. The title of the 1549 edition was *Certayne Psalmes chosen out of thee. vii. penytentiall Psalmes, drawen into englysshe meter by Sir Thomas Wyat knyght, whereunto is added a prologe of the auctore before every psalme, very pleasant and profettable to the godly reader.*

Basing his metrical version on the prose paraphrase of Aretino, Wyatt did not hesitate to depart from this when the Vulgate or the English Psalter suited his purpose, with the result that his *terza rima* is used with skill and effectiveness. Rathmell makes the following comment on the quality of Wyatt's Penitential Psalms:

> They are frankly personal, exhibit a wide and sophisticated vocabulary, and are plainly, and in the best sense, the work of a "courtly maker." Wyatt's terza rima is continually animated by the acting out of a personally experienced struggle. In his version of Psalm 130, a judiciously controlled rhetoric enforces dramatically the halting utterance of an anguished plea to God.[12]

Psalm 130. De profundis Clamavi

From depth off sin and from a diepe dispaire,
    From depth off deth, from depth off hertes sorrow,
    From this diepe Cave off darkness diepe repayre,
The have I cald, O lord, to be my borow;
    Thow in my voice, O lord, perceyve and here
    My hert, my hope, my plaint, my ouerthrow,
My will to ryse: and let by graunt apere
    That to my voyce thin eres do well entend.
    No place so farr that to the is not nere;
No depth so diepe that thou ne maist extend
    Thin ere therto: here then my wofull plaint.
    Ffor, lord, if thou do observe what men offend
And putt thy natyff mercy in restraint,

---

[11] Artur Weiser, *The Psalms: A commentary* 5th ed. (London, 1965) p. 77, "Of the seven penitential psalms of the Ancient Church (Pss. 6; 33; 38; 51; 102; 130; 143), only 38, 51 and 130 are proper penitential psalms."

[12] J. C. A. Rathmell, *The Psalms of Sir Philip Sidney and The Countess of Pembroke* (New York, 1963), p. xvi.

If just exaction demaund recompense,
Who may endure, O lord? Who shall not faynt
At such acompt? Dred, and not reuerence
Shold so raine large. But thou sekes rathr love,
Ffor in thi hand is mercys resedence,
By hope whereoff thou dost our hertes move.
I in the, Lord, have set my confydence;
My sowle such trust doth euermore aprove.
Thi holly word off eterne excellence,
Thi mercys promesse that is alway just,
Have bene my stay, my piller and pretence.
My sowle in god hath more desyrus trust
Then hath the wachman lokyng for the day,
By the releffe to quenche of slepe the thrust.
Let Israell trust vnto the lord alway,
Ffor grace and favour arn his propertie;
Plenteous rannzome shall com with hym, I say,
And shall redeme all our iniquitie.[13]

thrust] thirst

Wyatt elaborates on the phrase *de profundis* "out of the depths", in terms of his own immediate experience of despair and desolation heightened by the consciousness of his utter sinfulness. This expansion of the original is reinforced by the heavy alliteration of the opening verses; and the inter-locking of the *terza rima* together with the frequent run-on lines gives the whole an effect of unceasing supplication for God's mercy and love. "The judiciously controlled rhetoric [that] dramatically reinforces the halting utterance" of lines like

Thow in my voice, O Lord, perceyve and here
My hert, my hope, my plaint, my ouerthrow,
My will to ryse:. . .

gives the poem a colloquial directness like that of the Holy Sonnets of John Donne.

Although Wyatt's versions of the few psalms he translated were his first draft, which he doubtless would have revised if he had had the opportunity, their intrinsic quality has elicited praise from recent critics like Muir who remarks that "it may even be said that Wyatt

[13] Kenneth Muir, (ed.) *Collected Poems of Sir Thomas Wyatt* (London, 1949) pp. 223-224.

contrived to make better metrical versions of the psalms than either Sidney or Milton." [14] But whereas Wyatt's translations were in *terza rima*, those of Sir Philip Sidney and his sister, The Countess of Pembroke, were in a large variety of metrical forms, some no doubt influenced by the examples of Wyatt, and several others certainly by the French Marot-Bèze Psalter according to the recent editor of the Sidney Psalms:

> ... The work that most obviously served as a model to the Sidneys is the French psalter of 1562, a collection that had been completed at Geneva by Théodore de Bèze on the foundation of fifty psalms composed between 1532 and 1543 by Clément Marot. Marot, like Sidney, was a court poet and never envisaged initially that his versified psalms would be put to congregational use. It was no doubt the accomplishment and variety of the French poet's work that first suggested to Sidney the poetic potential of the Psalms. Sidney has done no more than Marot in bringing to bear on his psalmody all the verbal and rhythmical subtlety of his lyric art. It is significant, for instance, that there is not a single example among the Sidneian Psalms of the simple ballad stanza or "fourteener" so monotonously employed by Sternhold and Hopkins. What Sidney and the Countess have attempted to do is to create for every one of the 150 Psalms a unique combination of stanza pattern and rhyme scheme.[15]

Although the Sidney translations were not published until the nineteenth century for the first time, there are fourteen extant manuscripts, and there is no doubt that the translations were widely read in court circles and were known to such men as Fulke Greville, Samuel Daniel, Ben Jonson, Joseph Hall, Sir John Harrington, (possibly to George Herbert), and certainly to Donne who wrote a panegyric on the Sidney versions, shortly after the death of the Countess of Pembroke in 1621, which he said were as divinely inspired as the Hebrew originals:

Upon the translation of the Psalmes
by Sir Philip Sydney,
and the Countesse of Pembroke his Sister

Eternal God, (for whom who ever dare
Seeke new expressions, doe the Circle square,
And thrust into strait corners of poore wit

---

[14] *Ibid.*, p. xxii.
[15] Rathmell, *op. cit.*, p. xvii.

Thee, who art cornerlesse and infinite)
I would but blesse thy Name, not name thee now;
(And thy gifts are as infinite as thou:)
Fixe we our prayses therefore on this one,
That, as thy blessed Spirit fell upon
These Psalmes first Author in a cloven tongue;
(For 'twas a double power by which he sung
The highest matter in the noblest forme;)
So thou hast cleft that spirit, to performe
That work againe, and shed it, here, upon
Two, by their bloods, and by thy Spirit one;
A Brother and a Sister, made by thee
The Organ, where thou art the Harmony. . . .
* * * * * *
So though some have, some may some Psalmes translate,
We thy Sydnean Psalmes shall celebrate,
And, till we come th' Extemporall song to sing,
(Learn'd the first hower, that we see the King,
Who hath translated these translators) may
These their sweet learned labours, all the way
Be as our tuning, that, when hence we part
We may fall in with them, and sing our part.[16]

It is generally agreed that only the first forty-three Psalms were the translations of Sir Philip Sidney who died in 1586; and that the rest were done by the Countess of Pembroke between 1593 and 1600. "The earliest reference to her work is Samuel Daniel's notable tribute to her "Hymnes" contained in an address prefixed to his *Cleopatra* (Stationers' Register, October 1593)."[17] The tributes of Donne and Daniel are an indication of the superiority of the "Sydnean Psalmes" over the majority, if not all, of the English metrical Psalms of the sixteenth century. They are devotional poems in their own right informed by a fervent faith; and the poetic skill of the two translators is dedicated to the task of producing a Psalter worthy of the laments, hymns and praises of the Hebrew originals. These sensitive renderings were aided by a scholarship which, though lacking a knowledge of Hebrew, made use of various commentaries and translations. "It is clear that [Sidney and the Countess of Pembroke] carefully compared the versions of the Psalms found in the Prayer Book psalter and the two current versions of the Bible, the Geneva

---

[16] John Donne, *The Divine Poems* ed. Helen Gardner (Oxford, 1952), pp. 33-35.
[17] Rathmell, *op. cit.*, p. xxvi.

Bible of 1560 and the Bishops' Bible of 1568. They also consulted (in the English translations of Golding and Gilby) the elaborate commentaries on the Psalms of Calvin and Bèze."[18]

The dual authorship of the work under consideration is mentioned only in passing, for since the primary purpose of this chapter is to draw analogies to the Psalms from Hindi bhakti poetry, the "Sydnean Psalms" will henceforth be treated as a unified work: only "the highest matter in the noblest form" will be the subject of discussion.

The hymns, laments, thanksgivings, prayers, supplications, and didactic poems of the Psalms have their Hindi counterparts in collections of divine petition poems, *vinaya*, the most famous of which is the crowning glory of bhakti poetry, Tulasī Dāsa's *Vinaya Patrikā*, which may be translated—"An Epistle of [Divine] Petitions". This consists of 279 poems in a large variety of metres most probably written between 1609 and 1623, although 1582 has been put forward by Veṇī Mādhava Dāsa as the date of their composition.[19] The substance and style of the *Vinaya Patrikā* indicate that it is a work of the final stages of the poet's career when he was much afflicted by bodily and mental suffering. In this work he turned in deep humility, contrition and utter submission, in the *dāsya-bhāva* of bhakti, for succour and final salvation from earthly existences. His "petition" is symbolically forwarded through the associated divinities, relations and servants of his Lord, notably Hanumān—the personification of faithful and unwavering service—to whom twelve of the hymns (numbers 25-36) are addressed. The course of the poems runs through the praises of, and petitions to, the gods, persons and places associated with Rāma who is himself Viṣṇu incarnate: hymns are addressed specifically to the gods Ganeśa, Sūrya (the Sun), Śiva, Devī (or Pārvatī, the consort of Śiva); to the rivers Ganges and Jumna; to the pilgrimage shrines of Kāśi (Banaras) and Citrakūṭa; to Hanumān, the three brothers of Rāma and his wife, Sītā. These hymns lead progressively to a climax in the outpourings of the poet's soul in the main body of the *Vinaya Patrikā* as laments, hymns and praises addressed to Rāma, his *iṣta-deva*, the special God of his adoration and love.

Each of the *padas* or poems of the *Vinaya Patrikā* can stand by

---

[18] *Ibid.*, p. xix.

[19] See Rāmakumāra Varmā, *Hindī Sāhitya kā Alocanātmaka Itihāsa* [A Critical History of Hindi Literature] (Allahabad, 1958), p. 417.

itself as a finished and complete lyric even as the individual psalm of the Psalter and the metrical version of the Sidneys, or the sonnet of a sequence. However, the significance of such a unit, though meaningful and possibly satisfying by itself, is enhanced by the cumulative effect of the entire sequence of lyrics or sonnets to which it belongs. The form of the *Vinaya Patrikā*, thus regarded, is a unified work of art. Though it may strike many readers as repetitious and monotonous, especially in its numerous compound epithets and frequent kennings (in the manner of Sanskrit and Old English poetry), the poet's moods are subtly modulated, often imperceptibly shifting from one to the next, but occasionally marked by a strong contrast in tone and imagery employing the homely figures of the market place instead of the colours of conventional rhetoric.

Tulasī Dāsa added musical superscriptions, (as is the case with some of the Old Testament Psalms), to indicate the *rāga* or "musical mode", not tune, suited to the individual *padas*, for these lyrics of the *Vinaya Patrikā* are essentially Vaiṣṇava hymns. There are in this work twenty-one *rāgas*, the most commonly employed in order of frequency being *Kalyāna, Dhanāśrī, Bilāvala* and *Rāmakalī*. All these may be used for praise or petition, but some are more suitable for lyrics with a marked descriptive or allusive quality (generally associated with characters from the Epics and the *Purāṇas*); others are best for lyrics in which there is the prevailing feeling of love and assurance or the quietistic mood. Since the great majority of the *padas* express some aspect or the other of praise and petition, it serves no literary purpose to classify them according to their *rāgas*.[20] The following classification into thematic groups might be useful for a comparison with the Psalms: 1. Praise and prayer:- in which the composition of a *pada* generally progresses from an enumeration and praise of the special qualities of the object of devotion, in metaphors and allusions, to supplication in the final verse; 2. Songs of wisdom and ethics; 3. Vanity of the world; 4. Statements on intellectual

[20] See *The Legacy of India* ed. C. T. Garratt (Oxford, 1937),for an article by A. H. Fox Strangways (pp. 305-327) in which he states that "*Rāga*, or mode, is the glory of Indian music." He gives an interesting analogy in discussing the difference between *rāga* and tune: "When 'Ye banks and braes' is sung over to an Indian musician, he will say it is in *Kalyan*, and will play variations not on the tune but in the mode. This is a little disconcerting until the European recognises that to the Indian the *mode* is everything and tune nothing. . ."

In classical Indian music there are six primary *rāgas*; but each *rāga* has six *rāgiṇīs* regarded as its consorts, and their union produces several musical modes.

dispassion.[21] The majority of the Psalm "types" [22] are the laments which bear the closest resemblance to the hymns and petitions of the *Vinaya Patrikā*; but whereas Tulasī Dāsa always voices the contrition and supplication of the individual devotee, the psalmists are often the mouthpiece of the congregation of Israel engaged in the cultic worship of Yahweh. Some notable exceptions are found among the seven penitential psalms which have always had the greatest universal appeal because of their more personal tone. The *dāsya-bhāva* of the Lord-servant relationship of Tulasī Dāsa's *Rāma-bhakti* therefore, though in some ways akin to the reverence and worship of the Holy and Almighty expressed by the Hebrew psalmists, is, nevertheless, basically different from the awe-inspired sense of the numinous in the singers of Israel to whom Yahweh, majestic and sublime, stands essentially in a Creator-creature relationship.[23]

The belief in *avatāras* brings the godhead of Viṣṇu, incarnate as Kṛṣṇa and Rāma, into the humanity of Vaiṣṇava devotees who reverence and adore, but above all love their God become man,—a conception as much Christian as Hindu, except for doctrinal differences regarding, in the one case, the incarnation of God as a unique event and, in the other, as recurring in successive *avatāras*. Much Christian exegesis of the Psalms appears to be coloured by the belief of the commentators in the fulfilment of the Old Testament in the life and teaching of Jesus Christ. This is one of the reasons, at least, for the more frequent note of tenderness in adaptations of the Psalms than in the Hebrew originals.

The Christian colouring of the Psalms is deepest in Thomas Traherne's rhapsodic *Thanksgivings* which derive their initial impulse from the liturgical use of the Psalter in Christian worship. The portions of the Psalms serving as epigraphs, at intervals, to Traherne's prose-poems acquire an almost mystical reflection from his pervasive joy, in the human body and soul, that is reminiscent of his "felicity" in the *Centuries* of meditation with their strong metaphysical cast. Sidney's metrical psalms, though not metaphysically exploited by an eccentric fervour, like Traherne's,

---

[21] This classification is summarised from Rāmakumāra Varmā, *op. cit.*, p. 419.

[22] These are hymns, laments, thanksgivings, blessing and curse, wisdom and didactic poems.

[23] The sense of awe is also predominant in the theistic cults of Śiva and Devī; yet when Tulasī Dāsa addresses these deities in the opening hymns of the *Vinaya Patrikā*, it is their beneficent and loving aspect that is emphasised to reconcile them to the *Rāma-bhakti* of Vaiṣṇavism.

do, at least in one instance, depart from the meaning of the Hebrew. Significantly, this occurs in Psalm 8 a glory song of God's creation, the theme that most often accounts for Traherne's raptures and visions of a basic unity in the universe that is derived from the essence of God who, in the Vedantic formula, *saccidānanda*, is "being-consciousness-joy". The whole of Sidney's rendering is worth quoting to show how his metaphysical conception of divine "essence", in the third stanza, fits into the scheme of the Psalm:

PSALM 8 *DOMINE, DOMINUS*

O Lord that rul'st our mortall lyne,
How through the world thy name doth shine:
That hast of thine unmatched glory
Upon the heav'ns engrav'n the story.

From sucklings hath thy honor sprong,
Thy force hath flow'd from babies tongue,
Whereby thou stopp'st thine en'mies prating
Bent to revenge and ever-hating.

When I upon the heav'ns do look,
Which all from thee their essence took;
When Moon and Starrs, my thoughts beholdeth,
Whose life no life but of thee holdeth:

Then thinck I: Ah, what is this man
Whom that greate God remember can?
And what the race, of him descended,
It should be ought of God attended?

For though in lesse than Angells state
Thou planted hast this earthly mate;
Yet hast thou made ev'n hym an owner
Of glorious crown, and crowning honor.

Thou placest hym upon all landes
To rule the workes of thine own handes:
And so thou hast all things ordained,
That ev'n his feete, have on them raigned.

Thou under his dominion plac't
Both sheepe and oxen wholy hast;
And all the beastes for ever breeding,
Which in the fertill fieldes be feeding.

The Bird, free-burgesse of the Aire;
The Fish, of sea the native heire;
And what things els of waters traceth
The unworn pathes, his rule embraceth.
O Lord, that rul'st our mortall lyne,
How through the world thi name doth shine! [24]

This conception of creation as of the essence of the Creator who is both immanent and transcendent is often expressed in the *Vinaya Patrikā* and the *Rāma-carita-mānasa* of Tulasī Dāsa. Rāma is the Absolute *saccidānanda* "being-consciousness-joy" and the ground of the world of appearances, the sport (*līlā*) of the universe, produced by his creative power of *Māyā*. Tulasī Dāsa gives poetic expression to this concept of *Māyā* in what may be described as one of the metaphysical *padas* of the *Vinaya Patrikā*:

Pada 111
[Musical Mode] *Rāga: Vihāga Bilāvala*

O Kesava [Kṛṣṇa = Hari] I can find no words,
so how should I speak?
Seeing thy wondrous works, O Hari, inwardly
I understand and remain speechless.
The bodiless artist has, on the walls of the void,
without colours painted a picture
which cannot be washed away,
nor the pain it causes be destroyed;—
all this is to be discovered in this very body.
A most dreadful crocodile dwells in this mirage
And without a mouth swallows all things, moving
and unmoving, that go to drink therein.
Some say this [world] is real; some that it is an
illusion; yet others, that it is both.
Says Tulasī Dāsa, the person who rejects all three
views as erroneous,
he recognises his [true] self.

Kesava! kahi na jāi kā kahiye;
dekhata tava racanā vicitra Hari!
samujhi manahiṃ mana rahiye.
sūnya bhīti para citra, ranga nahiṃ,
tanu binu likhā citere;
dhoye miṭai na mare bhīti dukha,
pāiya ihi tanu here.

---

[24] Rathmell, *op. cit.*, pp. 16-17.

ravikara-nīra basai ati dāruna
makara rūpa tehi māhīṃ;
badana-hīna so grasai carācara,
pāna karana je jāhīṃ.
ko'u kaha satya, jhūṭha kaha ko'ū,
jugala prabala ko'u mānai;
Tulasi Dāsa pariharai tīna bhrama,
so āpana pahicānai.[25]

The trite Vedantic concept of the world and human existence as the illusory picture of Hari's *Māyā* is expressed with such simplicity of diction and directness of address that the lyric gains a colloquial, dramatic tone. At the same time, the implicit connexion between imagistic details and symbolic intention is reinforced by a multiple chain of ideas in the echoing of *vicitra, citra* and *citere*. The word *vicitra* has the various meanings of "variegated", "beautiful" "wonderful", "full of variety and surprises"; *citra* is "picture" or "painting", and *citere* is "painter". So alliteration and semantic echoes subtly reflect the image of the unreal as a painting in the void and a mirage with its imaginary crocodile—the phantasm of *Māyā*, the painter without form or substance.

The aim of Tulasī Dāsa's bhakti is to be liberated from the infatuation of the world of appearances which appeals to the physical senses; to remove the illusory wall with its paintings that separate him from the truth; to be safely ferried across the ocean of existence to the blessed haven where the individual self or being comes to rest in the Absolute Self.

Pada 115
[Musical Mode] *Rāga Vihāga Bilāvala*

Mādhava, how will this noose of infatuation [with the illusory] be broken?
No matter how many external means are employed, the knot within remains tied.
As long as the vessel is full of oil the reflection of the moon will be seen in it;
And the reflection will not be destroyed, though fuel and fire be applied for a hundred ages to make the vessel boil.
Just as the bird remains alive in the hollow of a felled tree,
So the mind, engaged in external rites without inward discrimination, remains unpurified.

---

[25] Tulasī Dāsa, *Vinaya Patrikā* ed. Devanārāyaṇa Dvidedī (Banaras, 1962), p. 204.

The mind within remains very foul with the desires of the senses, though the body be cleansed outwardly,
Just as the snake does not die in spite of all the means and blows applied to the outside of its hole.
Tulasī Dāsa, without the mercy of Hari and the guru, there cannot be clear discrimination;
And without [spiritual] discrimination no one can cross the terrible ocean of this world [of existence and rebirths].

Mādhava! moha-phāṃsa kyoṃ ṭūṭai;
bāhara koṭi upāya kariya,
abhyantara granthi na chūṭai.
ghṛta pūrana karāha antaragata
sasi pratibimba dikhāvai;
īndhana anala lagāi kalapa sata,
auṭata nāsa na pāvai.
taru-koṭara mahaṃ basa bihanga
taru kāṭai marai na jaise;
sādhana kariya vicāra-hīna
mana śuddha ho'i nahiṃ taise.
antara malina viṣaya mana ati,
tana pāvana kariya pakhāre;
mara'i na uraga aneka jatana
balamīki bibidha bidhi māre.
Tulasi Dāsa Hari-guru karunā binu
bimala bibeka na ho'ī;
binu bibeka saṃsāra-ghora-nidhi
pāra na pāvai koī.

In the world of the Psalmists this existence is real, and their tribulation and suffering are caused either by their human enemies or are the visitation of God's judgement because of sin. In the world of Tulasī Dāsa the ocean of existence is an illusion, and his enemy is ignorance (*avidyā*) from which spring the lusts of the mind as agents of suffering. Therefore, unlike the Psalmists, Tulasī Dāsa most often complains of his own sinfulness, and not of persecution by fellow human beings. This is most explicitly stated:

Pada 124
[Musical Mode] *Rāga Vihāga Bilāvala*

If thy mind discard desires and doubts, how can there be worldly pain, fear and untold sorrows that are born of dualism?
It is the stubborn mind that regards anyone as a foe, friend or neutral:
An enemy, like a snake, is dismissed [from the mind]; a friend, like gold, accepted; and the neutral person, like straw, disregarded.

As food, clothing, cattle, and all kinds of possessions dwell in a jewel [i.e., may be had for the purchasing with a jewel];
So do heaven, hell, and the many worlds of animate and inanimate things dwell in the midst of the mind.
As, yet unmade, the wooden puppet dwells in the tree; and in yarn the garment;
So, inherent in the mind are the many forms of things that body forth when the opportunity arises.
When the mind is washed clean by the water of Rāma-bhakti, the vision easily becomes clear;
[And then] says, Tulasi Dāsa, consciousness of this play of the universe, by gradual understanding, becomes [finally] comprehensible.

jau nija mana pariharai bikārā;
tau kata dvaita-janita saṃsṛti-dukha,
saṃsaya, soka apārā.
satru, mitra, madhyastha, tīni ye,
mana kīnheṃ bariāīṃ;
tyagana, gahana, upecchanīya,
ahi, hāṭaka, tṛna kī nāīṃ.
asana, basana, pasu, vastu vividha vidhi,
saba mani mahaṃ raha jaise;
saraga, naraka, car-acara loka bahu,
basata madhya mana taise.
biṭapa-madhya putarikā, sūta mahaṃ
kancuki binahiṃ banāye;
mana mahaṃ tathā līna nānā tanu,
pragaṭata avasara pāye.
raghupati-bhagati-bāri-chālita cita,
binu prayāsa hī sūjhai;
Tulasi Dāsa kaha cida-bilāsa
jaga būjhata būjhata būjhai.

The enemies of Tulasī Dāsa, in the practical terms of everyday life, were to be found not only in the creations of the mind, but also among the people around him in Banaras. "He was attacked by orthodox pandits for writing a sacred story [*Rāma-carita-mānasa*] in the vernacular, persecuted by Muslims, Śaivas and Vallabha Gosains, and towards the latter part of his life afflicted by boils." [26] Yet, in spite of all this, his constant petition is for liberation, through *Rāma-bhakti*, from the vices that are born of the desires in the mind. They are the thieves looting the mind that is his Lord's house. In the following lament he is overwhelmed by the feeling that he has

[26] W. Douglas P. Hill, *The Holy Lake of the Acts of Rāma* (London, 1952), pp. x-xi.

disgraced himself, and brought dishonour to his Master by letting the vices take possession of his mind.

Pada 125
[Musical Mode] *Rāga Vihāga Bilāvala*

To whom shall I declare my great affliction,
O! my beneficent and constant Lord, Śrī Raghuvīra?
Lord, my heart is thine house
Where many thieves have now come to dwell.
Very hard-hearted are they, and use great force,
They will not listen to my pleas and supplications.
Ignorance, infatuation, greed, egotism,
Drunken passion, anger, and lust the enemy of knowledge—
Lord, these are the thieves that greatly oppress me:
Knowing me to be without my Lord, they crush me down.
Alone I am, and the plunderers are innumerable:
There is no one to give heed to my cries.
Lord, though I flee, yet can I not be saved:
O! Raghunāyaka [Rāma], protect me.
Tulasī Dāsa says, "Hear, O! Rāma,
Thieves are looting thy homestead;
I am worried beyond measure
Lest dishonour come to thee."

maiṃ kehi kahauṃ bipati ati bhārī,
Śrī Raghuvīra dhīra hita kārī.
mama hṛdaya bhavana prabhu torā,
tahaṃ base āi bahu corā.
ati kaṭhina karahiṃ barajorā,
mānahiṃ nahiṃ vinaya nihorā.
tama, moha, lobha, ahaṃkārā,
mada, krodha, bodha-ripu mārā.
ati karahiṃ upadrava nāthā,
maradahiṃ mohiṃ jāni anāthā.
maiṃ eka, amita baṭapārā,
ko'u sunai na mora pukārā.
bhāgehu nahiṃ nātha! ubārā,
Raghunāyaka, karahu saṃbhārā.
kaha Tulasi Dāsa sunu Rāmā,
lūṭahiṃ tasakara tava dhāmā.
cintā yaha mohiṃ apārā,
apajasa nahiṃ ho'i tumhārā.

The reduplication or extension of an idea in several of these couplets, (a characteristic that is reminiscent of Hebrew parallelism), the subtly varied alliteration, assonance and rhyme,—all put to the service of the single mood of the consistently sustained metaphor, give this *pada* an unmistakable plangency in the Hindi. And it is interesting to observe that, in spite of the difference between Hindu and Christian theology, the personal laments of many of the Sidney versifications of the Psalms have a similar plangency of tone, of which the following is an example:

PSALM 51 *MISERERE MEI, DEUS*

O Lord, whose grace no limits comprehend;
    Sweet Lord, whose mercies stand from measure free;
To mee that grace, to mee that mercie send,
    And wipe, O Lord, my sinnes from sinfull mee
    O clense, O wash my foule iniquitie:
Clense still my spotts, still wash awaie my staynings,
Till staines and spotts in me leave no remaynings.

For I, alas, acknowledging doe know
    My filthie fault, my faultie filthiness
To my soules eye uncessantly doth show.
    Which done to thee, to thee I doe confesse,
    Just judge, true witness; that for righteousness,
Thy doome may passe against my guilt awarded,
Thy evidence for truth maie be regarded.[27]

Were it not for the fact that Hindi verse is quantitative, it might be said that the similarity of effect in this English metric version of Psalm 51: 1-2 has been achieved by exactly the same kind of poetic technique as that employed in *Pada* 125 of the *Vinaya Patrikā*. Rhyme, repetition and alliteration play subtle variations on the supplicating reiterations of

Clense still my spotts, still wash awaie my staynings,
Till staines and spotts in me leave no remaynings.

It is not surprising that Donne thought so highly of the "Sydnean Psalms". He himself did not versify any Psalms of the Old Testament, but his rendering of *The Lamentations of Jeremy, for the most part according to Tremelius*[28] has a very close affinity with the Penitential Psalms. Such a stanza as

---

[27] Rathmell, *op. cit.*, p. 120.
[28] John Donne: *The Divine Poems* ed. Helen Gardner (Oxford, 1952), pp. 35-48.

For these things doe I weepe, mine eye, mine eye
    Casts water out; For he which should be nigh
To comfort mee, is now departed farre,
    The foe prevailes, forlorne my children are.[29]

has the unmistakable tone of a Psalm of lament with its mood of utter desolation like Sidney's

My God, my God, why hast thou me forsaken?
    Woe me, from me, why is thy presence taken?
    Soe farre from seeing, mine unhealthfull eyes,
    Soe farre from hearing to my roaring cries.[30]

But Donne's poetic temperament, which inclined towards a concentration of argumentative thought and passion, could not find ample scope in the mere versification of biblical laments. However, much as he might be said to derive the intitial impulse in many of his religious lyrics from the meditative tradition of the *Spiritual Exercises*, the sense of his sinfulness and God's judgement upon him, is to some extent, informed with the penitential spirit of the Psalms.

Several of the dramatic openings, cries and ejaculations in his spiritual monologues recall the sentiment of many a verse from the Psalms, as Donne carries his thoughts and emotions in an unflinching candour before God. But these echoes from the Psalms gain new reverberations from the insights of Christian worship which is the ground of Donne's religious lyrics. *A Hymne to God the Father*, for example, has its starting point in Psalm 51:3, 5-

For I acknowledge my transgressions: and my sin is ever before me...
Behold, I was shapen in iniquity; and in sin did my mother conceive me;

but it concludes on the prayer for assurance in the resurrection:

A HYMNE TO GOD THE FATHER

I

Wilt thou forgive that sinne where I begunne,
    Which is my sin, though it were done before?

---

[29] *Ibid.*, p. 37.
[30] Rathmell, *op. cit.*, p. 46.

Wilt thou forgive those sinnes through which I runne,
And doe them still: though still I doe deplore?
When thou hast done, thou hast not done,
For, I have more.

II

Wilt thou forgive that sinne by which I wonne
Others to sinne? and, made my sinne their doore?
Wilt thou forgive that sinne which I did shunne
A yeare, or two: but wallowed in, a score?
When thou has done, thou has not done,
For, I have more.

III

I have a sinne of feare, that when I have spunne
My last thred, I shall perish on the shore;
Sweare by thy selfe, that at my death thy Sunne
Shall shine as it shines now, and heretofore;
And, having done that, Thou has done,
I have no more.[31]

Miss Gardner has justly maintained, in her notes on textual variants of this poem, that it is not necessary to adopt the tempting reading "at my death thy sonne/Shall shine as he shines now" of the concluding stanza, for fear of missing the intended pun on the word "Sunne". Indeed, the ambiguity is as necessary to the context and imagery, as it is to Donne's play on his own name throughout the verses, and to his characteristic wit which here connects an oblique allusion to original sin in the Old Testament with the redemption of man in the New Testament through Christ the Saviour.[32]

A great deal of the tension in Donne's religious poetry is due to this kind of opposition and reconciliation between his own old Adam and the new; and the two sets of "Holy Sonnets" are his expression of the dialogue between them. For *La Corona* he chose interlinked sonnets set in the frame-work of meditation on the Mysteries of the Annunciation, Nativity, Finding in the Temple, Crucifixion, Resurrection and Ascension. Beautifully and skilfully unified in conception and execution, the end of the sonnets like the circlet of a crown is literally in their beginning expressed by the identical words of the first and last verses of the entire sequence:

Deigne at my hands this crown of prayer and praise.

---

[31] John Donne: *The Divine Poems* ed. Gardner, p. 51.
[32] Some MSS. entitle this lyric *To Christ*: others, *Christo Salvatori*.

The second group of "Holy Sonnets" is more explicitly an expression of the spiritual conflicts which time and again, in diction, imagery and mood, recall the Psalms to recharge them with the fresh currents of the new dispensation of Christian experience. In these poems "the old subtle foe" presses hard upon the poet who, conscious of his own frailty and guilt, prays for redemption through God's grace manifested in Jesus Christ. Nearly all the sonnets end, like the *padas* of the *Vinaya Patrikā*, on a note of repentance or petition or a renewed assurance of God's mercy. But Donne's utterances do not have the tenderness of love that is present in the *Padas* of Tulasī Dāsa or George Herbert's psalm-like lyrics. The intellectual content of Donne's sonnets, packed with paradoxes (though no more profound than theirs), has the severity of an inexorable Old Testament prophet; but, at the same time, there is no mistaking the anguish of ḥis tormented soul. Mental, physical and spiritual suffering, sickness and the fear of death, hope alternating with despair—these are the usual themes on which the sonnets play variations as they progress in the meditative manner of an Ignatian "spiritual exercise". On occasions, prayers and self-communings are intermingled with an unusual detachment when it appears as though Donne has stepped out of his poem to see himself in a colloquy with God, as in Sonnet VI in which he witnesses the final scene of a morality drama:

3

This is my playes last scene, here heavens appoint
My pilgrimages last mile; and my race
Idly, yet quickly runne, hath this last pace,
My spans last inch, my minutes last point,
And gluttonous death, will instantly unjoynt
My body, and soule, and I shall sleepe a space,
But my'ever-waking part shall see that face,
Whose fears already shakes my every joynt:
Then, as my soule, to'heaven her first seate, takes flight,
And earth-borne body, in the earth shall dwell,
So, fall my sinnes, that all may have their right,
To where they'are bred, and would presse me, to hell.
Impute me righteous, thus purg'd of evill,
For thus I leave the world, the flesh, and devill. (VI) [33]

Death is the theme in several of the succeeding sonnets and the

[33] Donne, *op. cit.*, p. 7.

supreme death of God their climax, in which Christian doctrine complements the ideas and imagery of the Psalms. In Sonnet XII ("Why are wee by all creatures waited on?"), the wonder of God's providence expressed in "Thou madest him to have dominion over the works of thy hands; thou hast put all things under his feet" (Psalm 8:6), no less than the wonder of His glory is surpassed by the greater marvel of redemption through the suffering and death of the Creator:

8

Why are wee by all creatures waited on?
Why doe the prodigall elements supply
Life and food to mee, being more pure than I,
Simple, and further from corruption?
Why brook'st thou, ignorant horse, subjection?
Why dost thou bull, and bore so seelily
Dissemble weaknesse, and by'one mans stroke die,
Whose whole kinde, you might swallow and feed upon?
Weaker I am, woe is mee, and worse then you,
You have not sinn'd, nor need be timorous.
But wonder at a greater wonder, for to us
Created nature doth these things subdue,
But their Creator, whom sin, nor nature tyed,
For us, his Creatures, and his foes, hath dyed (XII) [34]

Death, the ever-present threat to man, is destroyed by the love of God which makes the human soul His bride. This is expressed in Sonnet XIV through the paradox of freedom in thraldom, and chastity through the ravishment by God.

10

Batter my heart, three person'd God; for, you
As yet but knocke, breathe, shine, and seeke to mend;
That I may rise, and stand, o'erthrow mee, 'and bend
Your force, to breake, blowe, burn and make me new.
I, like an usurpt towne, to'another due.
Labour to'admit you, but Oh, to no end,
Reason your viceroy in mee, mee should defend,
But is captiv'd, and proves weake or untrue,
Yet dearely' I love you, and would be lov'd faine,
But am betroth'd unto your enemie,
Divorce mee,'untie, or breake that knot againe,

[34] *Ibid.*, p. 10.

Take mee to you, imprison mee, for I
Except you'enthrall mee, never shall be free,
Nor ever chast, except you ravish mee. (XIV)[35]

In *A Litanie*, a series of nine-line lyrics, Donne glorifies the Trinity: first, through the Virgin Mary "That she-Cherubin,/Which unlock'd Paradise"; and then successively through praise of Angels, Patriarchs, Prophets, Apostles, Martyrs, Confessors, Virgins (of the celibate life) and Doctors of the Church. The litany ends with the final prayer to the Son of God. (How like the composition of the *Vinaya Patrikā* and its climax in Rāma's acceptance of Tulasī Dāsa's petition).

XXVIII

Sonne of God heare us, and since thou
By taking our blood, owest it us againe,
Gaine to thy selfe, or us allow;
And let not both us and thy selfe be slaine;
O lambe of God, which took'st our sinne
Which could not stick to thee,
O let it not returne to us againe,
But Patient and Physition being free,
As sinne is nothing, let it no where be.[36]

The religious poems of Donne and Tulasī Dāsa are grounded in worship; and the problems of their individual spiritual conflicts are only resolved by faith in the love of God. The metrical psalms of Sir Philip Sidney and the Countess of Pembroke, the divine songs and sonnets of Donne, and the *Vinaya Patrikā* are confessionals of the soul and essentially devotional in essence. The feelings, emotions and divine aspirations expressed in these works are, at one and the same time, the means and the end of a religious poetry inspired by the true spirit of bhakti.

---

[35] Donne, *op. cit.*, p. 11.
[36] *Ibid.*, pp. 25-26.

CHAPTER NINE

ALLEGORY AND THE RELIGIOUS EPIC

Spenser, Milton, and Tulasī Dāsa

In English religious poetry from the Middle Ages to the seventeenth century there were devotional lyrics as well as narrative poems of various lengths; but in Hindi bhakti poetry the long poem with a unified plot appeared when the Ṣūfī *santas* began producing their allegorical romances during the fifteenth century. These influenced more especially the *Rāma-bhakti* poems, the most famous of which is the *Rāma-carita-mānasa*, the epic by Tulasī Dāsa begun in 1574. *Kṛṣṇa-bhakti* and *nirguṇa-bhakti* generally found expression in detached *dohās* (couplets), *caupāīs* (quatrains) and *padas* of more than four verses. When these verse forms are used independent of any coherent narrative, and can each stand complete by itself (as in the *Sūra Sāgara*),[1] they are referred to as *muktaka* meaning "free" or "independent" as opposed to *prabandha*, i.e. "linked" or "connected" when used as the continuous verses of a unified narrative.

The Ṣūfī *prabandha kāvyas* have their English parallels in the medieval alliterative romances based on the Arthurian legends and the sixteenth-century *Faerie Queene* of Edmund Spenser. Tulasī Dāsa's *Rāma-carita-mānasa* has many elements in common with both *The Faerie Queene* and Milton's *Paradise Lost*: it has all the silvan charm and knight-errantry of Spenser with its allegorical import, and the spiritual pre-occupation of Milton in his portrayal of God and the holy angels opposing the wickedness of Satan and his companions for the sake of man's salvation. All three of these works are somewhat outside the range of the literary appreciation of the average, present-day English reader who has little understanding of the medieval and Renaissance world-view and the sensibility in this *genre* of the romantic and religious epic. Since the resemblance between the medievalism of *The Faerie Queene* and that of the Ṣūfī romances and the *Rāma-carita-mānasa* is very striking, it is possible that a comparison of the matter as well as the general poetic conventions of

[1] See chapter 4, p. 65.

the English and the Hindi poems might help to illuminate the common ground of Western and Eastern human experience and thus broaden the sympathy of the modern reader. The chief difference between Tulasī Dāsa and Spenser is the fact that the former as a devout religious poet explicitly sings, throughout his poem, the praises of Rāma, the *avatāra* on his earthly mission of destroying wickedness and upholding righteousness, (even as Milton the Christian poet sings of God and justifies His ways to men), whereas Spenser's moral and spiritual meaning is implicit in his allegory.

Before looking at *The Faerie Queene, Rāma-carita-mānasa* and *Paradise Lost* in some detail, a word might be said about the Ṣūfī romances of the sixteenth and early seventeenth centuries. As already suggested above, these have certain characteristics in common with the romantic epic of Spenser. The subject matter of their narrative is invariably the fortunes of royal lovers in an atmosphere of court intrigues, open-air adventure, and battles between rival kingdoms. A brief outline of the plot of Malik Muḥammad Jāyasī's *Padmāvat* (c. 1540), the most celebrated of the Ṣūfī *prema-gāthās* or love epics, will give some idea of the usual pattern of the *genre*. The main plot deals with the love of Ratna Sena, King of Chitor, for the beautiful Padmāvatī, the daughter of the King of Singhal, a fabled realm beyond the seas. Having heard of her matchless beauty through Hīrāmana, the parrot, Ratna Sena conducted by Hīrāmana, makes for Singhal encountering numerous adventures on the way. Aided by Śiva in battle, Ratna Sena finally wins Padmāvatī for his wife and returns with her to Chitor. Sometime later he is at war with Ala'uddin, the Sultan of Delhi, who inflamed by the beauty of Padmāvatī as described by the exiled Rāghava Cetana, has espoused the latter's cause against Ratna Sena. Unsuccessful at first in his siege of Chitor, Ala'uddin resorts to treachery and takes Ratna Sena captive to Delhi. However, Padmāvatī eventually secures the release of her husband. During Ratna Sena's captivity Deva Pāla, a rival prince, had sent messages of love to Padmāvatī in an attempt to win her over to himself. Learning of this on his return, Ratna Sena kills Deva Pāla in combat and is himself slain. Padmāvatī and the co-wife, Nāgamatī, immolate themselves as *satīs* on the funeral pyre.

After the conventional verses in praise of God, His prophet Mohammed, the four friends of the prophet, the poet's own *guru*, etc., Jāyasī gives the subject of the romance in a few preliminary verses, the substance of which is:

I have written this epic in the common language, (employing quatrains), about Padmāvatī, Queen of the island of Singhal, whom Ratna Sena brought to Chitor; and how Ala'uddin, Sultan of Delhi, hearing of her beauty from Rāghava Cetana, besieged the fortress of Chitor in the battle between Hindus and Muslims.

singhala-dīpa Padminī rānī,
ratanasena cita'ura gaṛha ānī;
alā'udīna dehalī sultānū,
rāghau cetana kīnha bakhānū.
sunā sāhi gaṛha cheṃkā āī,
hindū turukanha bha'ī larāī;
ādi anta jasa gāthā ahai,
likhi bhākhā caupāī kahai.[2]

Then he enters into his narrative proper, but interrupts its flow from time to time to remind the reader of its religious intention by singing the praises of God. Nevertheless, at the end he reinforces his message with a concise but explicit statement to the effect that the human body is the fortress of Chitor, the mind is King Ratna Sena, the heart is Singhal, wisdom is Padmāvatī and worldly affairs Nāgamatī, illusion is Ala'uddin, Satan is Rāghava Cetana, and the spiritual preceptor or *guru* is Hīrāmana, the parrot.[3]

Among other well-known Ṣūfī romances in Hindi of this period are Kutubana's *Mṛgāvatī* and Manjhana's *Madhumālatī* — both of the sixteenth century—and Usmān's *Citrāvalī* written in the first half of the seventeenth. Unlike Jāyasī, Usmān does not appear to have made use of any historical material for his plot which is extremely prolix and rambling; yet the poem has great appeal for many Indian readers because of its general descriptive quality, its indulgence in the marvellous, and above all, because of its mood of *viraha* or love-longing. Usmān himself especially mentions this last-named quality in his preliminary verses after the usual invocation.

Beauty, love and *viraha* are the main support of creation;
I shall speak of the secret of all three,—now, I begin my story.

rūpa prema virahā jagata, mūla sṛṣṭi ke thambha;
hauṃ tīnahu ke bheda kahuṃ, kathā karauṃ arambha.[4]

---

[2] Malik Muḥammad Jāyasī, *Jāyasī-Granthāvalī*, ed., Rāmacandra Śukla, (Allahabad, 1935), "Padmāvata", p. 11:24.

[3] These verses are regarded as an interpolation by some critics; but they appear in Śukla's edition and in Shirreff's translation.

[4] Saralā Śukla, *Jāyasī ke Paravarttī Hindī-Ṣūfī Kavi aura Kāvya* (Lucknow, 1956), p. 114.

It will be recalled that Jāyasī, in a typically mellifluous couplet made the following observation on the intimate connexion between love and *viraha*:

> In love itself dwells the savour of *viraha*,
> As in the honeycomb the elixir-like honey.
>
> *premahiṃ māṃha biraha rasa rasā,*
> *maina ke ghara madhu amṛta basā.*[5]

According to these Ṣūfī poets, love is impelled by beauty; and the ideal beauty is the Supreme Being whom all human souls long for in a state of *viraha*, the exquisite pain of separation from the Divine Lover. Spiritual progress is the quest for Him which entails many vicissitudes allegorically expressed in the adventures of the Ṣūfī romances. To express this spiritual progress graphically is the artistic aim of the poets who employ all the medieval machinery of dreams, disguises, transformations, birds that talk, and various orders of supernatural beings from fairies to gods. In doing so, the Ṣūfī Hindi poets exploit Hindu as well as Islamic and Hebrew theological ideas setting them in a background of geographical and social conditions, real or imaginary, that is largely Indian.

Spenser's intention, like that of the Ṣūfī Hindi poets, was to write a romantic epic with a moral significance. According to his original plan, *The Faerie Queene* was to be an allegory in twelve books, each dealing with one of the twelve moral virtues "as Aristotle hath devised." Prince Arthur as the perfect "gentleman or noble person fashioned in virtuous and gentle discipline" was to epitomise these virtues in himself as "Magnificence"; but the different books were each to have, in addition, some particular knight to represent one of the several virtues. The first six books that were completed tried to follow this broad plan in representing Holiness, Temperance, Chastity, Friendship, Justice and Courtesy; the Mutability Cantos most probably constitute the uncompleted seventh book with which *The Faerie Queen* ends.[6] Arthur, the questing Prince, and Gloriana, the Faerie Queene, are the rather tenuous links between the first six books which are connected to the seventh thematically in the ethical intention of the whole. As it actually turns out, the individual books

[5] See above—Chapter 6, p. 97.

[6] Graham Hough, *A Preface to The Faerie Queene* (London, 1962), Chapter V discusses the "Structure of *The Faerie Queene*."

instead of treating the representative knights as narrowly personifying single virtues, extend the scope of their character and conduct in a variety of adventures in which their paths sometimes cross. In this way the allegory of *The Faerie Queene* gains a variety and complexity in keeping with the mixed nature of human experience. Thus Saint George, the Knight of Holiness, incorporates in himself ideals of chivalry, religion and patriotism.

"The legende of the Knight of the Red Crosse, or of Holiness" of Book I, therefore, seems to stand by itself as a finished miniature epic, in which the qualities of a heroic romance are combined with a moral allegory. St. George as the Red Cross Knight, intended by Spenser to represent the soul in pursuit of Platonic Wisdom or Truth, turns out to be Everyman with the frailties and ideals of the questing hero. Similarly, Sir Guyon in Book II, through his various adventures, is realised more as a chivalric hero with a rounded personality than as a mere personification of temperance. As heroes of romance therefore, the Red Cross Knight and Sir Guyon resemble Ratna Sena of the *Padmāvat*. But, at the same time, Spenser's allegorical meaning, unlike that of the Ṣūfī romance, is inherent in the characters and events of his story; and, therefore, the books of Holiness and Temperance do not need to be explicated in the manner of a medieval *exemplum* as the *Padmāvat* is by Jāyasī at the end of his poem. Dame Celia, for example, in the House of Holiness is obviously the divine source of the cardinal virtues of faith, hope and love:

> Dame *Caelia* men did her call, as thought
> From heauen to come, or thither to arise,
> The mother of three daughters, well vpbrought
> In goodly thewes, and godly exercise:
> The eldest two most sober, chast, and wise,
> *Fidelia* and *Speranza* virgins were,
> Though spousd, yet wanting wedlocks solemnise;
> But faire *Charissa* to a louely fere
> Was lincked, and by him had many pledges dere.[7]
>
> (*F.Q.*, I, X, 4)

The allegory of Temperance guided by Reason is patent throughout the adventures of Sir Guyon in Book II.

---

[7] Edmund Spenser, *Faerie Queene* ed. J. C. Smith (Oxford, 1909). All quotations are taken from this edition.

Books III and IV are more in the nature of the romantic epic in which the kinds and degrees of love operate through a variety of characters ranging from the complex personality of the warrior maiden, Britomart, to the simpler representation of Florimell as beauty arousing desire in the beholder.

> Wonder it is to see, in diuerse minds,
> How diuersly loue doth his pageants play,
> And shewes his powre in variable kinds:
> The baser wit, whose idle thoughts alway
> Are wont to cleaue vnto the lowly clay,
> It stirreth vp to sensuall desire,
> And in lewd slouth to wast his carelesse day:
> But in braue sprite it kindles goodly fire,
> That to all high desert and honour doth aspire.
>
> (*F.Q.*, III, V, 1)

Though Spenser has named these books after Chastity and Friendship, his allegory is not as obvious as in the book of Temperance. It is the theme of love that predominates and the action is mainly concerned with the fate of various pairs of lovers worked out in an atmosphere of much violence and magic. And in this respect Books III and IV resemble the Ṣūfī romances. The frequent complaints of pining lovers, like that of Britomart for Artegall or Florimell for Marinell, are strikingly like the Hindi expressions of *viraha* or love-longing of Nāgamatī in the *Padmāvat*. Yet the allegorical meaning in *The Faerie Queene* is never completely lost; and the Platonic association of beauty and love with their divine source is expressed in the following apostrophe:

> Most sacred fire, that burnest mightily
> In liuing brests, ykindled first aboue,
> Emongst th'eternall spheres and lamping sky,
> And thence pourd into men, which men call Loue;
> Not that same, which doth base affections moue
> In brutish minds, and filthy lust inflame,
> But that sweet fit, that doth true beautie loue,
> And choseth vertue for his dearest Dame,
> Whence spring all noble deeds and neuer dying fame:
>
> (*F.Q.* III, III, 1.)

With love as their central theme the books of Chastity and Friendship deal with multiple quests of many lovers; but in Books V and VI Spenser returns to the pattern of the first two books, each having as its principal hero a character representing a particular moral concept as Justice, or the epitome of several traits in the Renaissance concept of Courtesy. Once more, however, the representative knights, Artegall and Calidore, rather than being abstractions personified as heroes, exhibit more comprehensive traits of human beings through a variety of exploits.

In the two Mutability Cantos, now accepted as a fragment of the uncompleted work, Spenser relates his fable of Mutability's claim to sovereignty over earth and heaven. Mother Nature pronounces her judgement that Mutability is not supreme, since Change is itself progress towards the changeless perfection of eternity.

> I well consider all that ye haue sayd,
> And find that all things stedfastnes doe hate
> And changed be: yet being rightly wayd
> They are not changed from their first estate;
> But by their change their being doe dilate:
> And turning to themselues at length againe,
> Doe worke their owne perfection so by fate:
> Then ouer them Change doth not rule and raigne;
> But they raigne ouer change, and doe their states maintaine.
> (*F.Q.*, VII, VII, 58).

> Then gin I thinke on that which Nature sayd,
> Of that same time when no more *Change* shall be,
> But stedfast rest of all things firmely stayd
> Vpon the pillours of Eternity,
> That is contrayr to *Mutabilitie*:
> For, all that moueth, doth in *Change* delight:
> But thence-forth all shall rest eternally
> With Him that is the God of Sabbaoth hight:
> O that great Sabbaoth God, graunt me that Sabaoths sight.
> (*F.Q.*, VII, VIII, 2)

This is the final note of *The Faerie Queene*, the note of religious didacticism which pervades the entire allegory.

Besides differing from the Ṣūfī romances in its emphasis on the allegorical structure, *The Faerie Queene* more consistently moves in the atmosphere of medieval romance without relating the more human experiences to any precise geographical or historical points of reference. It is true that there are echoes of contemporary politics in the adventures of Artegall as the Knight of Justice; and that the religious dissensions in England operate in some levels of the allegory where protestantism is championed against catholicism, but these are implicit only. In the Ṣūfī romances, on the other hand, the historical conflicts are obvious in the political wranglings of the Hindu princes and in their struggles against the Muslim conquerors. Some of the chief characters in the *Padmāvat* are certainly named after actual rulers; and the events of the story, however fantastic, are still tenuously related to historical incidents and sites in India.

In this respect the Ṣūfī romances resemble the romantic epics of Ariosto and Tasso rather than *The Faerie Queene*: and what C. S. Lewis has written of the Italian epics is largely true of the Ṣūfī tales:

> In the foreground we have fantastic adventure, in the middle distance daily life, in the background a venerable legend with a core of momentous historical truth.[8]

In the Ṣūfī romances, everyday life of Hindu society is fathfully reflected in the description of state affairs and the princely menage of the medieval palaces; and the awful sacrifice of the widowed queens, in the *Padmāvat*, on the funeral pyre as *satīs* is a grim reality. So it is evident that *The Faerie Queene* and the Ṣūfī romances, though having in common the medieval atmosphere of dreamlike incongruities, differ in the extent to which their narratives are related to the externals of the ethos of the societies in which the poems were produced.

As Spenser explicitly stated, in his letter to Sir Walter Raleigh, that he intended his poem to be "continued allegory or a dark conceit", it is reasonable to expect a definite moral strand to run throughout *The Faerie Queene*, although he did not finish the work or follow his original scheme of making each of the completed books a consistent allegory of the individual virtues that were to be integrated in Arthur as Magnanimity. But, as Graham Hough has pointed out, "much that is poetically important in *The Faerie Queene* is morally indifferent; and some things that are poetically important tend to run counter to the morality that is consciously invoked".[9] This is largely due to the fact that Spenser does not always harmonise the didactic with the emotional. Sometimes this is the result of his ambivalence between fidelity to his poetic sensibility and his responsibility to the morality of his allegory. For example, in his treatment of the Bower of Bliss,

---

[8] C. S. Lewis, *The Allegory of Love* (London, 1953), p. 309.

[9] Hough, *op. cit.*, p. 165.

the theme of *carpe diem* which expresses the transitoriness of youth and beauty, is so exquisitely sung that the note of censure is completely lost:

> The whiles some one did chaunt this louely lay;
> Ah see, who so faire thing doest faine to see,
> In springing flowre the image of thy day;
> Ah see the Virgin Rose, how sweetly shee
> Doth first peepe forth with bashfull modestee,
> That fairer seemes, the lesse ye see her may;
> Lo see soone after, how more bold and free
> Her bared bosome she doth broad display;
> Loe see soone after, how she fades, and falles away.
>
> So passeth, in the passing of a day,
> Of mortall life the leafe, the bud, the flowre,
> Ne more doth flourish after first decay,
> That earst was sought to decke both bed and bowre,
> Of many a Ladie, and many a Paramowre:
> Gather therefore the Rose, whilest yet is prime,
> For soone comes age, that will her pride deflowre:
> Gather the Rose of loue, whilest yet is time,
> Whilest louing thou mayst loued be with equall crime.
> (*F.Q.*, II, XII, 74-75)

It is not surprising that critics while agreeing on Spenser's general moral intention differ in their analysis of the effect of this famous key episode of Acrasia's Bower of Bliss in the book of Temperance. C. S. Lewis emphasising the allegory as expressive of evil and sterility, tends to denigrate the appeal of this set piece. Graham Hough, on the other hand, sees its poetic charm as due to the unresolved tension in Spenser's mind between the beauty of the sensuous and his moral intention. To him, therefore, the destruction of the Bower of Bliss tends to appear wanton and unconvincing.

The inconsistency in Spenser's presentation of some important characters may similarly partly be accounted for by his occasional disregard of the allegorical correspondence between the rational and emotional. Platonic wisdom or truth, for instance, cannot be reconciled with a romantic heroine whose relationship with the Red Cross Knight is not clearly defined. The result is that Una as the personification of an ideal is not wholly convincing.

Tulasī Dāsa, in contrast to Spenser's treatment of Una, gives the characters of Rāma and his wife, Sītā, a dialectical basis by identifying them with the Absolute Brahman and Śakti, the primal energy. This he does by his subtle treatment on the one hand, of the prototypes Śiva and Umā who look on at the earthly drama of incarnation; and on the other, of the *avatāras* who are the actors in that drama as Rāma and Sītā. Thus he harmonises the divine unity of the cosmic represented by the former pair in the spiritual sphere, with the conjugal love of the latter in the empirical sphere of human existence. For this reason he removes from the intimate relationship of both pairs any trace of the sensual found in Sanskrit drama or epic dealing with the wooing of Śiva and Umā; and Rāma, who in Vālmīki's *Rāmāyaṇa* is the mirror of princes, becomes in the *Rāma-carita-mānasa* the Supreme Person or Soul, (*Puruṣottama*), and Viṣṇu incarnate.

The *Rāma-carita-mānasa* like *The Faerie Queene*, has a rich variety of incidents but, at the same time, Rāma as the embodiment of infinite goodness, beauty and power (*śīla, saundarya, śakti*), is the central character throughout the poem of seven books, each representing a rung (*sopāna*) in the ladder of *Rāma-bhakti*, by means of which the devotee ascends in his worship to his spiritual consummation in *Hari-bhakti*. Owing something perhaps to the example of Jāyasī and other Ṣūfī Hindi poets, the *Rāma-carita-mānasa* has a complicated plot into which four main narratives are inter-woven having as their narrators the divine Śiva, the sage Yajñavalkya, the devout crow Kāga-bhuśuṇḍī, and Tulasī Dāsa himself as the omniscient author. All these narrators intersperse their stories with observations and discourses which expand the ethical and philosophical points of the general theme of bhakti. As in *The Faerie Queene*, there are in the *Rāma-carita-mānasa* stories within stories, mostly derived from the Sanskrit epic of Vālmīki and the *Purāṇas* in which the worlds of gods, men and nature shade into one another. Operating on this material, Vaiṣṇava dialectics and sensibility have, through the genius of the Hindi poet, transformed the older epic into the highly original art of a religious epic in the form of the *Rāma-carita-mānasa*, which however, still remains close in subject matter to Vālmīki's *Rāmāyaṇa*.

In the *Rāma-carita-mānasa* the romantic and the religious are both in the foreground; and they are often closely related to the realistic environment of life in the courts of the Hindu princes or of the hermitages of the forest sages. The childhood of Rāma and his brothers in the royal splendour of Ayodhyā, their religious and military training as youths, their courtship and marriage are all vividly described. Rāma occupies the central position as heir apparent before his exile, and after his return as king with Sītā as his consort. At the same time, Tulasī Dāsa continually reminds the reader of the true nature of Rāma as the *avatāra* of Viṣṇu to whom all devotion is due. Therefore, unlike Arthur and the other heroes of the various books of *The Faerie Queene*, Rāma, the embodiment of goodness, beauty and power (*śīla, saundarya, śakti*), pervades the Hindi epic.

Commenting on the character of Guyon, in Book II of *The Faerie Queene*, who according to Spenser represents Temperance, Hough writes, "... It is a virtue that consists chiefly of *not* doing things." [10] This concept of Temperance is totally different from that found in the *Bhagavad-Gītā* and the *Rāma-carita-mānasa* where it implies not inaction but dispassion. The Hindu ideal of human conduct is the dispassionate observance of one's own duty (*sva-dharma*) according to one's position in society determined by the caste into which one is born. This is expressed in the concept of Duty (*dharma*) which is central to the philosophy of the *Rāma-carita-mānasa*. These key concepts of Temperance and Duty in the Hindi epic have a close correspondence in practical terms with the ethical implications of Temperance and Courtesy in *The Faerie Queene*. Chastity may be regarded as being implicit in a life ruled by the principles of Duty, Temperance and Courtesy; and the remaining two Spenserian virtues, Friendship and Justice operate in a hierarchical society in which order and harmony are to be maintained. Temperance in *The Faerie Queene* is nearer to the Aristotelian golden mean than to the Platonic concept of dispassion which is the result of the rational element of the soul regulating and controlling all desire so that goodness is its own reward. This latter is very like the Hindu concept of dispassion which is the result of intellectual enlightenment by the highest reason.

Although Spenser's allegory of Guyon, the knight of Temperance accompanied by the palmer Reason, does not have a consistent dialectical basis like the *Rāma-carita-mānasa*, it nevertheless adumbrates the same fundamental principle of self-discipline as the rule of holy living in which ignorance born of desires is dispelled by the light of the highest reason or pure wisdom (*vimala vijñāna*). The grossest forms of desire are those of the physical senses, ambition and

---

[10] Hough, *op. cit.*, p. 155.

the love of wealth represented in *The Faerie Queene* by the attractions of Acrasia's Bower of Bliss and Mammon's realm. Guyon overcomes the temptations of Mammon, and with the help of Reason finally destroys the Bower of Bliss although he had earlier succumbed briefly to voluptuousness in the absence of Reason. The Castle of Alma in which Guyon is instructed in Temperance, (and the House of Holiness in Book I), have their counterpart in the various *āshrams* or hermitages visited by Rāma and Sītā during their forest sojourn and the discourses of the sages whom they meet. All these discourses aim at the intellectual enlightenment of the devotee and serve as a means of *Rāma-bhakti* in which the true *bhakta* is immersed by contemplating the deeds of Rāma (*Rāma-carita*) reflected in the holy lake (*mānasa*):

> The four beautiful and noble dialogues, composed with thought and understanding, are the four charming *ghats* of this pure and lovely lake. The seven parts are the beauteous steps that delight the soul when viewed with the eyes of wisdom.[11]
>
> *suthi sundara saṃbāda bara birace buddhi bicāri,*
> *tei ehi pāvana subhaga sara ghāṭa manohara cāri*
>
> *sapta prabandha subhaga sopānā,*
> *gyāna-nayana niraṣata mana mānā.*

Hence the name of Tulasī Dāsa's religious epic: *Rāma-carita-mānasa*—

> Its name is the Holy Lake of Rāma's Acts, and those who listen to it are refreshed; a soul that burns with the fever of worldly desire, like an elephant in a forest fire, is happy if it plunge into this Lake.[12]
>
> *Rāma-carita-mānasa ehi nāmā,*
> *sunata sravana pāiya bisrāmā;*
> *mana-kari viṣaya-anala-bana jaraī,*
> *hoi sukhī jau ehi sara paraī.*

The aim of Tulasī Dāsa and Spenser is to instruct and edify hearers or readers by the ideals set forth in the *Rāma-carita-mānasa* and *The Faerie Queene*; and though the latter has not had such reverence

---

[11] Tulasī Dāsa, *The Holy Lake of the Acts of Rāma*, translation of *Rāma-carita-mānasa* by W. D. P. Hill (London, 1952), p. 23.

[12] Hill, *op. cit.*, p. 23.

accorded it in England as the *Rāma-carita-mānasa* has for centuries enjoyed in North India, Milton in his *Areopagitica* has paid noble tribute to Spenser as moral teacher and poet:

> ... Our sage and serious poet Spenser, whom I dare be known to think a better teacher than Scotus or Aquinas, describing true temperance under the person of Guyon, brings him in with his palmer through the cave of Mammon and the bower of earthly bliss, that he might see and know, and yet abstain.[13]

The moral and poetical qualities of *The Faerie Queene* struck a most responsive chord in Milton's heart for he himself had long contemplated

> what resounds
> In Fable or Romance of *Uthers* Son
> Begirt with *British* and Armoric Knights. . .[14]
> (*P.L.*, I, 579-583)

as the subject of an English epic. However, he finally decided on the biblical story of the Fall as the subject of his epic, and the result was *Paradise Lost* (1667). It is interesting to observe that Spenser had already treated as a lyrical subject the Creation, Fall and Redemption in his *Hymn of Heavenly Love* (1596); and that both the subject matter and style of *The Faerie Queene* and the *Four Hymns* had influenced such works as Giles Fletcher's *Christ's Victory and Triumph* (1610), before Milton himself wrote *On the Morning of Christ's Nativity* (1629) which may be regarded as the prelude to his *Paradise Lost*. The ode celebrates the dispossession of the heathen gods:

> Our Babe to shew his Godhead true,
> Can in his swadling bands controul the damned crew.

But the full redemption of man and nature is yet to be accomplished:

> The Babe lies yet in smiling Infancy,
> That on the bitter cross

[13] John Milton, *Complete Poems and Major Prose* ed. M. Y. Hughes, (New York, 1957), pp. 728-729.

[14] John Milton, *The Poetical Works*, Vol I *Paradise Lost* ed. Helen Darbishire (Oxford, 1952). All quotations are taken from this edition of *Paradise Lost*.

Must redeem our loss;
So both himself and us to glorifie...

Milton's long deliberation on the choice of a subject for his epic, and his hesitation in choosing a specifically religious subject in preference to a strictly historical one or the legendary Arthur of *The Faerie Queene*, may account for some of the tension that exists in *Paradise Lost* between his Christian and Pagan interests. His mingling of the biblical and classical, for example, in the conventional epic similes and the association of the appeal to the Muses with his more devout invocations, produces a tension between the scriptural and non-scriptural in an explicitly Christian poem. This very tension, however, contributes towards the emotional quality of the epic that might otherwise have been dryly didactic and moralising. For example, in his description of the Garden of Eden, Milton by comparing it with the fair field of Enna, evokes a feeling of the tragic inevitability of human innocence and beauty being marred by the powers of darkness:

Not that faire field
Of *Enna*, where *Proserpin* gathring flours
Her self a fairer Floure by gloomie *Dis*
Was gatherd, which cost *Ceres* all that pain
To seek her through the World; nor that sweet Grove
Of *Daphne* by *Orontes*, and th'inspir'd
Castalian Spring, might with this Paradise
Of *Eden* strive;...

(*P.L.*, IV, 268-275)

This pain of Ceres, like an impending doom, is obliquely referred to again later in Book IX when Eve, for the first time, goes off by herself half apprehensive of the fatal consequences:

Thus saying, from her Husbands hand her hand
Soft she withdrew, and like a Wood-Nymph light
Oread or *Dryad*, or of *Delia*'s Traine,
Betook her to the Groves, but *Delia*'s self
In gate surpassd and Goddess-like deport,...
Likest she seemd, *Pomona* when she fled
Vertumnus, or to *Ceres* in her Prime,
Yet Virgin of *Proserpina* from *Jove*.

(*P.L.*, IX, 385-396)

In *Paradise Lost* Milton thus often achieves a poetic blending of feeling and thought by the suggestive power of such imagery as exploits the divers experiences derived from his wide reading of Christian and pagan literature. In the *Rāma-carita-mānasa* there is no such conflict as there appears to be in Milton, since the source of every literary allusion is regarded as orthodox Hindu scripture; and the Vaiṣṇava poet is able to reconcile the intellectuality of the Upaniṣads with his emotional surrender to the mythology of the *Purāṇas.*

However, both in the case of Milton and Tulasī Dāsa, what the poets believe is central to the theme of their epics, and an understanding of their religious beliefs is essential to a just appreciation of their poetic achievement. C. S. Lewis, in *A Preface to Paradise Lost,* writes:

> . . .I should warn the reader that I am myself a Christian, and that some (by no means all) of the things which the atheist reader must 'try to feel as if he believed' I actually, in cold prose, do believe. But for the student of Milton my Christianity is an advantage. What would you not give to have a real, live Epicurean at your elbow while reading Lucretius? [15]

For the Hindu reader, Tulasī Dāsa is at his elbow; and, if he himself is also a Vaiṣṇava, then the poet is even nearer than breathing in their common expression of faith, *Rāma-bhakti,* which includes the singing of and listening to the praises of the Lord. (The *Rāma-carita-mānasa* is generally chanted or recited in communal worship). The voice of the poet is a necessary element in both the Hindi and English epics since it helps to attune the reader's response to the poet's interpretation of the story as a spiritual experience or devotional exercise. Professor Martz has noted this fact in connexion with Milton whose

> ... voice is indeed everywhere in the poem, advising, exhorting, warning, praising, denouncing, lamenting, promising, judging, in all ways guiding us (or, as some have complained, attempting to manipulate us) by his strong evaluative comments ... Thus in Book 3 his voice seems subtly to emerge at the close of the angelic hymn in Heaven, praising the offer of the Son of God to sacrifice himself for mankind's good:
>
> O unexampl'd love,
> Love no where to be found less then Divine!

[15] C. S. Lewis, *A Preface to Paradise Lost* (London, 1956), p. 64.

> Hail Son of God, Saviour of Men, thy Name
> Shall be the copious matter of my Song
> Henceforth, and never shall my Harp thy praise
> Forget, nor from thy Fathers praise disjoine.
>
> [3.410-15]
>
> Likewise, at the close of the great morning-psalm in Paradise, the individual voice of the bard seems to join the voices of Adam and Eve:
>
> Witness if I be silent, Morn or Eeven,
> To Hill, or Valley, Fountain, or fresh shade
> Made vocal by my Song, and taught his praise.
>
> [5.202-04]
>
> ...Everywhere in the poem we hear this human, flexible, responsive voice of an individual living in a great tradition, interpreting the discoveries of his "unpremeditated Verse", and encouraging us to read the poem as the progress of an interior journey, toward the center of the soul.[16]

To this end the poet addresses himself to his task in the spirit of earnest devotion seeking the inspiration and support of the God he worships. This is clearly indicated in the opening verses of the first, third and seventh books of *Paradise Lost.*

> And chiefly Thou O Spirit, that dost preferr
> Before all Temples th'upright heart and pure,
> Instruct me, for Thou know'st; Thou from the first
> Wast present, and with mighty wings outspred
> Dove-like satst brooding on the vast Abyss
> And mad'st it pregnant: What in mee is dark
> Illumin, what is low raise and support;
> That to the hight of this great Argument
> I may assert Eternal Providence,
> And justifie the wayes of God to men.
>
> (*P.L.*, I, 17-26)

> Hail holy Light, ofspring of Heav'n first-born,
> Or of th' Eternal Coeternal beam
> May I express thee unblam'd? since God is Light,
> And never but in unapproached Light
> Dwelt from Eternitie, dwelt then in thee,
> Bright effluence of bright essence increate.
> Or hear'st thou rather pure Ethereal stream,
> Whose Fountain who shall tell? before the Sun,

[16] Louis L. Martz, *The Paradise Within* (New Haven, 1964), pp. 107-110.

Before the Heav'ns thou wert, and at the voice
Of God, as with a Mantle didst invest
The rising world of waters dark and deep,
Won from the void and formless infinite.
Thee I re-visit now with bolder wing,
Escap't the *Stygian* Pool, though long detaind
In that obscure sojourn, while in my flight
Through utter and through middle darkness borne
With other notes then to th' *Orphean* Lyre
I sung of *Chaos* and *Eternal Night*,
Taught by the heav'nly Muse to venture down
The dark descent, and up to reascend,
Though hard and rare: thee I revisit safe,
And feel thy sovran vital Lamp; but thou
Revisit'st not these eyes, that rowle in vain
To find thy piercing ray, and find no dawn:
So thick a drop serene hath quencht thir Orbs,
Or dim suffusion veild.

(*P.L.*, III, 1-26)

So much the rather thou Celestial Light
Shine inward, and the mind through all her powers
Irradiate, there plant eyes, all mist from thence
Purge and disperse, that I may see and tell
Of things invisible to mortal sight.

(*P.L.*, III, 51-55)

DESCEND from Heav'n *Urania*, by that name
If rightly thou art calld, whose Voice divine
Following, above th' *Olympian* Hill I soare,
Above the flight of *Pegasean* wing.
The meaning, not the Name I call:for thou
Nor of the Muses nine, nor on the top
Of old *Olympus* dwellst, but Heav'nlie borne,
Before the Hills appeerd, or Fountain flowd,
Thou with Eternal wisdom didst converse,
Wisdom thy Sister, and with her didst play
In presence of th'Almightie Father, pleas'd
With thy Celestial Song.

(*P.L.*, VII, 1-12)

. . .still govern thou my Song,
Urania, and fit audience find, though few:
But drive farr off the barbarous dissonance
Of *Bacchus* and his Revellers, the Race
Of that wilde Rout that tore the *Thracian* Bard
In *Rhodope*, where Woods and Rocks had Eares
To rapture, till the savage clamor dround

Both Harp and Voice; nor could the Muse defend
Her Son. So fail not thou, who thee implores:
For thou art Heav'nlie, shee an empty dreame.

(*P.L.*, VII, 30-39)

The classical convention of invoking the muse of poetry as a matter of form, is used in these invocations not as part of a poetical exercise, but to convey the significant and earnest appeal of Milton, Christian bard and hierophant, for spiritual support and inspiration. Hence there is in these verses a tone of devout self-dedication and a sense of the poet's inadequacy while his "adventurous Song... pursues/Things unattempted yet in Prose or Rhime". Milton prays for the light of divine wisdom and for the inspiration of the heavenly muse, which produces celestial song in the presence of the Almighty. Only in the measure in which this prayer is answered will the poet be able to understand and sing of the divine purpose in the world of human beings.

Tulasī Dāsa begins his epic with Sanskrit verses in homage to Vāṇī and Vināyaka. The former, the goddess of speech and wisdom also called Sarasvatī, is the equivalent of Milton's Urania or the heavenly muse of poetry; and the latter, popularly known as Ganeśa, is the patron god of all scribes and poets.

Homage to Vāṇī and Vināyaka, inventors of letters and
all their significance, of styles and metres, too, and of auspicious prayers.[17]

varṇānāmarthasanghānām rasānām chandasāmapi,
mangalānām ca karttārau vande vāṇīvināyakau.

Tulasī Dāsa's belief in the existence and influence of Sarasvatī is real; and his appeal to her at the very beginning of his poem is due to the fact that for him the essence of bhakti is identical with the aesthetic pleasure derived from poetry, "the breath and finer spirit of all knowledge". Sarasvatī as Divine Wisdom can so inspire the poet that his art becomes the means of apprehending the Absolute, *saccidānanda*, "being-consciousness-joy". Though Milton's invocation of Urania does not have the directness and simplicity of Tulasī Dāsa's homage to Sarasvatī, it nevertheless voices a positive belief in the inspiration of "celestial song" by the heavenly muse that derives from

[17] W. D. P. Hill, *op. cit.*, p. 1.

the Almighty Father. The *Rāma-carita-mānasa* and *Paradise Lost* must, therefore, be regarded as works in which history, legend and myth are intended to be welded together to give form to a poetic vision illuminated by Divine Wisdom. This vision, of necessity, is communicated through the medium of the senses, but the senses at the service of the questing soul in an unhappy world.

Milton sees the post-lapsarian world of the Bible as the product of disobedience. Tulasī Dasa's world is dominated by *karma*, that is, destiny determined by the fruit of past action in previous existences. There is a similarity between the Christian doctrine of sin and the Hindu concept of *karma* since both depend upon the cause-effect nexus intimately bound up with the moral law of the universe. Both in *Paradise Lost* and in the *Rāma-carita-mānasa* this law operates through a system of order in a divinely-constituted hierarchy within which harmony is preserved by adherence to duty (*dharma*). Infringement of the secular and religious duty appropriate to one's status in this hierarchy, contributes to the disorder, confusion and conflicts of the Iron Age, the *Kaliyuga* so often mentioned by Tulasī Dāsa. It disturbs the harmony of individual and cosmic existence, mars every kind of orderly relationship, and disrupts the human-divine communion.

Dealing with the story of the Fall, *Paradise Lost* attempts a poetic interpretation of the central dilemma of the human condition and its tragic consequences arising from the interaction of free-will and moral obligation. Divine justice and grace operating through redemptive love seem to resolve this dilemma on the purely dialectical level of christian theology as demonstrated in the speeches of God the Father and His Son in Book III. Man of his own free will has chosen to disobey, and therefore he must die. This, according to divine justice, is the inevitable consequence of violating the moral law of the universe

> Die hee or Justice must; unless for him
> Som other able, and as willing, pay
> The rigid satisfaction, death for death.
> Say Heav'nly Powers, where shall we find such love,
> Which of ye will be mortal to redeem
> Mans mortal crime, and just th' unjust to save?
> Dwels in all Heaven charitie so deare?
>
> (*P.L.*, III, 210-216)

To this question of God, the Son replies:

Father, thy word is past, Man shall find Grace;
And shall Grace not find means, that finds her way,
The speediest of thy winged messengers,
To visit all thy creatures, and to all
Comes unprevented, unimplor'd, unsought,
Happie for Man, so coming; hee her aide
Can never seek, once dead in sins and lost;
Attonement for himself or offering meet,
Indebted and undon, hath none to bring:
Behold mee then, mee for him, life for life
I offer, on mee let thine anger fall;
Account mee Man; I for his sake will leave
Thy bosom, and this glorie next to thee
Freely put off, and for him lastly die
Well pleas'd; on mee let Death wreck all his rage;
Under his gloomie power I shall not long
Lie vanquisht;. . .

(*P.L.*, III, 227-243)

Through Christ's resurrection death will be disarmed of its mortal sting:

But I shall rise Victorious, and subdue
My Vanquisher, spoild of his vanted spoile;
Death his deaths wound shall then receive, and stoop
Inglorious, of his mortal sting disarmd.
I through the ample Air in Triumph high
Shall lead Hell Captive maugre Hell, and show
The Powers of darkness bound.

(*P.L.*, III 250-256)

The fall of man and the atonement through the incarnation are the cardinal points on which the whole of Milton's theology turns. Yet man is not absolved from all responsibility for the Christian believer although the suffering of all mankind may be bound up with the legacy of original sin. However, the destiny of every individual being is worked out in a single existence between the boundaries of birth and death on this planet. In the *Rāma-carita-mānasa* the concept of *karma* and the belief in metempsychosis appear to lay an additional burden upon the individual human soul. To a large extent this accounts for the apparently defeatist attitude of the Hindu mind in the face of an inexorable "fate". But the moral law, which operates throughout the material and supra-mundane, is common to both epics. Another special concept of Hindu metaphysics which pervades

Tulasī Dāsa's poem is that of *māyā*. To most western readers this is entirely synonymous with the idea of illusion; but the word *māyā* has several shades of meaning according to the different contexts in which it is used, and sometimes its connotation is very vague indeed. However, it is worth remembering some salient points about the doctrine of *māyā* in order to follow the theology of Tulasī Dāsa as reflected in the *Rāma-carita-mānasa*, and to compare his ideas with those of Spenser and Milton.

It should be borne in mind that although Tulasī Dāsa's devotion is centred on *Rāma-bhakti*, he sings both of the *saguṇa* and *nirguṇa* Brahman since he is essentially a believer in the qualified non-dualism (*viśiṣṭādvaita*) of Rāmānuja who considered the phenomenal world and individual human souls to be real, but at the same time maintained that they could not exist independently of the one Absolute Brahman. Tulasī Dāsa therefore repeatedly states that Rāma is simultaneously both the conditioned *avatāra* and the God Viṣṇu himself, identified with the unconditioned Brahman. Sītā is the incarnation of Viṣṇu's consort, Lakṣmi or *śakti*, the creative energy of God; so she is also the divine mother of the universe. This *śakti* is also called *māyā* and, in concept, is not unlike Spenser's Venus representing the fecundity of nature in the Garden of Adonis in *The Faerie Queene*; and his Sapience, the cause of creation, in the *Hymn of Heavenly Beauty*:

> There in his bosome *Sapience* doth sit,
> The soueraine dearling of the *Deity*,
> Clad like a Queene in royall robes, most fit
> For so great powre and peerelesse maiesty.
> And all with gemmes and iewels gorgeously
> Adornd, that brighter then the starres appeare,
> And make her natiue brightnes seem more cleare.
>
> And on her head a crowne of purest gold
> Is set, in signe of highest soueraignty,
> And in her hand a scepter she doth hold,
> With which she rules the house of God on hy,
> And menageth the euer-mouing sky,
> And in the same these lower creatures all,
> Subiected to her powre imperiall.
>
> Both heauen and earth obey vnto her will,
> And all the creatures which they both containe:
> For of her fulnesse which the world doth fill,

They all partake, and do in state remaine,
As their great Maker did at first ordaine,
Through obseruation of her high beheast,
By which they first were made, and still increast.
(lines 183-203)[18]

In *Paradise Lost*, at the behest of God the Father, the Son as theWord fills the role of creative energy:

And thou my Word, begott'n Son, by thee
This I perform, speak thou, and be it don:
My overshadowing Spirit and might with thee
I send along, ride forth, and bid the Deep
Within appointed bounds be Heav'n and Earth,
Boundless the Deep, because I am who fill
Infinitude, not vacuous the space...
(*P.L.*, VII, 163-169)

Mean while the Son
On his great Expedition now appeerd,
Girt with Omnipotence, with Radiance crownd
Of Majestie Divine, Sapience and Love
Immense, and all his Father in him shon.
(*P.L.*, VII, 192-196)

Tulasī Dāsa frequently uses the word *māyā* to denote the power that produces the endless cycle of generation, growth and dissolution; he also uses it to mean the show of things, nature, which deceives only those who, labouring under the delusion of ignorance (*avidyā*), fail to identify all time and being and *māyā* herself with the Absolute Brahman. Hence like Spenser's Mutability, Tulasī Dāsa's *māyā* also stands for the concept of change in fixity.

Divine Wisdom enables the devotee of Rāma to realise intuitively the truth of unity in multiplicity epitomised in the identity of Sītā and Rāma:

> I do homage to the feet of Sītā and Rāma, who dearly love the afflicted and who are truly one, as the word is one with its meaning, and water with the wave, though they are distinguished in speech.[19]

girā aratha jala bīci sama kahiyata bhinna na bhinna,
banda'uṃ sītārāmapada jinhahiṃ parama priya khinna.

---

[18] Edmund Spenser, *Minor Poems* ed. E. de Sélincourt (Oxford, 1910), p. 469.
[19] W. D. P. Hill, *The Holy Lake of the Acts of Rāma*, p. 14.

In a subsequent passage Tulasī Dāsa writes:

> You are the guardian of the bounds of revelation,
> O Rāma, Lord of the world, and Jānakī [Sītā] is Illusion,[20]
> who at the nod of her gracious lord creates,
> preserves or destroys the world;
> and he who supports the earth, the thousand-headed
> Serpent King, is Lakṣmaṇ, sovereign of all created things.
> As a king have you come to slay the demon host
> and accomplish the purpose of the gods.
>
> Your true form, Rāma, transcends speech and reason,
> incomprehensible, ineffable, infinite, called ever by the Veda "Not thus, not thus"!
> The world is visible and you are he who watches its play;
> Brahmā, Hari and Śambhu you make to dance like puppets.
> Not even they can comprehend your mysteries;
> who else, then, can know you as you are?
> He only knows you to whom you grant that knowledge;
> and when he knows you, he becomes one with you.
> It is by your grace, Raghunandana [Rāma], that your votary
> knows you, who touch the votary's heart like cooling sandalwood.
> Your body is True Thought and Bliss, immutable;
> they know it who have won the right to know it.
> Yet to accomplish the purpose of saints and gods you have put on the form of man
> and speak and act as does a human king.[21]
>
> *sruti-setu-pālaka rāma tumha jagadīsamāyā Jānakī,*
> *jo sṛjati jagapālati harati rukha pāi kṛpānidhāna kī.*
> *jo sahasasīsu ahīsu mahi dharu laṣanu sa-carācara-dhanī,*
> *surakāja dhari nararāja tanu cale dalana khala-nisicara-anī.*
>
> *rāma-sarūpa tumhāra bacana'agocara buddhipara,*
> *abigata akatha apāra neti neti nita nigama kaha.*
>
> *jaga pekhana tumha dekhanhihāre,*
> *bidhi-hari-sambhu-nacāvanihāre;*
> *teu na jānahiṃ maramu tumhārā*
> *a'ura tumhahiṃ ko jānanihārā.*
>
> *soi jāna'i jehi dehu janāī,*
> *jānata tumhahiṃ tumhahiṃ hoi jāī;*
> *tumharihi kṛpā tumhahiṃ raghunandana,*
> *jānahiṃ bhagata bhagata-ura-candana.*

---

[20] Hill translates *māyā* as "illusion".
[21] Hill, *op. cit.*, pp. 212-213.

cidānandamaya deha tumhārī,
bigatabikāra jāna adhikārī;
naratanu dhareu santa-sura-kājā,
kahahu karahu jasa prākṛta rājā.

It is evident from these quotations that the metaphysical concept of *māyā* as an aspect of the Brahman is quite different from the popular notion of it as mere illusion or magic, although the word *māyā* also has these secondary meanings and is so used on occasions by Tulasī Dāsa himself.

The realisation of the truth of the unity of all being may justify Tulasī Dāsa's homage and prayer to Śiva in the invocations of the several books of the *Rāma-carita-mānasa* of which the hero is the *avatāra* of Viṣṇu or Hari; but when he says that Rāma makes "Brahma, Hari and Śambhu [Śiva]... dance like puppets", Tulasī Dāsa's non-dualism shades into polytheism. So there appears to be an inherent ambiguity in his philosophy of Brahman and *māyā* although many Hindu critics would maintain with Pāṇḍeya that polytheism and pantheism have their ground in non-dualism.[22] Hill's reading of the poem seems fair:

> But in the main Tulasī Dāsa, like all Vaiṣṇava theists, held Viṣṇu to be infinitely superior to Brahmā and Śiva, one with the Absolute and performing all the functions normally assigned to the other two members of the triad. As the chief *avatāra* of Viṣṇu, Rāma is credited with all his powers, and the hymns of praise addressed to Rāma observe no distinction between the two.[23]

Throughout his poem Tulasī Dāsa sings of Rāma as supreme virtue, beauty and power (*śīla, saundarya, śakti*) extolling him above all other gods in order to instil in the hearts of his readers and hearers the *Rāma-bhakti* which gives to the *bhaktas* or saintly devotees of all castes final salvation from earthly existences, thus uniting them with Rāma forever. Devotion to Rāma is, in the first place, dependent upon his grace bestowed upon his servants, therefore Tulasī Dāsa's verses are charged with the *dāsya-bhāva*. This is the mood of loving adoration and submission that comes from the servant-master relationship in which there is, on the part of the devotee, no other desire than to love and serve the Lord, Rāma, even

---

[22] Rāmaniranjana Pāṇḍeya, *Rāma-bhakti Śākhā* (Hyderabad, 1960), p. 351—"Bhārata meṃ bahudevavāda aura sarvavāda donoṃ advaitavāda se anuprāṇita haiṃ."

[23] Hill, *op. cit.*, p. xxvi.

as the monkey Hanumān does in the story. Further, Rāma and Sīta both absolutely pure in thought, word and deed, are represented as the ideal of conjugal love that is at once human and divine, with a warmth of feeling that is absent from the Father-Son relationship in the empyrean of *Paradise Lost.* The mood of devotion of the *dāsya-bhāva* and the poetic sentiment (*rasa*) arising from it are the things of central importance in the reading of the *Rāma-carita-mānasa.* The theology is only useful in so far as it helps to reinforce this mood.

In *Paradise Lost* Milton makes the Son of God the epitome of the power and wisdom co-eternal with the Almighty:

> O Son, in whom my Soul hath chief delight,
> Son of my bosom, Son who art alone
> My Word, my wisdom, and effectual might. . .
>
> (*P.L.,* III, 168-170)

His power already demonstrated in the rout of the rebellious angels, is to be further revealed in his role as saviour of mankind when, as grace and love incarnate, he will finally vanquish sin and death. Nature too will be redeemed:

> for then the Earth
> Shall all be Paradise, farr happier place
> Then this of *Eden*, and farr happier daies.
>
> (*P.L.*, XII, 463-465)

Although the incarnation of Jesus, having the doctrine of atonement behind it, differs basically from that of the Hindu doctrine of *avatāra*, the divine intention is the same: to restore the harmonious relationship of Creator and creature which Adam, before the Fall, was sure lay in the power of God:

> Thou in thy secresie although alone,
> Best with thy self accompanied, seekst not
> Social communication, yet so pleas'd,
> Canst raise thy Creature to what hight thou wilt
> Of Union or Communion, deifi'd. . .
>
> (*P.L.*, VIII, 427-431)

It is to this "union or communion" that Milton's poetry as religious meditation can raise the mind of the responsive reader.

Once we are aware that we may find controversial asides and doctrinal

> discrepancies, we can afford to treat them with the passing interest they deserve, and concentrate on the main purpose, which is not to expound a theological thesis but to reinforce a mystical mood. The poem is a survey of the whole scheme of Providence by which [Milton] hopes to attune the human to the Divine Mind, and thus purify the human heart and elevate it to God.[24]

Fr Cormican's Christian interpretation of *Paradise Lost*, summarised in the above paragraph, is remarkably like that given of the *Rāma-carita-mānasa* by Tulasī Dāsa himself: the seven books are progressive steps in bhakti, which is granted by the grace of Rāma to his devotees who immerse themselves in contemplation of the holy lake of his deeds. It is clear that for both Milton and Tulasī Dāsa their works are poetic statements of spiritual facts, and that the characters and action of their stories are symbols of reality. Hence though their narrative may appear in parts implausible, it must nevertheless be regarded as the basis of a symbolic vision. What Fr Cormican calls "a mystical mood" corresponds to the *bhakti-rasa* of Vaiṣṇava experience; and, in so far as *Paradise Lost* and the *Rāma-carita-mānasa* succeed in eliciting the desired poetic sentiment, these poems are successful as works of religious devotion.

For the devout, as well as for the unbelieving but sympathetic student, a number of striking correspondences appear between the English and Hindi narrative religious poems of the sixteenth and seventeenth centuries. The above discussion has attempted to show how *Paradise Lost* and *The Faerie Queene* on the one hand, and on the other, the *Rāma-carita-mānasa* illuminate one another in the search for the ideal truth and beauty through allegory and symbol.

---

[24] L. A. Cormican, "Milton's Religious Verse" in *From Donne to Marvell* ed. B. Ford (Harmondsworth, 1956), p. 180.

CONCLUSION

In the foregoing chapters an examination has been attempted of the poetic forms, in two literatures, given to the general theme of man's constant search for self-fulfilment through some ideal experience, which reveals his humanity as essentially related to the other-worldly and divine. From this examination it appears that the quest for union with the divine is pursued both on the emotional and the intellectual planes; and that though the expression of this quest in English and Hindi poetry generally inclines either more towards feeling or more towards thought, there is a marked tension between the two modes of religious experience in several of the poems considered in this study. The spirit of the earlier English lyrics is similar to that of *saguṇa* bhakti which gives prominence to feelings associated with the worship of a personal loving God manifested in His incarnation. The metaphysical poetry found in the English lyrics of the late sixteenth and the seventeenth centuries is seen as being more akin to that of *nirguṇa* bhakti with the emphasis upon the speculative.

On the whole, the voice of the individual poets is not so easily distinguishable in Hindi religious poetry as that of the individual poets in English. This may be due either to the fact that Hindi bhakti poetry is more constantly and consciously ethical in its intention, or that the poets place more reliance upon stock responses because of the need to conform to the set *bhāvas* of bhakti poetics. As far as the ethical is concerned, Kabīr may be considered by virtue of his robust individualism an exception to this general observation. Pre-eminently the Hindi poet of democracy and equality, he castigates all those who uphold caste distinctions, sectarianism, and organised religion of any kind. Tulasī Dāsa lays great emphasis upon social service and brotherhood as the fruits of *Rāma-bhakti*, but he supports the caste system and orthodox Hinduism. The devotees of Kṛṣṇa, immersed in their raptures, are not much concerned with social or moral problems. But it should be noted that the great Kṛṣṇa *bhaktas*, like Caitanya, advocated high ethical standards of human conduct and condemned the sensualities of the extremists in the Kṛṣṇa cult.

Yet even in Kabīr and Tulasī Dāsa, the matter of paramount importance is absorption in devotion to the Supreme Being, for they are primarily *bhaktas* or saints and incidentally preachers. The non-didactic aspect of their poetry is therefore intended chiefly to evoke the kind of sensations that are identical with spiritual rapture. According to the theorists of Hindi and Sanskrit poetics, such rapture is achieved by enjoying the *rasa* derived from the *bhāvas* or emotional conditions induced by the poetry. The usual translation of *rasa* is "sentiment" as in the following quotation from Keith, which is taken from a passage in which he states the theory of *rasa* as promulgated in classical Sanskrit criticism:

> The process of apprehension of sentiment [*rasa*] is comparable to the piercing of a hundred lotus leaves with one needle; there is a process by which the factors [in poetry] induce the sentiment, but it is so rapid as to seem instantaneous. It is clear also that the rising up of sentiment is not the result of inference; it can come into being only in a person who has had in previous lives experience which gives him aesthetic susceptibilities, makes him a feeling heart or connoisseur (*sahṛdaya*), and in him it arises as a perfectly unique emotional experience, comparable only to the bliss of cognition of the absolute, a transcendental (*alaukika*) joy.

In a footnote Keith adds:

> This [joy] is, we must remember, identic with the bliss which is part of the absolute as one, being, thought, joy.*

Hence the emphasis in Hindi criticism is placed upon the enjoyment of poetry through savouring the *rasa* of the various *bhāvas* of bhakti. *Rasa* literally means "juice" or "sap" of some substance. The English word "sentiment" does not convey the exact connotation of the Hindi so well as the word "gusto" in Keats's sense of immersion in some poetic experience through that "negative capability" which enables the poet to identify himself entirely with objects and experiences imaginatively in a "life of sensations".

The codification of *bhāvas* and their corresponding *rasas* was conducive to establishing stereotypes of natural descriptions, character and action which led to a conventionalisation of imagery aiming at stock responses. For example, the human soul is attracted to the divine like bees to nectar-filled blossoms, moths to the flame, rivers to the sea; the agony of separation is compared to the state of

* A. Berriedale Keith, *A History of Sanskrit Literature* (London, 1955), pp. 388-89.

the fish out of water and the serpent deprived of its crest jewel; and the ecstasy of union is ineffable like the bliss of the dumb man who enjoys the choicest delicacies without being able to describe their sweetness. In spite of this, however, Sūra Dāsa, Mīrāṃ Bāī and Tulasī Dāsa, working within the conventional framework of *Kṛṣṇa-bhakti* or *Rāma-bhakti*, time and again give their lyrics the stamp of their own personality by the ardour of their devotion. In doing so they remind one of the more pronounced personal accents in the work of Herbert, Vaughan and Donne.

Paradise Lost and the *Rāma-carita-mānasa* combine fervent devotion with theological and philosophical abstractions. They may, therefore, justly be regarded as poetic elaborations of the two main strands of the emotional and the intellectual in the religious experience which inspired the English lyrics and Hindi *muktaka* verses from the late fourteenth century to about the end of the seventeenth century. Although the works of the English Metaphysical poets of the seventeenth century, or of Sūra Dāsa and Kabīr, provide examples of poetry in which feeling and thought are sometimes integrated, there is not in them the comprehensiveness that is found in the epics of Milton and Tulasī Dāsa. Even Spenser, who is not so much a poet of religious experience as he is of religious didacticism, shows this tendency to bring thought and feeling together, with greater amplitude than the Metaphysicals, in his *Hymn of Heavenly Love* and *Hymn to Heavenly Beauty* as well as in the two *Mutability Cantos* of *The Faerie Queene*. Milton propounds Christian doctrine in parts of *Paradise Lost* with dull and heavy pedantry; but in some of the more emotional passages—where he invokes the divine wisdom, harmony and light, or in which he identifies himself with Adam and Eve in their psalms of adoration,—his poetry rises to the pitch of spiritual exaltation. Tulasī Dāsa, in the *Rāma-carita-mānasa*, combines metaphysical discursiveness with the fervour of Sūra Dāsa's bhakti and the baroque richness of Spenser. Thus the expansiveness of the romantic and religious epic forms gives the poets ample scope for their versatility, inventiveness and devotional fervour; and the longer narrative poems in English and Hindi are, in fact, the climax of the religious poetry reviewed in this study.

BIBLIOGRAPHY

I. Primary Sources

1. *Poetry and Prose Texts (chiefly) English*

Allberry, C. R. C. (ed.), *A Manichaean Psalm-Book* (Stuttgart, 1938).

Bottral, M. (ed.), *The Way to Blessedness: Thomas Traherne's Christian Ethicks* (London, 1962).

Britt, M. (ed.), *Hymns of the Breviary and Missal* (London, 1924).

Brittain, F. (ed.), *The Penguin Book of Latin Verse* (Harmondsworth, 1962).

Brook, G. L. (ed.), *The Harley Lyrics* (Manchester, 1948).

Brown, C. (ed.), *English Lyrics of the XIIIth Century* (Oxford, 1932).

— —, *Religious Lyrics of the XIVth Century* (Oxford, 1924).

— —, *Religious Lyrics of the XVth Century* (Oxford, 1939).

Comper, F. M. M. (ed.), *Spiritual Songs from English MSS. of the Fourteenth to Sixteenth Centuries* (London, 1936).

Crashaw, Richard, *The Poems English Latin and Greek*, ed. L. C. Martin (Oxford, 1927).

Davies, R. T., *Medieval English Lyrics: A Critical Anthology* (London, 1963).

Donne, John, *The Poems of John Donne*, ed. Sir Herbert Grierson (London, 1957).

— —, *The Divine Poems*, ed. Helen Gardner (Oxford, 1952).

Gaselle, S. (ed.), *The Oxford Book of Medieval Latin Verse* (Oxford, 1937).

Greene, R. L. (ed.), *The Early English Carols* (Oxford, 1935).

Grierson, Sir Herbert, (ed.), *Metaphysical Lyrics and Poems of the Seventeenth Century* (Oxford, 1921).

Herbert, George, *The Works of George Herbert*, ed. F. E. Hutchinson (Oxford, 1945).

Hopkins, G. M., *The Sermons and Devotional Writings*, ed. C. Devlin (London, 1959).

Love, Nicholas, *The Mirrour of the Blessed Lyf of Jesu Christ*, (ed.) L. F. Powell (Oxford, 1908).

Milton, John, *The Poetical Works of John Milton, Vol. I, Paradise Lost*, ed. Helen Darbishire (Oxford, 1952).

St John of the Cross, *Poems of St John of the Cross* with a translation by Roy Campbell (London, 1960),

Sidney, Sir Philip, *The Poems of Sir Philip Sidney*, ed. W. A. Ringler, jr. (Oxford, 1962).

Sidney, Sir Philip and The Countess of Pembroke, *The Psalms of Sir Philip Sidney and The Countess of Pembroke*, ed. J. C. A. Rathmell (New York, 1963).

Southwell, Robert, *The Complete Poems of Robert Southwell*, ed. A. B. Grosart (London, 1872).

Spenser, Edmund, *Spenser's Faerie Queene* 2 vols., ed. J. C. Smith (Oxford, 1909).

— —,*Spenser's Minor Poems*, ed. E. de Sélincourt (Oxford, 1910).

Surrey, Henry Howard, Earl of, *The Poems*, ed., F.M. Padelford (Seattle, 1928).

Traherne, Thomas, *Thomas Traherne: Centuries, Poems and Thanksgivings* 2 vols., ed. H. M. Margoliouth (Oxford, 1958).

Vaughan, Henry, *The Works of Henry Vaughan*, ed. L. C. Martin, (2nd. ed. Oxford, 1957).

Wyatt, Sir Thomas, *Collected Poems of Sir Thomas Wyatt*, ed. Kenneth Muir (London, 1949).

2. *Hindi Poetry and Prose Texts (original and translation)*

Ādi Granth (English). Selections from Sacred Writings of the Sikhs, trans. Trilochan Singh *et al.* (London, 1960).
Śrī Guru-Granth Sāhib (English). Trans. Gopal Singh (Delhi, 1960-62).
Āḷvāra Prabandham (English). *Hymns of the Aḷvārs.* Trans. J. S. M. Hooper (Calcutta, 1929).
Aṣṭachāpa, [short biographical sketches of eight Vaiṣṇava poets— Sūra Dāsa, Kṛṣṇa Dāsa, Paramānanda, Kumbhana, Nanda, Caturbhuja, Chīta, and Govinda Svāmī—taken from the works of Gokula Nātha containing respectively biographies of 84 and 252 Vaiṣṇavas] ed. Dhirendra Varmā (4th ed. Allahabad, 1950).
Bhagavad-Gītā, (Sanskrit text and English translation) S. Rādhākrishnan (2nd. ed. London, 1949).
Dādū, *Vānī* of Dādū (English) in *A Sixteenth-Century Indian Mystic* by W. G. Orr (London, 1947).
Gorakha Nātha, *Gorakha Vānī*, ed. P. D. Baṛathvāla (Allahabad, 1960).
Jāyasī, Malik, Muhammad, *Padmāvat* (English). Trans. A. G. Shirreff (Calcutta, 1944).
——*Jāyasī Granthāvalī*, ed. Rāmacandra Śukla (Allahabad, 1935).
Kabīr, *The Bījak of Kabīr.* (English). Trans. Rev. Ahmad Shāh (Allahabad, 1917).
——, *Kabīra.* Hazārī-Prasāda Dvivedī (7th ed. Bombay, 1964). *Kabīr au Cabaret de l'Amour.* A selection of verses trans. into French by Charlotte Vaudeville (Paris, 1959).
——, *Kabīra Granthāvalī (dohā).* Trans. into French by Charlotte Vaudeville (Pondicherry, 1957).
——, *Kabīra Granthāvalī*, ed. Śyāmasundara Dāsa (9th ed. Banaras, 1964).
——, *Kabīra Granthāvalī*, ed. Pārasanātha Tivārī (Allahabad, 1961).
——, *Santa Kabīra*, ed. Rāmakumāra Varmā (4th ed. Allahabad, 1957).
Mīrāṃ Bāī, *Mīrāṃ Bāī kī Padāvalī*, ed Paraśurāma Caturvedī (11th ed. Allahabad, 1962).
Nābhā Dāsa, *Bhakta Māla*, ed. Sītā Rāmaśaraṇa Prasāda (Lucknow, 1926).
Nārada-Bhakti-Sūtra, Sanskrit text with Hindi commentary by H. P. Poddar (11th ed. Gorakhpur, 1963).
Prem Sagar., Hindi rendering of the 10th chapter of the *Bhāgavata Purāṇa* by Lallu Lāl, ed. E. B. Eastwick (Hertford, 1851).
Śāṇḍilya-Bhakti-Sūtra., Sanskrit text with Hindi commentary by Rāmanārāyaṇa Datta Śāstri (4th ed. Gorakhpur, 1963).
Santa-Kāvya Saṃgraha., ed. Ganeśa Prāsada Dvivedī, 1939; revised Paraśurāma Caturvedī (2nd ed. Allahabad, 1952).
Sūra Dāsa., *Sūra-Sudhā*, ed. Miśra-Bandhu (Banaras, 1923).
Tulasī Dāsa., *The Holy Lake of the Acts of Rāma* (English). Trans. W. D. P. Hill of the *Rāma-carita-mānasa* (London, 1952).
——, *Kavitāvalī* (English). Trans. F. R. Allchin (London, 1964).
——, *The Petition to Rām* (English). Trans. F. R. Allchin of the *Vinaya Patrikā* (London, 1966).
——, *Vinaya Patrikā*, ed. Bhagavān-dīna and Viśvanātha Prasāda Caube (Allahabad, 1949).
——, *Vinaya Patrikā*, ed. Devanārāyaṇa Dvivedī (2nd ed. Banaras, 1962).
——, *Vinaya Patrikā*, ed. Viyogī Hari (6th ed. Banaras, 1950).
——, *Tulasī Granthāvalī* 3 vols., ed. Rāmacandra Śukla, Bhagavān-dīna and Vraja-ratna Dāsa (Banaras, 1923).

II. The Religious and Intellectual Background and Literary Criticism

Allen, P. S., *The Romanesque Lyric 50-1050 A.D.* (Chapel Hill, 1928)
Baṛathvāla, P. D., *The Nirguṇ School of Bhakti Poetry* (Banaras, 1936).
Bhattachārya, S., *The Philosophy of the Śrīmad-Bhāgavata* (Santiniketan, 1960-1962).
Bouquet, A. C., *Comparative Religion* (6th ed. London, 1962).
Brittain, F., *The Medieval Latin and Romance Lyric to 1300 A.D.* (2nd ed. Cambridge, 1951).
Broadbent, J. B., *Poetic Love* (London, 1964).
Bullough, G., *Mirror of Minds: Changing Psychological Beliefs in English Poetry* (London, 1962).
Bush, D., *English Literature in the Earlier Seventeenth Century 1600-1660*, Oxford History of English Literature, Vol. V (2nd ed. Oxford, 1962).
Campbell, J., *Masks of Gold* (London, 1962).
Campbell, L. B., *Divine Poetry and Drama in Sixteenth-Century England* (Berkeley, 1959).
Carpenter, J. E., *Comparative Religion* (London, 1913). *Theism in Medieval India* (London, 1921).
Chambers, R. W., *On the Continuity of English Prose from Alfred to More and his School* (London, 1962).
Copleston, F., *A History of Philosophy—Vol. III Ockham to Suarez* (London, 1953).
— —, *A History of Philosophy—Vol. IV Descartes to Leibnitz* (London, 1958).
Cross, F. L. (ed.), *Oxford Dictionary of the Christian Church* (Oxford, 1957).
de Mourgues, O., *Metaphysical, Baroque and Précieux Poetry* (Oxford, 1953).
Daniélou, A., *Hindu Polytheism* (London, 1964).
Dāsgupta, S., *A History of Indian Philosophy* 4 vols. (Cambridge, 1922-45).
De, S. K., *Early History of the Vaiṣṇava Faith and Movement in Bengal* (2nd ed. Calcutta, 1961).
Eliot, T. S., *Selected Essays* (3rd ed. London, 1951).
Farquhar, J. N., *Modern Religious Movements in India* (London, 1929). *Outline of the Religious Literature of India* (London, 1920).
Religious literature of India (London, 1920).
Frost, M., *Historical Companion to Hymns Ancient and Modern* (London, 1962).
Garner, R., *Henry Vaughan—Experience and the Tradition* (Chicago, 1959).
Garratt, G. T., *The Legacy of India* (Oxford, 1938).
Gillman, F. J., *Evolution of the English Hymn* (New York, 1927).
Gilson, E., *The Spirit of Medieval Philosophy* (New York, 1940).
Greene, R. L., *The Early English Carols* (Oxford, 1935).
Grierson, Sir G.A., *The Satsaiya of Bihārī* (Calcutta, 1896).
Hiriyanna, M., *The Essentials of Indian Philosophy* (London, 1949).
Hitti, P. K., *History of the Arabs* (4th ed. London, 1949).
Hough, G., *A Preface to the Faerie Queene* (London, 1962).
Husain, I., *The Mystical Element in the Metaphysical Poets of the Seventeenth Century* (Edinburgh, 1948).
Husain, Y., *Glimpses of Medieval Indian Culture* (2nd ed. Bombay, 1959).
James, W., *Varieties of Religious Experience* (London, 1902).
Jennings, E., *Ever Changing Shape* (London, 1961).
Julian, J. (ed.), *Dictionary of Hymnology* (2nd ed. London, 1907).
Keay, F. E., *Kabīr and his Followers* (Calcutta, 1931).
Keith, A. B., *A History of Sanskrit Literature* (London, 1953).
Knowles, D., *The English Mystical Tradition* (London, 1955).
Koestler, A., *The Lotus and the Robot* (London, 1960).

Leff, G., *Medieval Thought—St Augustine to Ockham* (London, 1959).
Leishman, J. B., *The Metaphysical Poets—Donne, Herbert, Vaughan, Traherne* (New York, 1963).
Lewis, C. S., *The Allegory of Love* (Oxford, 1936).
——, *English Literature in the Sixteenth Century excluding Drama*—Oxford History of English Literature, Vol. III (Oxford, 1954).
Macnicol, N., *The Making of Modern India* (Oxford, 1924).
Mahadevan, T. M. P., (ed.) *A Seminar on Saints* (Madras, 1960).
Mahood, M. M., *Poetry and Humanism* (London, 1950).
Martz, L. L., *The Paradise Within* (New Haven, 1964).
——, *The Poetry of Meditation* (New Haven, 1954).
Messenger, R. E., *Ethical Teachings in the Latin Hymns of Medieval England* (New York 1930).
——, *The Medieval Latin Hymn* (Washington, 1953).
Neil, S., *Christain Faith and Other Faiths* (London, 1961).
Nicholson, R. A., *The Mystics of Islam* (London, 1914).
Otto, R., *The Idea of the Holy* (Oxford, 1924).
——, *India's Religion of Grace and Christianity* (New York, 1930).
——, *Mysticism East and West* (London, 1932).
Owst, G. R., *Literature and Pulpit in Medieval England* (Cambridge, 1933).
Parrinder, E. G., *Upanishads, Gītā and Bible* (London, 1962).
—— *Worship in the World's Religions* (London, 1961).
Pieper, J., *Scholasticism* (London, 1961).
Raby, F. J. E., *A History of Christian-Latin Poetry from the Beginnings to the Close of the Middle Ages* (2nd ed. Oxford, 1953).
Rādhākrishnan, S., *Eastern Religions and Western Thought* (2nd ed. Oxford, 1940).
——, *Indian Philosophy* 2 vols. (2nd. ed. London, 1951).
——, *The Principal Upaniṣads* (London, 1953).
Salter, K. W., *Thomas Traherne—Mystic and Poet* (London, 1964).
Sen, S., *History of Bengali Literature* (New Delhi, 1960).
Smart, N., *The Yogi and the Devotee: the Interplay between the Upanishads and Catholic Theology* (London, 1968).
Summers, J., *George Herbert: His Religion and Art* (London, 1954).
Tuve, R., *Elizabethan and Metaphysical Imagery: Renaissance Poetic and Twentieth-Century Critics* (Chicago, 1947). *A Reading of George Herbert* (London, 1952).
Underhill, E., *Mysticism* 1st ed. 1911 (12th ed. reprinted London, 1960).
Underhill, M. M., *The Hindu Religious Year* (Calcutta, 1921).
Wade, G. I., *Thomas Traherne* (London/New Jersey, 1946).
Warnke, F. J., *European Metaphysical Poetry* (New Haven/London, 1961).
Warren, A., *Richard Crashaw: A Study in Baroque Sensibility* (London, 1959).
Westcott, G. H., *Kabir and the Kabir Panth* 1st ed. 1907 (reprinted Calcutta, 1953).
White, H. C., *The Metaphysical Poets—A Study in Religious Experience* 1st ed. 1936 (reprinted New York, 1956).
Wilson, H. H., *Religious Sects of the Hindus* 1st ed. 1861 (reprinted Calcutta, 1958).
Wilson, R. M., *Early Middle English Literature* (London, 1939).
Zaehner, R. C., *Hindu and Muslim Mysticism* (London, 1960). *Mysticism Sacred and Profane* (Oxford, 1957).
Zimmer, H. R., *Myths and Symbols in Indian Art and Civilization* (New York, 1946).

2. *Works in Hindi*

Baṛathvāla, Pitāmbara Datta, *Hindī Kāvya meṃ Nirguṇa Sampradāya* (Lucknow, 1950?)
Caturvedī, Paraśurāma, *Kabīra-Sāhitya kī Parakha* (Allahabad, 1954). *Uttarī Bhārata kī Santa-Paramparā* (2nd ed. Allahabad, 1964).

Dīkṣita, Rājapati, *Tulasī Dāsa aura unkā Yuga* (Banaras, 1952).
Dvivedī, Hazārī-Prasāda, *Kabīra* (7th ed. Bombay, 1964).
Gupta, Dīnadayālu, *Aṣṭachāpa aura Vallabha Sampradāya* (Lucknow, printed Allahabad, 1947).
Gupta, Mātā-Prasāda, *Tulasī Dāsa* (Allahabad, 1946).
Miśra-Bandhu, *Hindī Navaratna* (2nd ed. Lucknow, 1924).
Mohammad, Malik, *Āḷavāra Bhaktoṃ kā Tāmila-Prabandham aura Hindī Kṛṣṇa-Kāvya* (Agra, 1964).
Pāṇḍeya, Rāma-Niranjana, *Rāma-bhakti Śākhā* (Hyderabad, 1960).
Śarmā, Munśirāma, *Bhakti kā Vikāśa* (Banaras, 1958).
Śarmā, Vinaya-Mohana, *Hindī ko Maraṭhī Santoṃ kī Dena* (Patna, 1957).
Siṃha, Bhagavati Prasāda, *Rāma-bhakti meṃ Rasika Sampradāya* (Balaramapura, 1957).
Siṃha, Motī, *Nirguṇa Sāhitya kī Saṃskṛtika Pṛṣṭhabhūmi* (Banaras, 1962).
Siṃha, Sāvitrī, *Braja-bhāṣā ke Kṛṣṇa-bhakti Kāvya meṃ Abhivyanjana-śilpa* (Delhi, 1961).
Siṃha, Udayabhānu, *Hindī ke Svīkṛta Śodha-prabandha* (2nd ed. Delhi, 1963).
— —, *Tulasī Darśana Mīmāṃsā* (Lucknow, 1961).
Snātaka (Vijayendra), *Radhāvallabha Sampradāya: Siddhānta aura Sāhitya* (Delhi, 1957).
Śukla, Rāmacandra, *Sūra Dāsa* (5th ed. Banaras, 1964).
Śukla, Saralā, *Jayasī ke Paravarttī Hindī-Ṣūfī Kavi aura Kāvya* (Lucknow, 1956).
Tivārī, Rāmapūjana, *Ṣūfī-mata Sādhanā aura Sāhitya* (Banaras, 1956).
Trigunāyata, Govinda, *Hindī kī Nirguṇa Kāvya-dhārā aura uskī Dārśnika Pṛṣṭhabhūmi* (Kanpur, 1961).
Upādhyāya, Ayodhyā Siṃha, *Hindī Bhāṣā aura uske Sāhitya kā Vikāśa* (Patna, 1934).
Upādhyāya, Baladeva, *Bhāgavata Sampradāya* (Banaras, 1953).
Upādhyāya, Viśvambhara Nātha, *Santa-vaiṣṇava Kāvya para Tāntrika Prabhāva* (Agra, 1962).
Varmā, Rāmakumāra, *Hindī Sāhitya kā Alocanātmaka Itihāsa* (4th ed. Allahabad, 1958).
Vaudeville, Charlotte, *Tulasī Dāsa Racita Rāma-carita-mānasa kā Mūlādhāra va Racanaviṣayaka Samālocanātmaka: eka Adhyayana*—trans. from the original French by J. K. Balbir—(Pondicherry, 1965).

INDEX

DATE DUE

36177

PR
508 Ramsaran
.R4 English and Hindi religious
R3 poetry
1973